Y0-BTB-060

Imants Baruss
Psychology Dept
Kings College
266 Epworth Av
London, Ontario
Canada N6A 2M3
(519) 433-3491
ibaruss @ UWO. ca

THE PERSONAL NATURE OF NOTIONS OF CONSCIOUSNESS

A Theoretical and Empirical Examination of the Role of the Personal in the Understanding of Consciousness

Imants Baruss

UNIVERSITY
PRESS OF
AMERICA

Lanham • New York • London

Copyright © 1990 by
University Press of America®, Inc.
4720 Boston Way
Lanham, Maryland 20706

3 Henrietta Street
London WC2E 8LU England

Library of Congress Cataloging-in-Publication Data

Baruss, Imants, 1952–
The personal nature of notions of consciousness : a theoretical
and empirical examination of the role of the personal in the
understanding of consciousness / Imants Baruss.
p.   cm.
Originally presented as the author's thesis
(doctoral—University of Regina).
Includes bibliographical references.
1. Consciousness.   I. Title.
BF311.B33   1990   153—dc20   89–29559 CIP

ISBN 0–8191–7707–5 (alk. paper)

The paper used in this publication meets the minimum requirements of
American National Standard for Information Sciences—Permanence
of Paper for Printed Library Materials, ANSI Z39.48–1984.

ACKNOWLEDGEMENTS

This book is essentially my doctoral dissertation submitted to the University of Regina. First and foremost, I would like to thank my supervisor Dr. R. J. Moore for directing me and for participating in this work. His relentless enthusiasm and optimism, particularly in the course of the empirical investigation, have made this work enjoyable. I would like to thank Dr. C. Stark-Adamec, the Head of the Department of Psychology, for the wise guidance of my academic maturation, and Dr. C. Blachford and Dr. D. Secoy of the Faculty of Graduate Studies and Research for overseeing my studies. I would like to thank the remaining members of my examining committee, Dr. J. Schner, Dr. P. Engstrom and Dr. J. Osborne for their support and contributions to my work.

I thank the Faculty of Graduate Studies and Research for the financial support that I have received from the University of Regina and the Government of Saskatchewan. I would like to thank the University of Regina for making funds from the University of Regina President's Fund available to my supervisor, Dr. Moore, in order to finance the empirical investigation. In addition, I would like to thank Campion College for making funds available to Dr. Moore from the College's SSHRC grant in order to facilitate the production of the questionnaire and the analyses of data. Finally, I thank King's College, affiliated with The University of Western Ontario, for equipment and research funds used in the preparation of this book.

I gratefully acknowledge permission to reprint the following material:
Chapter 3 of this book is a revised version of I. Baruss, "Metanalysis of definitions of consciousness," which appeared in *Imagination, Cognition and Personality*, Volume 6, Number 4, pages 321 – 329.
© 1987, Baywood Publishing Co., Inc.
Reprinted by permission of Baywood Publishing Company.
Part of Chapter 4, Section 4.1 is a revised version of Section 1 of I. Baruss, "Categorical modelling of Husserl's intentionality," which appeared in *Husserl Studies*, Volume 6, pages 25 – 41.
© 1989 Kluwer Academic Publishers. Printed in the Netherlands.
Reprinted by permission of Kluwer Academic Publishers.
Parts of Chapter 5 are revised passages from a book chapter by I. Baruss and R. J. Moore, "Notions of consciousness and reality," to appear in

Imagery 5 – Current perspectives.
Reprinted by permission of the editors J. E. Shorr, M. Wolpin, J. Connella and P. Robin.

I am grateful for permission to quote from the following sources:
D. A. Helminiak, "Consciousness as a subject matter," *Journal for the Theory of Social Behaviour*, Volume 14, Number 2.
© 1984 Basil Blackwell Limited.
Reprinted by permission of Basil Blackwell Limited.
The philosophy of consciousness without an object by F. Merrell-Wolff, published by The Julian Press, Inc.
Copyright © MCMLXXIII by Franklin F. Wolff.
Reprinted by permission of Random House.
R. Sperry, "The new mentalist paradigm and ultimate concern", *Perspectives in Biology and Medicine*, Volume 29, Number 3, Part I.
© 1986 by The University of Chicago. All rights reserved.
Reprinted by permission of The University of Chicago Press.
R. N. Walsh, "Journey beyond belief," *Journal of Humanistic Psychology* (Volume 24, Number 2) pp 30–65, copyright 1984 by Association for Humanistic Psychology.
Reprinted by permission of Sage Publications, Inc.
D. C. Dennett, "How to study consciousness empirically or nothing comes to mind," *Synthese*, Volume 53, pages 159 – 180.
Copyright © 1982 by D. Reidel Publishing Co., Dordrecht, Holland, and Boston, U.S.A.
Reprinted by permission of Kluwer Academic Publishers.
Godel, Escher, Bach: An eternal golden braid by D. R. Hofstadter.
Copyright © 1979 by Basic Books, Inc.
Reprinted by permission of Basic Books, Inc.
Wilder Penfield, *The mystery of the mind: A critical study of consciousness and the human brain.*
Copyright © 1975 by Princeton University Press.
Reprinted by permission of Princeton University Press.
W. James, *The principles of psychology*, published by Harvard University Press.
Copyright (c) 1981 by the President and Fellows of Harvard College.
Reprinted by permission.

In addition, I would like to thank the following people for the contributions that they have made to this work: Dr. D. Blewett, Dr. H. Lyons-Young, Dr. H. Korte, M. Lake, D. Anderson, M. Cooper, K. Costain, Dr. P. Herman, Dr. R. Morecock, Dr. E. Taylor, L. Nevett, Professor J. Campbell, M. Gardner, the editors at University Press of America and the respondents to the various consciousness questionnaires without whom the empirical work would not have been possible.

TABLE OF CONTENTS

LIST OF FIGURES AND TABLES

CHAPTER 1

INTRODUCTION

When we have to do with anything, the mere seeing of the Things which are closest to us bears in itself the structure of interpretation, and in so primordial a manner that just to grasp something free, as it were, of the 'as', requires a certain readjustment. (Heidegger, 1926/1962, p. 190; emphasis in original)

The researcher approaching the study of the nature of consciousness for the first time is often bewildered by the plethora of viewpoints and lack of consensus in this area of study. Why does this situation exist? The problem lies in the disparity and incompatibility of firmly held ideas about the nature of consciousness and the manner in which it is to be studied. Many of these ideas are defended by their proponents, not only as the only legitimate ideas about consciousness, but as the only existent ones. What appears to be accepted in theory, but fails to be appreciated in practice, is the recognition that these various versions of consciousness are correlated with a given person's purported experience and their personal beliefs about reality. The purpose of this book, then, is not to try to give an account of the nature of consciousness, but to examine in a scientific manner, both theoretically and empirically, the role of the personal in the understanding of consciousness. It is hoped that such an investigation would clarify the field of consciousness studies and facilitate the study of the nature of consciousness.

The first section of this chapter illustrates this state of affairs in consciousness studies by presenting a number of the diverse ways in which consciousness is understood, along with some examples of statements concerning personal beliefs and purported experiences that appear to be relevant to a person's understanding of consciousness. Section 2 restates the thesis of this book and discusses the nature and scope of the project; Section 3 gives an outline of the contents of the book.

1.1 Disparity of views concerning consciousness

There is heuristic support from the psychological literature that the area of consciousness studies is in a state of confusion. Toulmin has characterized it as a "tangled thicket(s)" (1982, p. 56). White has pointed out that "consciousness . . . has been investigated from a bewildering variety

of points of view in the years since it emerged from the shadow of be-
haviourism" (1988, p. 42). He has added that this variety, may, in part, be
due to the fact that different problems have been addressed. This confusion appears to be reflected in the use of the term consciousness itself:
Roberts (1984) has said that few people are clear about its use, and that
it seems to have meanings that overlap; Miller and Buckhout (1973) have
maintained that the term has many uses; Klein (1984) has argued that the
term does not refer to a single concept; Helminiak (1984) has stated that
it is used as an umbrella term. According to Miller and Buckhout (1973),
most psychologists have admitted that they do not know what consciousness is. Despite the confusion, there are many who have maintained that
a notion of consciousness is necessary (e.g., Mandler, 1975, 1985; Osborne,
1981; Pugh, 1976; Walsh, 1984a). As Csikszentmihalyi has said, "psychology
without a lively theory of consciousness is a rather lifeless discipline"
(1978, p. 337).

To demonstrate the disparity of opinions concerning the nature of
consciousness, some examples are given here. The first of these is from
the enigmatic James who insisted in his paper, "Does consciousness exist?"
that consciousness does not exist, that thoughts exist, but that thoughts
are just the breath:

> I am as confident as I am of anything that, in myself, the stream of
> thinking (which I recognize emphatically as a phenomenon) is only a
> careless name for what, when scrutinized, reveals itself to consist
> chiefly of the stream of my breathing. The 'I think' which Kant said
> must be able to accompany all my objects, is the 'I breathe' which
> actually does accompany them. There are other internal facts besides
> breathing (intracephalic muscular adjustments, etc., of which I have
> said a word in my larger Psychology), and these increase the assets
> of 'consciousness,' so far as the latter is subject to immediate
> perception; but breath, which was ever the original of 'spirit,'
> breath moving outwards, between the glottis and the nostrils, is, I
> am persuaded, the essence out of which philosophers have con-
> structed the entity known to them as consciousness. *That entity is
> fictitious, while thoughts in the concrete are fully real. But thoughts
> in the concrete are made of the same stuff as things are.* (James,
> 1904a, p. 491; emphasis in original)

Another figure famous in the history of psychology as the progenitor
of behaviorism, Watson, denied utility to the notion of consciousness:

> The present volume does some violence to the traditional classifica-
> tion of psychological topics and to their conventional treatment. For
> example, the reader will find no discussion of consciousness and no
> reference to such terms as sensation, perception, attention, will,
> image and the like. These terms are in good repute, but I have
> found that I can get along without them both in carrying out

investigations and in presenting psychology as a system to my students. I frankly do not know what they mean, nor do I believe that any one else can use them consistently. (Watson, 1919, p. viii)

Watson has not been the only one to relegate consciousness to the dust bin. A recent movement in philosophy, eliminative materialism, has also sought to do the same:

The 'spirits' and 'principles' of alchemy, the 'crystal spheres' of pre-Galilean astronomy, 'daemonic possession' of Medieval medicine, 'phlogiston', 'ether', and 'signatures', are now nought but dry bones of an earlier intellectual ecology. The theme of this paper is that a similar fate may befall concepts respected and revered in our own prevailing conception of how humans works [sic], and the concept on which I mean to focus is consciousness. (Churchland, 1983, p. 80)

Part of some authors' versions of consciousness is an avoidance of the clarification of the referent of the term consciousness. In his book *The concept of consciousness*, Klein has sidestepped committing himself to a definition of consciousness. The closest that he has come has been to remark, almost parenthetically, that "Equating consciousness with information dissipates the mystery associated with consciousness seen as an entity" (Klein, 1984, p. 175). The definition and explanation of consciousness in terms of information is a strategy also utilized in cognitive science, currently the predominant paradigm in psychology.

Pope and Singer seem to have been more comfortable with characterizing consciousness as being, at least in part, mysterious:

The contributions in this volume represent efforts to study the stream of consciousness with a deep appreciation and respect for its rich diversity, its continuous, often quirky movement, its immediacy in the lives of us all, and ultimately its mystery. (Pope & Singer, 1978, p. 3)

Such a notion of consciousness may be faithful to the experience of consciousness, but what shape can one's experience take? For instance:

In meditation that changeable mental content − historically accumulated mental artefacts [sic] − is periodically cleansed in order to obtain a lucid consciousness. . . . It is only through 'pure consciousness,' unconditioned, that one's perception becomes direct, approaching the world as it is. So perceived, the world transcends the categories of parochial psychology and mortality; reality is assumption-free and conflict-free. (Chang, 1978, p. 113)

These and similar notions of consciousness could be labelled phenomenological and transcendental.

As presented here, these examples of diverse notions of consciousness appear to be self-contained. They do not exist in a vacuum, however, but are to be found within and follow from the larger context of the author's thought. The following, slightly longer passages, give clear indication of this. In the first case, the discussion is not about consciousness per se but mental events more generally, although, if the authors were to discuss consciousness, it would likely be in the same manner as their discussion of mind.[1] The authors' reasons for rejecting dualism[2] reveal their beliefs about the nature of reality and what they consider to be acceptable means for studying that reality.

> There have been recent attempts to revive the dualistic view. This we find, as scientists, difficult to accept.
> Many scientists consider that two important corollaries will ultimately follow from a dualistic view. Firstly, because mind becomes on such an analysis a kind of 'mystical entity', it cannot, by definition, be studied by other than mystical methods; i.e. the central problem of neurobiology cannot be tackled scientifically! If this were to be the case, we would have to agree that either (a) the problem cannot be approached scientifically, in which case we should abandon neurobiology since it would be an empty exercise, or (b) that we may learn about mind 'properties', but not as a scientific problem. The latter implies that *explanation regarding some aspects of living systems may be obtained by means other than the scientific method.* Wide acceptance of such a view would engender a devastating anti-intellectual attitude and a lapse into the form of mysticism known to generate fortune-tellers and witch-hunts, even in modern times. (Llinas & Pellionisz, 1984, p. 2; emphasis in original)

Llinas and Pellionisz clarify their position concerning the mind. To the question, "Can mind be understood in physiological terms?" they respond:

> Our own point of view regarding this question is optimistic. The kinds of explanation-sketches that come to mind here relate to the problem of emerging properties, but only in the sense that emergentism may be considered reductionistic. If one were to ask then,

---

[1]It should be pointed out that it is not clear precisely what is meant by mind, just as it is not clear what is meant by consciousness. The two are often identified, but there is no reason to suppose, except where one is deliberately defined in terms of the other, that the relationship between the two is at all clear. For example, one can conceive of mental activity which is not conscious although it's harder to conceive of consciousness which is not mental.

[2]The philosophical position that mind can exist independently of the brain.

'What are the parameters of importance in the generation of mind': the answer would be 'those that generate brain'. (Llinas & Pellionisz, 1984, p. 3)

Llinas and Pellionisz are not lost in academic backwaters, but are highly regarded for their tensor-algebraic analyses of brain processes. Their version of a supervenience thesis[3] is shared by many intellectuals and is clearly correlated with their understanding of mind.

A similar form of materialism appears in cognitive science. Hofstadter is one of the popularizers of this form of materialism, maintaining that consciousness emerges from neural networks, with self-consciousness the result of reflexive processes:

> My belief is that the explanations of 'emergent' phenomena in our brains − for instance, ideas, hopes, images, analogies, and finally consciousness and free will − are based on a kind of Strange Loop, an interaction between levels in which the top level reaches back down towards the bottom level and influences it, while at the same time being itself determined by the bottom level. In other words, a self-reinforcing 'resonance' between different levels − quite like the Henkin sentence which, by merely asserting its own provability, actually becomes provable. The self comes into being at the moment it has the power to reflect itself. . . . In order to deal with the full richness of the brain/mind system, we will have to be able to slip between levels comfortably. Moreover, we will have to admit various types of 'causality': ways in which an event at one level of description can 'cause' events at other levels to happen. (Hofstadter, 1979, p. 709)

But these emergent properties are nonetheless deemed to be ultimately explicable in terms of physical processes:

> Though no one of us will ever be able to step back far enough to see the 'big picture', we shouldn't forget that it exists. We should remember that physical law is what makes it all happen − way, way down in neural nooks and crannies which are too remote for us to reach with our high-level introspective probes. (Hofstadter, 1979, p. 710)

As a final example, the notion of consciousness without an object is considered. In this case Merrell-Wolff not only has a set of beliefs that accompany his notion of consciousness, but claims to have had experi-

---

[3]Supervenience theses are a recent form of stating a materialist position, e.g., that differences or changes in reality are not possible without physical differences or changes (Gemes, 1987).

    .   5   states of consciousness that are consistent with his
ness and beliefs about reality:[4]

> The consciousness to be sought is the state of pure subjectivity
> without an object. This consideration rendered clear to me the
> emphasis, repeatedly stated by the manuals, upon the closing out of
> the modifications of the mind. But I had never found it possible
> completely to silence thought. So it occurred to me that success
> might be attained simply by a discriminative isolation of the subjec-
> tive pole of consciousness, with the focus of consciousness placed
> upon this aspect, but otherwise leaving the mental processes free to
> continue in their spontaneous functioning – they, however, remaining
> in the periphery of the attentive consciousness. Further, I realized
> that pure subjective consciousness without an object must appear to
> the relative consciousness to have objects. Hence Recognition did
> not, of itself, imply a new experiential content in consciousness. I
> saw that genuine Recognition is simply a realization of Nothing, but
> a Nothing that is absolutely substantial and identical with the SELF.
> This was the final turn of the KEY that opened the DOOR. I found
> myself at once identical with the Voidness, Darkness, and Silence,
> but realized them as utter, though ineffable, Fullness, in the sense
> of Substantiality, Light, in the sense of Illumination, and Sound, in
> the sense of pure formless Meaning and Value. The deepening of
> consciousness that followed at once is simply inconceivable and quite
> beyond the possibility of adequate representation. To suggest the
> Value of this transcendental state of consciousness requires concepts
> of the most intensive possible connotation and the modes of expres-
> sion that indicate the most superlative value art can devise. Yet the
> result of the best effort seems a sorry sort of thing when compared
> with the immediate Actuality. (All language, as such, is defeated
> when used as an instrument of portrayal of the transcendent.)
> (Merrell-Wolff, 1973b, pp. 36 - 37; emphases in original)

The foregoing examples have illustrated both the variety of notions
of consciousness in the academic literature and the heuristically obvious
observation that *these notions of consciousness were embedded in the
beliefs about reality and purported personal experiences of their authors.*

1.2 Thesis, nature and scope of the project

As a result of these observations, the present project took on as its goal
the explication of the role of the personal in the understanding of
consciousness. The contention here is that *significant correlations exist
between conceptualizations of consciousness, beliefs about reality and*

---

[4]Footnotes that appear in the course of quotations are omitted in
this book.

purported personal experiences and that these relationships must be
adequately taken into account in discussions of consciousness. At the
most general level, for example, it was thought that those who believed
that only that which is physical is real, and that science is the only way
to gain an understanding of reality, would characterize consciousness as a
physically derived process. At the other extreme, those who would claim
to have had a mystical experience would be unwilling to conceptualize
consciousness as a physical process but to understand it in transcendent
terms. These differences of understanding, involving differences in beliefs
about reality and personal experiences, it was believed, would be bound to
influence the effort to give an account of the nature of consciousness
within the intellectual community.

If it seems apparent that one's beliefs and experiences are correlated with one's understanding of consciousness, then what is the purpose
of carrying out a study such as this? There are a number of answers to
this question. First, what seems, not always is. The very problem itself,
that discussions concerning consciousness often involve firmly held,
fantastic statements, suggests that one cannot be too careful about
making assertions in this field of endeavor. Secondly, it is not just the
purpose here, to seek evidence for the thesis, but to further clarify and
provide insight into the nature of the relationships in question, to bring
the issue into sharper focus, so that its configuration can be seen. Lastly,
and perhaps most importantly, this study can serve a pedagogical purpose,
by informing intellectuals of views of consciousness other than their own,
and by demonstrating the relationship of their views to their personal
beliefs and purported experiences. As such, it could help to organize the
study of consciousness to bring about a more fruitful interchange between
various factions.

This last point is an important one because it addresses the potential significance of this study. In the academic literature, discourses
concerning consciousness are carried out in a manner disconnected from
the author's personal life. One's personal beliefs and experiences are supposed to remain personal and not play a role in such discussions. The
academic and the personal are to be played out within separate spheres
of activity.

This disjunction of the academic and the personal may work well for
the physical sciences: it does not matter whether or not one believes in
life after death if one is interested in the trajectory of a nuclear missile
or the operation of the sodium-potassium pump. However, as soon as the
content area of one's beliefs intersects the content area of one's research, as is the case for the study of consciousness, it seems clear that
one will inescapably influence the other.

This contention is illustrated in the following comments by
Szentagothai and Sperry. Szentagothai has insisted that the personal and

academic remain separated.

> I am simply a humble neurobiologist who wants to understand how the nervous system operates. In doing so I feel committed to stay within the strictest rules of natural science, though admitting that these are in continuous change and development. I have indicated my personal stand in the ultimate questions of existence, but this is beyond scientific reasoning. (Szentagothai, 1984, p. 2)

On the other hand, Sperry, in addressing the separation of scientific from religious matters, has said:

> I personally find this kind of thinking leaves much to be desired. If two systems of belief concerning such vital things as the nature and origins of humankind, life, the universe, and the kinds of forces in control are perceived to stand in direct contradiction to each other and to be indeed 'mutually exclusive,' then certainly something must be seriously wrong! (Sperry, 1986, p. 415)

Materialist and religious views, as they stand, are not compatible, no matter how much one may wish to keep peace in the academic family.

These statements concerning incompatibility draw attention to the volatility of the subject area. This project itself has come under criticism from a number of directions. There are those who have apoplectically insisted that this is "behaviorist research" and that consciousness can never be understood using behavioral methods. Others have intimated that this study is unscientific because it includes the examination of non-materialistic beliefs about reality. There are also those who have insisted that the entire study is misguided and that something else should have been done instead. In each case, different notions of consciousness and beliefs about reality have been involved that have come in conflict with one another and with the direction of this research.

The purpose of this research is not to jump into the fray, but to examine it using the standard methods of investigation in theoretical and social psychology. In particular, no effort is made to advocate one version of reality over another. That is simply irrelevant to this work. It is true that this research is carried out entirely within the traditional scientific framework and that thereby, it, itself, implicitly represents a scientific world-view. For this research project, the standard methods of research used in the behavioral sciences are appropriate.

No one has carried out a project such as this. While there are many who have tackled the problems that consciousness presents, only Natsoulas (1978a, 1983a, 1986-87) has extensively addressed the ways in which consciousness is conceptualized. More specifically, with regard to the empirical aspect of this work, although there has been increasing nomothetic work carried out regarding beliefs about reality (e.g., Krasner & Houts, 1984; Unger, Draper & Pendergrass, 1986), no one has attempted to carry out an empirical investigation of the relationship between notions of consciousness and beliefs about reality.[5] Thus, this work is not only original in content, but is also original in that it seeks to open up a new way of looking at studies in consciousness.

Finally, it is necessary to discuss briefly, some of the terminology in this book. A number of key phrases have been used without comment, e.g., "notion of consciousness", "beliefs about reality", and "the personal". Each of these will be addressed in turn.

There is as yet no literature in academic psychology that adequately deals with abstract concepts, understanding, beliefs and the like. Indeed, the problems with these notions are not unrelated to those of consciousness, and they suffer from the same confusion that surrounds the notion of consciousness. As a result, in this book these words will have meanings that the words usually have in the metalanguage of psychology. The term "notion", specifically, is used to refer not only to concepts, but to some of the implied properties or characteristics of that which is conceptualized, and in that sense already links concepts to beliefs. The term "consciousness" is similarly used in a loose way until Chapter 3 when the possible referents of the term are sorted out and a working definition becomes possible.

Another way of clarifying what is meant by the "notion of consciousness", and of putting the current work into perspective, is to consider the following distinctions that must be kept in mind when discussing the understanding of consciousness. One approach would be to look at the use of the term "consciousness". This is touched on in Chapter 3 which is concerned with the phenomena and concepts to which the term is referring. A second area of endeavor would be concerned with the ways in which consciousness is conceived, or the ways in which it is understood. This is the interest and concern of this project. Finally, one could ask questions about the nature of consciousness directly, given that one has verbally and conceptually isolated what one means by consciousness. While it is not the purpose of this work to clarify questions concerning the nature of consciousness, some discussion of the possible nature of consciousness is necessary in order to talk about the ways in which it is conceptualized. In essence, these distinctions may not amount to much, but hopefully they will help to clarify the scope of this project.

Which are the "beliefs about reality" that are to be potentially correlated with notions of consciousness? The following passage not only

---

[5]Sternberg (1979) has carried out a study similar to this one for the concept of God.

reinforces the relevance of such beliefs but also indicates the kinds of beliefs that may be important:

> From the standpoint of the brain's cognitive processing, one can hardly overrate the central control power of the belief system as a shaper of both individual and social behavior. What we believe determines what we value, what we choose, and how we act. . . . The beliefs that count most are not those about ordinary day-to-day concerns and basic subsistence but, rather, the higher religious, philosophic, and ideologic beliefs; the kind people live and die for, beliefs that concern life's purpose and meaning, beliefs about God, the human psyche, and its role in the cosmic scheme. Such beliefs determine a society's judgement of how things ought to be in the world, the cultural sense of value, of moral right and wrong and social justice. The force of belief in thousands of millions of minds, determining how people think, what they value and decide, shapes the course of history and is in no small part responsible for the current precarious state of the human condition. (Sperry, 1986, p. 414)

It is evident from the discussion thus far, that one of the critical dimensions of belief is that of materialism versus transcendentalism. Related to this are beliefs regarding the status and efficacy of the mind. Epistemological beliefs would also appear to be relevant, e.g., is science the only way to gain knowledge of reality, or are other means possible? Finally, extraordinary beliefs, such as religious beliefs or belief in parapsychological phenomena, the importance of the issue of meaning for one's life, and attitudes towards life and death, may be important.

The term "the personal" is used to refer to that which reflects on the individual. This includes beliefs about reality that a person may hold, as well as claims to unusual or mystical experiences. The personal also subsumes demographic data, such as age, sex, educational background, profession and religious' or spiritual orientation. While there may be other aspects of a person that are correlated with their notions of consciousness, only the above aspects of the personal are considered in this investigation.

In addition to these key phrases, this project is referred to as being both theoretical and empirical in nature. The term theoretical refers to the metatheory within which all discussions in psychology take place and is not meant to designate any specialized activity other than that.[6]

---

[6]In particular, it is not the purpose of this project to carefully reconstruct the convoluted arguments that have been presented in the history of the philosophy of mind. Where some of that material is important for this study it has been presented in summary fashion.

In some sense, the theoretical material of Chapters 1 through 4 can be considered a lengthy introduction to the empirical work, necessitated by the abstract nature of the subject matter of this project, even though Chapters 2 to 4 stand on their own merit as discussions of particular issues concerning consciousness. The term empirical, in the context of the methodology of this research, has its usual meaning. Since every empirical study does involve both a theoretical and empirical component, this study, involving both, is no different in kind from other studies in psychology, but different by virtue of the additional attention given to the theoretical aspect. This balance can be seen from the next section, which describes in more detail the organization of this book.

1.3 Outline

The course of this book follows a natural movement through Chapters 1 to 4 culminating in the empirical study in Chapter 5 and discussion of the implications of the results of this project in Chapter 6. The following section provides a brief outline and justification for the order of this work.

It has been noted in Section 1, that there is confusion in the academic literature concerning consciousness. Chapter 2 discusses the problem of consciousness. Why is it that the subject matter of consciousness poses such difficulties for the modern investigator? An answer is proposed in Section 1, that this problem stems from the apparent subjectivity and subjective immediacy of consciousness. Because science has traditionally been concerned with that which is objective and publicly observable, the applicability of science to the study of consciousness has been called into question, contributing to the confusion in this area of study. Section 2 considers some of the features of science that bear on the investigation of consciousness as well as some of the suggestions that have been made of ways in which the scientific enterprise could be modified to accommodate the phenomenon of consciousness. These issues of subjectivity and methodology which create problems in the understanding of consciousness appear to be related to personal aspects of the authors who discuss consciousness. In Section 3, the literature in which this is suggested is reviewed.

At this point in the book it becomes clear that an empirical examination of the role of the personal in the understanding of consciousness would be useful and consistent with the current trend in psychology to study empirically the academic research endeavor itself. Before proceeding however, it is necessary to clarify the different uses of the term consciousness and to catalogue the notions of consciousness that are to be found in the literature. This is the purpose of Chapters 3 and 4.

In Chapter 3, the question of the referent of the term consciousness is addressed. What are the phenomena that one seeks to designate when one uses the term consciousness? A metanalysis is carried out which examines the work of those who have sought to define the term consciousness. Five possibly separate meanings of the term are isolated. It is suggested that *consciousness$_1$* refer to the characteristic of an organism in a running state which entails the registration and processing of and acting upon information; *behavioral consciousness$_2$* refer to the explicit knowledge of one's situation, mental states or actions, as demonstrated by one's behavior; and *subjective consciousness$_2$* refer to subjective awareness as characterized by intentionality. The sense of existence of the subject of mental acts, at the root of the problem of subjectivity, is to be the referent of *consciousness$_3$*. Finally, the original Latin *conscientia* is to be retained to mean shared knowledge, or participation in a shared plan. It is through the use of such categories that the various meanings of the term consciousness are clarified.

In Chapter 4, some of the notions of consciousness are more closely examined. The development of James's understanding of consciousness, characterized by his explanations of mental events in terms of human physiology, is discussed in Section 1. Section 2 is concerned with the relationship between the physicality of the world and consciousness. Some attention is paid to the eliminative materialist position as well as to the search for the physiological substrates of consciousness. The notion of consciousness entertained by cognitive science is the subject of Section 3: the Turing test, Dennett's arguments for a computational theory of consciousness and Searle's "Chinese room" are discussed. Section 4 is concerned with phenomenalist versions of consciousness. These include the phenomenological tradition, whereby conscious mental acts are deemed to be characterized by intentionality, and humanistic and transpersonal versions of consciousness in which self-transformation is purported to be a means of gaining access to transcendent states of consciousness. In Section 5, the contention that there has been a "consciousness revolution" is introduced, as are other contexts, issues and perspectives concerning consciousness that have not been mentioned in the previous parts of this chapter.

Chapters 2 to 4, by introducing the problem of consciousness, clarifying the different definitions of consciousness, and introducing the variety of notions of consciousness, clear the way for the empirical study of Chapter 5. This begins with a summary of the literature directly relevant to the investigation. Section 2 describes the development of the survey instrument and its implementation in an empirical study. The results of this research are given in Sections 3 and 4.

Section 1 of Chapter 6 introduces the discussion of the thesis of the book by briefly reviewing essential material from earlier chapters. How the role of the personal in the understanding of consciousness has tacitly been recognized, and how this book facilitates this process, is presented in Section 2. Section 3 offers proposals for further research.

CHAPTER 2

THE PROBLEM OF CONSCIOUSNESS

Where There's Smoke, There's Smoke (Wheeler, 1981, p. 101)

What exactly is the problem? Why is there so much difficulty involved in the study and understanding of consciousness? One does not have to look far to find the problem of consciousness.[7] According to the customary understanding of the nature of science, only that which is publicly observable, and hence materially present to the human senses, is accepted as scientific data. On the basis of such an account, mental phenomena are reducible to, or explained by, observable physical proper-ties and correlates of the brain, with little or no room left for an individual's world of subjective experience which cannot, by its very nature, so it is alleged, be examined objectively. Personal experience appears to attest to the existence of one's consciousness. However, it would seem that this experience cannot be witnessed by another as it can by oneself. The problem of consciousness arises from the conflict between the strict methodological demands of conventional science as to what is and what is not observable "scientifically" and the "subjective" nature of one's own conscious experiences. Toulmin has made this point clearly:

> The contrast between, on the one hand, the seemingly *inward* character typical of so many of the relevant phenomena and, on the other hand, the *public* criteria for judging the correctness or incorrectness of their descriptions, has exposed us to a recurrent tension between the supposedly private, inward character of personal thought, experience, mental life, or consciousness and the public, interpersonal language in which thought, experience, and so forth have to be described. (Toulmin, 1982, p. 53; emphasis in original)

Given this subjective nature of conscious experiences, any putative scientific account of them would seem to require less restrictive methodo-

---

[7]It should be noted that to speak of *the* problem of consciousness is somewhat misleading. That which is described here is considered to be the essential problem of consciousness by the author. For an explicit discus-sion of other problems of consciousness, one can refer to Natsoulas (1981).

logical rules as to what is and is not scientifically observable.

The sense in which consciousness is characterized by a subjective aspect and the difficulty that that entails are discussed in the first section of this chapter. In the second section, the nature of conventional science and its limitations for the investigation of consciousness are discussed first, followed by an examination of proposed alternative methodologies. The latter part of this second section includes a discussion of introspection. The third section is devoted to an exposition of reasons for considering the contention that beliefs about reality are correlated with different notions of consciousness.

It is important to note that it is not a matter here of developing a philosophical argument, but of clarifying the apparent discrepancy between the subjective nature of experience and the objective methods of science by recounting some of the relevant information found in the literature. As such, this chapter takes the form of a mosaic rather than a flow of thought.

2.1 The subjective nature of consciousness

The purpose of this section is to elucidate the seemingly subjective nature of consciousness in an effort to more clearly define the problem of consciousness. This effort will include further discussion concerning the discrepancy between the subjective and objective as well as some of the strategies that have been used in order to try to resolve the discrepancy.

To illustrate the issue of the subjective aspect of consciousness, suppose that one were to succeed in building a machine that would appear to be like a human being and act like a human being in every way, so that it would be behaviorally indistinguishable from a human being. Would something still be missing? Would the machine necessarily be conscious? Let the term "zombie" denote a machine, extra-terrestrial or other organism that differs from a normal human being only in that "consciousness" is missing.[8] Would such a machine, behaviorally indistinguishable from a human being, have a sense of its own existence? Or would such a machine be a zombie?

This question helps to bring into focus the immediate sense of existence that seems to be privately present to normal human beings. This experience of a sense of existence, is not better expressed than by a philosopher cited by James:

---

[8]This "zombie" terminology is that used by Dennett (1982).

Consciousness is inexplicable and hardly describable, yet all conscious experiences have this in common that what we call their content has this peculiar reference to a center for which 'self' is the name, in virtue of which reference alone the content is subjectively given, or appears. . . . While in this way consciousness, or reference to a self, is the only thing which distinguishes a conscious content from any sort of being that might be there with no one conscious of it, yet this only ground of the distinction defies all closer explanations. The existence of consciousness, although it is the fundamental fact of psychology, can indeed be laid down as certain, can be brought out by analysis, but can neither be defined nor deduced from anything but itself. (Natorp, quoted in James, 1904a, p. 479)

Merrell-Wolff, describing the results of experiences in altered states of consciousness, has had this to say:

The inner core of the 'I', like Nirvana, is not an objective existence but is, rather, the 'thread' upon which the objective material of consciousness is strung. Relative consciousness deals with the objective material but never finds the 'thread' as an object. Yet it is that 'thread' that renders all else possible. In fact, it is the most immediate and ever-present reality of all. (Merrell-Wolff, 1973b, p. 31)

One does not have to cite passages from the history of psychology or from the literature concerning altered states, to find descriptions of the sense of self that is at issue here. Helminiak, with reference to ordinary waking consciousness, has this sense of existence of the self in mind, with his definition of consciousness$_4$:

Consciousness$_3$ is the subject's awareness of *an object*. Consciousness$_4$, the condition and concomitant of awareness of any object, is the subject's awareness of self *as subject*. Again, awareness of an object is a reflexive function. It sets the subject over and against something else, an object. . . . On the other hand, the subject's awareness of self as subject is not reflexive. It does not set the subject over and against anything, not even self, but constitutes the subject as immediately present to him- [*sic*] or herself. This is consciousness as 'conscious' . . . that is, consciousness as aware – aware, namely, of itself; it is awareness of awareness. That of which it is aware is obviously not an object but is awareness itself, subjectivity itself. It is the subject's awareness of him- [*sic*] or herself precisely as subject. It is non-reflexive consciousness. (Helminiak, 1984, p. 214; emphasis in original)

Thus, this "subjective sense of existence" has been introduced here as a private characteristic of consciousness.

There are a few points that should be made about this "subjective sense of existence". To begin with, one has to be careful to make the distinction between the experience of the subjective sense of existence and its verbal assertion. A human being, machine, or zombie can lie and claim to have a subjective sense of existence when in fact, they do not.

A second point concerns the status of this subjective sense of existence. The fact that one has ongoing subjective experience may appear to be self-validating for some persons who might be inclined to regard it as an "empirical fact in good standing" rather than as a "theorist's fiction" in the terminology of Dennett (1986, p. 20). For Dennett, subjective events have the same status as the fictional characters of a novel and hence do not require any consideration or explanation as real facts (Dennett, 1982, 1986). Similarly, in contemporary cognitive science, it is generally accepted that there is no continuous subjective self (Lycan, 1986), allusions to such a self being considered matters of failed reference (Natsoulas, 1983b).

This entire discussion brings to light an old problem that keeps resurfacing. From a materialist perspective, reality is material and subjective events must necessarily be explained in objective terms. From a subjectivist point of view, experience is the only existent and material reality is a way of organizing and conceptualizing certain experiences. The dilemma created by the incompatibility of these two poles pervades much of contemporary philosophical thought (Dancy, 1988; Nagel, 1986).

There is a variety of ways of dealing with this problem. For example, Rorty has claimed that the "'purportedly metaphysical "problem of consciousness"'" is really only 'the epistemological "problem of privileged access"'" and since privileged access is just a language game, it cannot give rise to an ontological gap between supposed events of consciousness and "purely physical events of the central nervous system" (Levison, 1987, p. 381).

An alternative is to try to characterise private experience in public terms. But how does one carry out this project purely in the public domain without reference to subjective events? For example, in trying to simulate consciousness on a computer, Mandler (1985) has remarked that one must know what it is that one is trying to simulate. Similarly, in trying to find syntactic criteria for statements about mental events, one revises such criteria on the basis of an *a priori* notion of what it is that one is characterising (Marras, 1972). Thus, it has been argued that the very effort to simulate or objectify mental events lends credence to their existence and to the fact that there is some understanding of their subjective nature.

What evidence is there that one would be successful in disregarding the subjective aspects of consciousness and of successfully characterising them in objective terms? Ironically, empiricism falls on both ends of the objective-subjective spectrum. On the one hand, in practice, one assumes that an objective world exists that can be observed by independent observers; on the other hand, one could argue that, in theory, observation is the experience of certain events and hence within the subjective domain (e.g., Pribram, 1982). How one understands empiricism itself appears to depend upon other variables, so that it does not seem likely that a homogeneous version of empiricism could be found to decide this question. Thus, the answer one adopts becomes an "overbelief", in the terminology of Barrett (1978), a metaphysical position that cannot be determined by empirical means.

Another way out would be to look for some kind of "neutral monism" that could accommodate both objective and subjective positions (Armstrong, 1987; Kurtzman, 1987; Pribram, 1986). Neutral monism has been characterized as a doctrine according to which "mind and matter are simply different ways of organizing and marking off overlapping bundles of the same constituents" (Armstrong, 1987, p. 491). Kurtzman (1987) has pointed out that this was the position of psychophysical parallelism held by Wundt. In other words, psychophysical parallelism does not involve separate mental and physical domains of existence, which run in perfect synchrony, but a single existent, experience, which can be interpreted as material or mental. The problem with this approach is revealed when one considers what must occur at the time of physical death. Does experience cease or continue? Either answer to that question means that neutrality has been lost.

To make matters more difficult, Jackendoff (1987) has maintained that there is not one ontological gap, but two. There is a gap between the neurophysiological and computational levels and again between the computational and experiential levels. In other words, it is not clear what the neurophysiological processes are which allow for the computational domain postulated in cognitive science, nor is it clear how computation can result in lived personal experience.

Finally, the supposed existence of private, subjective events has led to the problem of the existence of other minds. Whether or not one purports to experience the subjective sense of existence, one cannot know that others are not zombies.[9] This is not the same as saying that it does

---

[9]There are suggestions that it is possible to know directly that others are conscious. Marcel (1976), for example, has introduced the notion of mystery to characterize an authentic mode of existence whereby the distinction between within and without disappears. Assagioli (1965) has discussed the notion of communion whereby a breakdown of the boundaries between two personalities becomes possible. One can also consider experiences from altered states of consciousness such as those

not matter whether or not others are zombies, but that one must deal with the problem of privileged access if only to show that it is a pseudo-problem.

The fact that one cannot normally know that another is conscious in the same manner as oneself, can be extended to another's subjective experience more generally. This is a simple point, but one which has serious consequences. Philosophers and psychologists alike have labored under the assumption that other's experiences are like their own and have used their own experience as a criterion for making pronouncements about the nature of the mind, without explicitly acknowledging that those pronouncements are based on the database of their own experience, and, as such, are constrained by what they have experienced. Thus, for example, Natsoulas (1983a) following the tradition in phenomenology, has maintained that consciousness is always consciousness of or about something. Merrell-Wolff (1973a; 1973b), because of what he has claimed to have experienced, would disagree, and would maintain that it is possible to isolate the subjective element of consciousness so that consciousness without an object becomes possible. One's contentions about the nature of consciousness appear to be relative to one's experience.

The privacy of experience poses a problem for the application of the scientific method to the study of consciousness. In 1801, Whitney demonstrated to the United States government the manufacture of firearms with interchangeable parts made possible by the introduction of the notion of tolerance (Green, 1956). This interchangeability of machined parts is an analogue of the interchangeability of observers in science. The necessity for tolerance translates into the necessity for each scientific observer to be committed to a Procruste's bed which strips her of her uniqueness. The result of this process is the production of a scientific community within which, at least in principle, one observer can be replaced by another without jeopardizing the stability of the body of knowledge that gets generated. This assumption of interchangeability gets tacitly carried over into descriptions of consciousness, even though such an assumption is unwarranted. The supposition that another's experience is the same as one's own is aggravated by the fact that consciousness itself may be part of the individual's uniqueness that is lost in the process of accepting an individual as part of the scientific community. In terms of the analogy from mechanical engineering, personal differences with regard to consciousness get lost in the tolerance.

Thus, while one may, rightly or wrongly, be certain for oneself that one has a sense of existence, the problem of the existence of other minds implies that one cannot carry over assumptions based on one's own

---

induced by some forms of meditation in which direct identification of the object of meditation is deemed to be possible (Baker, 1975).

experience to others whose experience may differ in significant ways. This feature of apparent subjectivity, which causes problems for the scientific investigation of consciousness, will be seen to be a pervasive theme in the discussion concerning methodological issues in the next section.

2.2 Methodological considerations in the study of consciousness

In Section 1 the problem of consciousness was identified as a difficulty in reconciling the apparently subjective nature of consciousness with the objective methods of conventional science. Section 2 first examines the nature of science and the study of consciousness and, second, discusses alternatives to a conventionally conceptualized science that have been advocated for the study of consciousness. The purpose here is not to make evaluative statements about the methodology to be used in the study of consciousness but to display some of the points of view that have been held in that regard.

2.2.1 Science and the study of consciousness

The discussion in this subsection touches on a number of issues. The fact that science imposes restrictions on the understanding of consciousness is mentioned initially. It is further suggested that the actual practice of science is a distortion of its ideal practice. Science is not, in fact, a homogeneous enterprise, and three aspects of science are introduced as a means of organizing the consideration of the practice of science. A little bit of the history of the interface between science and psychology is given before discussing more generally the role of beliefs about reality in shaping science. The subsection concludes by considering one sense in which science is personal in nature.

It is worthwhile to start this discussion with some of the statements of researchers who have systematically studied consciousness and found the scientific world-view wanting in the study of consciousness. For example, Harman has asked the question: "Why throughout the development of science hasn't there been more emphasis on research in human consciousness?" (Harman, 1981b, p. 1) He has suggested a number of reasons for this. First, he has pointed to the methodological problems that consciousness poses. Second, he has remarked that there are fashions in science, with the possibility of ridicule and hostility being directed to those who explore the unfashionable. Third, he has suggested that scientists may be ambivalent about gaining knowledge in this area, demonstrating an approach-avoidance conflict with respect to self-understanding. More recently Harman has said: "Spreading *accelerando* over the past quarter century has been the realization that somehow science seems to miss important aspects of human experience" (Harman, 1987b, p. 23) and that an "extended science" is necessary which would encompass and investigate a wider spectrum of personal experience.

Advocates of cognitive science themselves have expressed concerns about the contemporary study of consciousness. Dennett has said that "any proper scientific account of the phenomenon of consciousness must inevitably take this somewhat doctrinaire step of demanding that the phenomenon be viewed as objectively accessible, but one may still wonder if, once the step is taken, the truly mysterious phenomenon will be left behind" (Dennett, 1987, p. 162). Johnson-Laird has criticized more specifically the methodology used in cognitive psychology, "I believe that we are not going to understand the mind if cognitive psychologists simply go on doing experiments and building theories that consist of little boxes with arrows between them" (quoted by Groeger, 1987, p. 296).

Pelletier has made the claim that science, as it is practiced, does not correspond to the authentic endeavor of science. "There's a wholesale preoccupation with only those things that can be seen or touched, defined or measured, in a very limited version of science that's not really the scientific method – it's really a scientific dogma" (Pelletier, 1985a, p. 3).

Sperry, has been concerned about the deeper implications of science:

> For me, as a scientist, the great crisis of contemporary belief is that science, so demonstrably successful and in touch with reality in most respects, increasingly teaches that we and our world are but the product of a passing fluke of physics, ultimately lacking in purpose or meaning. Science seems further to insist that the whole of our conscious existence is merely an accessory, impotent, and superfluous attribute, aspect, or epiphenomenal correlate of brain physiology, arising out of and ending in oblivion. (Sperry, 1986, p. 415)

The tendency of many of those who support a scientific world-view is to say that mental activity and, along with it, consciousness, can be fully accounted for in material terms using the conventional methods of science. This appears to constrain the notion of consciousness in the manner in which Sperry has indicated. Tart (1985) has argued that such adherence to materialism for the explanation of human nature, although possibly correct, leads to such a dismal outlook on life that most scientists themselves are not willing to accept it.

Science, however, should not be construed as a homogeneous enterprise. Perhaps the following tripartite scheme can prove to be useful in understanding the heterogeneity of science. First of all, what is the essence of science? Science is ultimately concerned with correctly understanding the nature of reality rather than being satisfied with holding opinions or merely speculating about it. In other words, it has to be decided what is to be meant by knowledge and what constitutes an adequate explanation of a phenomenon. Second, science involves the problem of methodology. Given that one seeks knowledge, how is that knowledge to be acquired? What methods are to be considered valid for substantiating contentions about the nature of reality? Third, science comes with a world-view, with a framework of beliefs about reality, within which science itself functions. Part of the reason for the heterogeneity of science results from the interdependent decisions that have to be made at each of these three levels as to what constitutes science.

For example, with regard to the first aspect of science, in the behavioral sciences is one to be satisfied having found information about the contingency of two events or does one wish to know the reason for the contingency, perhaps by explicating the mechanisms involved? With regard to the second, is one, for example, willing to accept the procedures that have been traditionally used as the means for acquiring knowledge in a specific subject area, or does one think that other methods are applicable? An historical example illustrates the importance of decisions made regarding the world-view of science: an eighteenth century committee decided that meteorites did not exist because "there are no stones in the sky to fall" (quoted in Harman, 1987b, p. 25).

These three aspects of science appear to be hierarchically arranged in order of resistance to change. Thus, the purpose of science, which is to question speculations, takes precedence over the specific methods used, which themselves are more important than the world-view one adopts. To illustrate this, the eighteenth century world-view of science that there were no stones in the sky presumably had to give way after careful observations were made of those stones. A number of those who seek to understand consciousness, claim that the methodology of the behavioral sciences does not adequately allow them to seek knowledge concerning subjective experiences. These investigators have been unwilling to presuppose that consciousness is a byproduct of neural activity and have sought to modify investigative procedures so that that speculation could be tested. Some of these proposed modifications of science are discussed in the next subsection. The point here is that the essence of science appears to lie in the replacement of opinion with knowledge and that this is more important than loyalty to specific investigative procedures.

Despite the foregoing heuristic, science is not simple in nature. However, this does not pose a problem for most scientists who have their own working sense of what science is about. They know the research methods that are applicable to their area of expertise and they have, usually, an unexamined world-view within which they function. By and large, they would have neither the time, nor the interest, to engage in serious philosophical discussions about the nature of science.[10] As Hillner

---

[10]Such is the case, for example, in the queen of sciences, mathematics. Most mathematicians remain oblivious of the issues in mathematical foundations. The joke is, that mathematicians are Platonists on

has remarked, "Most practicing scientists do not let the philosophy of science get in the way and conduct their activities according to their own implicit criteria" (1985, p. 323). It is important to note, then, that there may be differences between the way science is ideally conceptualized in the philosophy of science, and the way in which it is understood in practice. In particular, the thread between the philosophy of science and psychology has been tenuous and, historically, this has had a serious impact on the study and understanding of consciousness. It may be worthwhile to consider briefly the origins of the relationship between science and psychology.

The advances in science and technology of the industrial revolution of the eighteenth century resulted in a wave of optimism that characterized the cultural climate of that time. These advances in material well-being were translated into a philosophical program, that of positivism, which became a powerful influence in the western world in the last half of the nineteenth century and early part of the twentieth. According to the original formulations of positivism, the scientific method was the only valid means of investigation and facts the only possible objects of knowledge. Positivism denied the existence or intelligibility of anything other than facts or laws ascertained by science. Philosophy itself was constrained by the methods of science and the application of these principles to human affairs, including ethics, politics and religion (Abbagnano, 1967).

Clearly, the strength of this philosophical position rested on the notion of "facts". For the empiricocritical branch of positivism which developed before the turn of the century, facts were understood to be stable aggregations of sensations. These sensations were constituents of both physical bodies and mental events and, as such, were neutral, neither physical not psychical (Abbagnano, 1967).

The attempt to found our knowledge in a systematic way, to check its credentials thoroughly, seemed to require that we unearth some

---

weekdays and formalists on Sundays. That is to say, they go ahead blithely proving theorems as though there were real ideal entities, the mathematical constructions, to be found and manipulated. However, if they were asked to profess their faith, they would reply that, no, of course there are no such things as mathematical entities, that all they are really doing, is pushing symbols around on the blackboard in accordance with arbitrary rules. Furthermore, some of them probably believe that somewhere in the world there is a group of logicians who specialize in the foundations of mathematics who could justify everything that they are doing on a blackboard. Such a group of logicians does not exist. Today there are no satisfactory solutions to the problems in the foundations of mathematics.

ultimate foundations which would not in turn need further grounding. The notion of the 'idea' or the 'impression,' an intramental
representation of extramental reality, seemed to fill this requirement
perfectly. All our knowledge of the 'external world' must come to us
through such 'ideas,' or else this knowledge can have no rational
foundation at all. (Maybe it has no such foundation anyway, even
though based on 'ideas', as many were tempted to argue, or feared
might be the case, but the only hope of a rational foundation lay in
this kind of grounding.) (C. Taylor, 1982, p. 38)

James, one of the influential figures in the history of western
experimental psychology, rejected some of the tenets of positivism. By the
time James was 28 years of age, he was paralyzed by a sense of malaise
and repelled by positivism. At that time, he read a number of essays by
Renouvier concerning the nature of the mind, and decided to believe in
the efficacy of free will (Miller & Buckhout, 1973). James rejected that
part of the package of positivism that regarded the world as completely
determined and mechanical in nature. Thus, even though James's notion of
consciousness changed in the course of his life,[11] human mental activity
was always understood by him to be a subject that required understanding
and explanation.

The major movement in North American experimental psychology was
not to follow James's lead in that regard, but to emulate the physical
sciences as they were understood in the nineteenth century. As Watson,
conscious of generating a movement in North American psychology
(Boring, 1929), expressed it:

The key which will unlock the door of any other scientific structure
will unlock the door of psychology. The differences among the
various sciences now are only those necessitated by the division of
labor. Until psychology recognizes this and discards everything
which cannot be stated in the universal terms of science, she does
not deserve her place in the sun. (1919, p. vii)

Emphasis was placed on that which could be studied objectively, and the
study of human psychology became the study of human and animal
behavior, with an effort to discover the laws relating stimuli and responses. The search for contingencies between stimuli and responses had
a conceptual basis in the physiological notion of a reflex arc, which had,
however, already come under criticism as a strategy in psychology before
the turn of the century (Hilgard, 1987). Under such a version of science,
there was no room for consciousness, or for mental events more generally. This way of conceptualizing human nature is still to be found today.
For example, the recent model of Llinas and Pellionisz, cited in Chapter

---

[11]As discussed in Chapter 4.

1, also depicts human mental activity as a glorified reflex arc.

Although psychology has changed over the years, most noticeably by readmitting mental events back into the domain of psychology in the 1950s, it turns out that these changes in psychology were relatively independent of the rise and fall of logical positivism in the period from 1930 to 1950 (Hilgard, 1987).[12] As mentioned previously for scientists more generally, by and large, psychologists have been unaffected by theories of science. They carry on the everyday business of the enterprise of science which seems to them well-established and straightforward (Hilgard, 1987).

However, whether made explicit or not, the various versions of science that are practiced appear to depend upon a substratum of beliefs. Rather than being an artefact of poor science, such a relationship appears to be inherent in the nature of the process of acquiring knowledge itself. Maxwell, for example, has maintained that there is a continuum between foundational principles and empirical generalizations, and that "there are no statements of much scope, interest, or importance that are decidable or, even, confirmable or disconfirmable on the basis of only the data plus logic" (1976, p. 333). Osborne has pointed out that there is no neat split between facts and values:

> Any attempt to discriminate between facts and values is itself an unavoidable statement of value. Many psychologists overlook this issue by taking current paradigms as immutables which determine appropriate values for scientific conduct. Perhaps we need to increase awareness of the sociological and value-laden evolution of our paradigms and the relationship between 'facts' and values. (1981, p. 286)

It should not be surprising that science rests on beliefs about the nature of reality and beliefs about what is and is not important, for it has grown out of, and finds its roots in, common sense.

Physicists have had to give up a number of common sense notions in order to adequately account for phenomena in the physical world. For example, the assumption of determinism, whereby cause-effect relation-ships could be postulated to exist in principle, had to give way to probabilistic explanations for subatomic events. Similarly, scale modelling of processes in the small had to be given up in favor of the complemen-tarity principle. In other words, it is not correct to imagine that events at quantum levels are just like events at the people-sized level only in miniature. It does not make sense, for example, to think of an electron

---

[12]Logical positivism is a form of positivism emphasizing language and logic.

exclusively as a particle. Sometimes an electron behaves like a wave (Blanpied, 1969). In fact, some of the investigators in physical science feel that descriptions of consciousness in terms of the theory of quantum mechanics are more accurate than those of traditional psychology (e.g., Jahn & Dunne, 1986; Wolf, 1984). What is known about psychological questions, is still represented at the common-sense level of discourse (Natsoulas, 1978a) and it appears that, at least in the case of consciousness, research in psychology rests upon a common-sense understanding of reality, the underlying assumptions of which have not been explicitly formulated (White, 1982, 1986).

The tenets of science are not themselves the product of science, but rather of human culture and thought. As Brennan has remarked: "Before undertaking any psychological study, one must assume a basic belief in the specific nature of life, which is a philosophical exercise" (1985, p. 125). These basic beliefs can, in practice, be a caricature of empirical investigation. Such is the case with the position of Llinas and Pellionisz, given in the quotation of Chapter 1, a position sometimes referred to as scientism (e.g., Maslow, 1966; Pelletier, 1985b). Such a constricted view of science is seen to operate in the same manner as a religion (Osborne, 1981) and has been accused of impeding the development of understanding (Eccles, 1976b). Perhaps the defining feature of scientism is the notion that science itself must not be questioned. As Osborne has pointed out:

> The two usual preconditions in modern science for acceptance of an interpretive theory are that it be: (1) logical and self-consistent, and (2) empirically testable. An unstated third precondition is that the new theory not challenge the world-view implicit in the first two conditions. (1981, p. 288)

The purpose of science is to remove the impediments to knowledge, rather than to replace one dogmatic system with another. Yet this latter situation is sometimes the result in the practice of science, and when the scientism involves a "sticks and stones" materialism that refuses to acknowledge the possible existence of anything which cannot be readily seen or touched, it cramps the study of human consciousness.

As a corollary to the foregoing, beliefs and values which govern any version of science determine the direction that research takes. James believed in the efficacy of the mind and promoted its exploration. Watson did not believe in the mind and, not only was it not studied, but it was not mentioned in textbooks of psychology during the behaviorist reign from 1930 to 1950 (Webb, 1981). This point has been made often (e.g., Rheingold, 1982; Unger, 1983; Watson, 1967) but bears restating here because of its importance for the study of consciousness.

The preceding discussion concerning beliefs and values in science suggests that science is not as impersonal as it is sometimes thought to be. Polanyi has discussed at length the manifestly personal nature of science.

> Any account of science which does not explicitly describe it as something we believe in is essentially incomplete and a false pretense. It amounts to a claim that science is essentially different from and superior to all human beliefs that are not scientific statements – and this is untrue. (Polanyi, 1974, p. 51)

Hsu (1972) has considered the supposed differences between beliefs and knowledge and finds them both to be aspects of the personal. Beliefs are not, generally, carefree presuppositions about reality, but are, in a sense, the best judgement that can be made about it at any given time. But knowledge is of the same form, although the decision to accept a proposition about reality may be based on the results of procedures carried out to verify that proposition. Neither Polanyi nor Hsu maintained a strictly subjectivist or relativist position. They believed that there was a "universal" which was to be discovered as much as possible. But they have returned the investigator to the centre of the picture by asserting the personal nature of beliefs and knowledge and the active role of the investigator in the process of acquiring knowledge.

> We are not only claiming that knowledge is a product of our knowing activity, but also that the resultant knowledge has the irreducible impression of the personal participation of the knower. This is in a way a restating of the Kantian view that our knowledge is informed by the categories of our understanding and the forms of our sensibility. (Hsu, 1972, pp. 109 - 110)

In psychology, there has been greater awareness of these issues, and attempts have been made to study the beliefs and values of scientists. This can be done in a number of ways. One can study the psychological characteristics of scientists, one can analyze the influence of social forces on the behavior of an individual scientist, or one can study the assumptions made by individual investigators in various disciplines (Gergen, 1985). Considering the last of these, not surprisingly, it has been found that behaviorists differ from randomly selected contemporaries with regard to basic assumptions about psychology and science. In particular, behaviorists endorse factual, quantitative, empirical, objectivist approaches to psychology, while the comparison group acknowledge more humanistic and subjective approaches (Krasner & Houts, 1984). Alternatively, these two groups can be characterized by their acceptance or non-acceptance of various investigative procedures. Psychologists associated with the natural sciences believe that the most important scholarly values are scientific, that knowledge is acquired through observation, that the appropriate setting for investigation is the laboratory, that laws should be nomothetic and that one should seek to analyze the world into its constituent elements. Those who are not so identified, believe that the most important scholarly values are humanistic, that intuition is the basic source of knowledge, that field studies and case histories are the appropriate means of gathering information, that laws should be idiographic and that one should analyze the functioning of whole systems rather than breaking them up into parts (Kimble, 1984). Thus, at least within psychology, one can identify two groups which differ in terms of the values they bring to bear on the study of human nature.

Discussion of the limitations of science as a methodology for studying consciousness led in this subsection to a more careful examination of the nature of science as a heterogeneous enterprise. This heterogeneity may be due, at least in part, to the personal nature of the scientific endeavor, discussed in the last part of this subsection. The apparent context-dependent and personal nature of notions of consciousness is discussed in the next section. Before doing that, however, some of the alternative methods that have been suggested for the study of consciousness are mentioned.

2.2.2 Alternative approaches to the study of consciousness

Two streams of thought come together in this subsection. Not only does the understanding and practice of science depend, in part, on the personal, but some of the alternative approaches to the study of consciousness consider the understanding of consciousness to be a personal matter. More generally, however, the aim in this subsection is to point out some of the suggested approaches to the study of consciousness that would embrace the purportedly subjective features of experience.

Dilley (1975) and Osborne (1981) have suggested that any investigation must be adapted to the phenomenon that it seeks to study. It has also been suggested that philosophy play a greater role in the investigation of consciousness (Mandler, 1975; Robinson, 1976) and that new conceptual paradigms are needed (Csikzentmihalyi, 1978). Osborne has pointed out that a logical inquiry need not be the only manner in which consciousness can be explored, although it certainly should be employed to the extent that it proves useful in understanding consciousness. Messer (1985) has argued for increased humanistic methods in psychology.

Provision for more scope in the study of consciousness has been given by Battista (1978), who has catalogued three types of data about consciousness: phenomenological data which result from the direct experience of consciousness; psychological data which are the product of the "observation of the conditions under which particular states of consciousness occur in other individuals" (Battista, 1978, p. 62); and what Battista has called "empirical data about consciousness" (1978, p. 64), gathered by examining the physical correlates of conscious states. It would appear that Battista has been referring to data from self-report when he has been referring to "conscious states," so that from the point of view of an outside observer, his third type of data is an example of the second.

Phenomenological methods have also been advocated by Keen (1975), Pekala and Levine (1981-82), and Barrell, Aanstoos, Richards and Aarons (1987), for the study of human psychological nature. For example, Keen has maintained that a phenomenological investigation should not adhere to a rigid methodology, but must remain open and loyal to the event, "The goal of every technique is to help the phenomenon *reveal itself more completely* than it does in ordinary experience" (Keen, 1975, p. 41; emphasis in original).

Such admonitions do not sit well with those who advocate methodological behaviorism and would exclude data from subjective experiences or from processes that are not publicly observable (Armstrong, 1987). On this basis Natsoulas, for example, has said that "The very idea of a subjective science should be repudiated" (Natsoulas, 1978b, p. 269). Others have expressed the fear that encouraging more liberal methods in the study of consciousness would result in chaos:

> Opening the doors to a freer exploration of mental activities, although a virtue to those who are disciplined to scientific procedures and values, may turn into a vice for those who see the new freedom as an opportunity for free-floating uncritical fantasies about mental life. (Hilgard, 1980, p. 15)

This raises an important point. Thus far in science, the personal integrity of an investigator has not been an issue. The criterion of public observability has acted as a safeguard to protect the body of accumulated scientific knowledge from false or mistaken reports of events. Methodologies that are more sensitive to subjective events may well involve serious problems. This does not mean that they should not be introduced, just that science would become a more complicated enterprise as a result of having to consider the personal experiences and beliefs of specific investigators as part of the assessment of the validity of any specific investigation.

The paradigmatic example of a more liberal methodology is the process of introspection. Introspection literally refers to the observation of one's own mental states and was the preferred method of observation for Wundt and James, the originators of Western psychology in its scientific form. However, there has been a problem historically with introspection, which fell into disrepute because of the inconsistencies of introspective reports and the public inaccessibility of the mental events that were supposedly being observed.

It is not the purpose here to recite the history of the problem of introspection, nor to suggest a solution for it. The current position in cognitive science emphasizes the fact that people do not simply perceive their own mental events in some unproblematical way. On the other hand, there is not sufficient evidence yet that people do not have any information about their own mental states.

Lyons has given an account of the history of the problems concerning introspection in philosophy and psychology and has come to the conclusion that introspection gives one access to a personal collection of "myriad public performances, edited and 'replayed' according to largely stereotyped views about our cognitive life" (1986, p. 148). In other words, the biological organism that one is, within which there are mental processes, can access various scripts of oneself and others and distort, change, and "replay" them for oneself within one's cognitive system. This position is similar to that of Mandler (1985) who has maintained that, while introspection gives one the best available, albeit distorted, information about one's mental processes, such introspection cannot substitute for objective observation. In 1977 Nesbitt and Wilson proposed that introspective access to mental processes was not possible. Reviewing ten years of research, White (1988) has not found adequate evidence to support Nesbitt and Wilson's proposal. White has found that the term "process" itself has not been adequately defined and that the reliance on verbal reports as indicators of introspective access has resulted in a failure of the internal validity of the studies attempting to verify the proposal.

There is no question that many people have claimed to have access to their mental events, and that they have some form of subjective sense of existence as a concomitant of every mental act. For example, Helminiak has made the following statement:

> I am suggesting that there are two distinct but concomitant aspects of consciousness. Most will grant the one: by consciousness I am aware of some object. But some will ask for proof of the other: in every act of awareness of some object I am simultaneously aware of myself as the aware subject. To ask for proof is to miss the point here. My concern is not to prove that there are two aspects of consciousness. My concern is to suggest that only acknowledgement of two distinct aspects allows an adequate articulation of the phenomenon, consciousness. In other words, my beginning point is one's own experience. My goal is adequately to articulate that experience. If I were to reach my goal, others who are also conscious would be able to recognize their own experience of consciousness in my articulation of that phenomenon. If such a happy coincidence is 'proof', it is 'proof' only in this, that we recognize that a particular articulation squares with the data of experience. That is, we recognize that we have understood correctly. But I doubt that this will satisfy those asking for proof. Most likely they will object

that what I speak of is not part of their experience. They do not recognize themselves in my words. In effect, they ask that I convince them, against their own experience, that what I describe really exists. In this case, the prospect of success is bleak indeed. For either they are not aware of some dimension of their experience which is, despite their oblivion to it, nonetheless real; or they are aware of it but conceptualize it differently and so do not recognize it in my articulation; or they are aware of it but for reasons known only to them – or perhaps for reasons unknown to them, usually presuppositional choices on which rise and fall whole systems and schools of thought – they do not consider it; or my own articulation, in fact, misses the mark. Obviously I do not accept the final alternative. So, in being asked to supply proof of my position, I am being asked to supply for the others the experience or the insight which they do not have. So it is that to ask for proof misses the point here. Unlike in any other subject matter, here I cannot point out this or that or some other thing over there and so make my point. For non-reflexive consciousness is precisely not some sensibly observable object over and against which the subject stands. One cannot point it out to another such that the other could walk over and examine it and so be convinced of its reality. The sole possible source of experience of pre-reflexive consciousness lies in the experience of the experiencer him- [sic] or herself. No one can supply the desired evidence where these data are missing or overlooked. Thus, the issue is not to prove that pre-reflexive consciousness does exist. The issue is not to provide logical argument that leads to unavoidable conclusion. The issue is rather to judge whether or not the notion of pre-reflexive consciousness helps to articulate the phenomenon in question, human consciousness. At stake is further understanding and so more adequate articulation of a given phenomenon and not the demonstration of the existence of something postulated by abstract definition nor 'proof' about some out-there reality. The subject's own insight into the subject's own self as subject is at stake here. One's understanding of one's self is at stake here. The stakes are very high, indeed. (Helminiak, 1984, pp. 215 - 216)

Hillner has stated the same point more briefly, "You either know what it is to be self-aware or you do not know" (1985, p. 261).

Both Helminiak and Hillner appear to have found their subjective experiences to be convincing. The conviction itself, however, is not necessarily an indication of the correctness of the information conveyed in that experience.

Now the person, whatever a person is, is undeniably having his/her own conscious experience and is in some sense intimately associated with it in a way in which no outsider could be. But this is not to deny the possibility that there can exist incorrect 'knowledge' about conscious experience while it is going on, that incorrect beliefs and opinions can be formed about it, that things can fail to be noticed or realized about it, that incorrect inferences can be made about it, that things not consciously experienced can be reported, and that something can be reported as not being conscious when it is, or as being conscious when it is not. (White, 1982, pp. 10 - 11)

Thus far, the assumption has been that introspection functions at the same capacity in each person. That assumption may not be correct and may not be verifiable using the conventional methods of research. An alternative would be to regard it in the same light as most observational techniques, such as, for example, techniques in nuclear physics, which require a particular set of beliefs, a specific interpretive framework and half a lifetime of schooling and training in order to carry them out successfully. "Self-observation may be a highly disciplined skill which requires longer and subtler training and guided experience than any other skill we know" (Needleman, 1965, p. 98). Successful introspection may require prolonged, intensive practice: "When one spends twenty hours a day in this practice, the mind eventually settles itself and another profound rearrangement of consciousness occurs" (Brown, 1988, p. 15).

Other authors have argued that attempted observation of one's inner processes is not enough in order to fully understand one's subjective consciousness. One may need to become an active participant in a way that involves the whole person.

It soon became clear, if this search in a new direction was to be successful, I had to reach beyond anything contained within the academic circles of the West. The manuals demanded a life-practice or attitude that involved the whole man, and thus the requirements were incompatible with the attitude of a tentative *trying*, while part of the man stood back enclosed in a sort of reserve. (Merrell-Wolff, 1973b, p. 21; emphasis in original)

The importance of the experiential component has been repeatedly mentioned in the literature concerning consciousness. Walsh and Vaughan have said that "Intellectual comprehension demands an experiential foundation. Experiential knowledge is clearly a limiting factor for conceptual understanding" (1980, p. 173). This has been repeated again by Walsh (1984a) and emphasized by Tart (1985), who has maintained that what one appears to know changes between states of consciousness, and Roberts (1983), who has suggested that alterations of consciousness be used as a strategy for studying it. This last suggestion has been made also by Dane and DeGood in their review of *The handbook of states of consciousness*, "The seeming hiatus in research . . . may actually be a necessary step in developing a cadre of investigators with adequate personal experience and expertise in states of consciousness" (1987, p. 98).

If one's own experience is to serve as both the background and subject matter of one's investigations, then the words of Keen, written in another context, are relevant here:

> What is needed is not the development of research techniques but rather the development of researchers. The next step in the methodological development of phenomenological psychology should perhaps involve not concentration on how to obtain the data but rather how to train researchers to be sensitive, self-critical, truth-seeking people. (Keen, 1975, p. 58)

There is a corollary that grows out of this emphasis on personal experience. One may be able to intellectually pose the problem of consciousness for oneself. However, in order to obtain an answer to that question, one may need to undergo some form of self-transformation that involves experiences that allow one to understand the matter in question. For example, Walsh has said, "these issues are resolvable – more accurately, transcendable – by a transformation of one's state of consciousness and sense of identity such as can occur through the practice of meditation or yoga" (1988, pp. 1 – 2).

Ornstein has made the same point in the opening paragraphs of his book, *The psychology of consciousness*:

> I suppose many people who read this book have asked themselves, 'What is consciousness?' only to end up unsure of the answer and a bit confused. In my own wonderings, I began to read psychology and philosophy, hoping to find the answer there. Instead, I encountered a bewildering array of ideas, beginning with a definition of consciousness as 'awareness of awareness,' on up to facile cosmic pronouncements, and down to those who maintain that these wonderings are not meaningful. To ask 'What is consciousness?' does not appear to be unreasonable; yet the question does not seem to be fully answerable in reasonable terms. So, along with questions like 'What is God?' and 'What is life?' we generally rule out consciousness from scientific inquiry.
>
> After long searching for answers in many places, I have come to feel that these compelling questions *can* be answered, but, unfortunately, not fully within the mode of reason or intellection. There is no way to simply write down the answer, as we might give a textbook definition. The answers must come personally, experientially. (Ornstein, 1972, p. ix)

This focus on personal experience and self-transformation has suggested to some writers a distinction between knowledge, that is a matter of having information about something, and understanding, which implies that a meaningful synthesis of information has taken place that is not just experienced as more information. For example, Osborne has said,

"There is a qualitative dimension of consciousness that can transform knowledge to understanding. Such a dimension is always a personal experience" (1981, p. 278). Sloan (1980) has wanted to reverse the importance of insight and verification in science, suggesting that insight is the more important of the two.

There have also been suggestions that there are modes of understanding latent within a person that are superior to rational thought. Tart, for example, has said, "In many ASC's, one's experience is that one is obviously and lucidly experiencing truth directly, without question" (1980, p. 210).[13] However, in addition to White's caveat concerning convictions about self-evident knowledge, Mandell (1980) has argued that chronic induction of altered states of consciousness leads to a degeneration of hippocampal CA_3 cells with the result that the brain fails to recognize novel information, misinterpreting it as that which is already known, hence giving a person a sense of conviction about the nature of reality.

Whatever the case may be in that regard, for any given individual, convictions concerning subjective experiences may be comparable to convictions concerning the objective world. "In the limited confines of individualistic consciousness, the experimental datum is just as objective (or subjective) as that associated with the overt behavior of a group of organisms" (Hillner, 1985, p. 256). According to Hillner, reports concerning consciousness given by a person are applicable only to the understanding of the psychological reality of that person. Osborne (1981) has maintained that one can compare one's own experiences against the report given by others, thereby gaining further insight into one's own experiences. In either case, public observability has been replaced with a collection of solo efforts in the understanding of consciousness.

This subsection, after identifying alternative methods suggested for the study of consciousness, discussed specific suggestions for greater use of introspective and experiential techniques. These coincide with the personal aspects of the understanding and practice of science. This personal characteristic that surfaces in considerations of the methods for studying consciousness is implicated in the next section in a more general discussion concerning belief systems and their relation to notions of consciousness.

2.3 Notions of consciousness in the context of beliefs

In Section 1 of this chapter, the issue of subjectivity and the apparent gap between subjectivity and objectivity were discussed. Some of the perceived limitations of the conventional practice of science and sug-

---

[13]The acronym ASC refers to "Altered State of Consciousness."

gested alternative methodologies were discussed in Section 2. In both sections it was indicated that the understanding of subjective experience and the means used for expressing it appeared to be, at least in part, a personal matter. In this final section the issue of the personal is not discussed as such. However, earlier remarks concerning the context of beliefs within which intellectual understanding functions, are taken up again, and some of the literature is reviewed that discusses this issue both generally and more specifically with regard to the notion of consciousness.

The importance of the interpretive aspect of understanding has been emphasized by a number of authors. "Outside of any frame of reference the world has neither nature nor limits" (Gemes, 1987, p. 317). And again, "the forms and the laws in our worlds do not lie there ready-made to be discovered but are imposed by world-versions we contrive − in the sciences, the arts, perception, and everyday practice" (Goodman, 1984, p. 21). Greenman (1987) has argued that the philosophical positions that philosophers hold are dependent upon the particular authors whom they have read, which have determined the direction that their understanding has taken. Kornblith (1987) has argued that those induced to acquiesce to hold certain beliefs in Asch's experiments concerning conformity were justified in holding them, even though their beliefs were not integrated into their larger body of beliefs. Thus, it has been maintained that there is a wide scope for the interpretation of one's experience and that such interpretation may depend upon influences that one cannot fully control. Newell has discussed the consequences of this:

> Once we admit that ways of reasoning vary with the ways of the reasoners, the scope for common ground seems too narrow to escape relativism, and the admission marks the fact that there are different institutions, different practices and different styles in approaching the world. Tolerance we may have, but no claim to universality for our own ways. (1986, p. 101)

The impact that differences in beliefs can have, is perhaps best illustrated in the case of religion. As Neusner has argued, both theologues and secularists have conspired to make religion a personal matter, yet "most of the world is what it is today because of religion" (1988, p. 23).

Perhaps the most fundamental beliefs about reality are revealed by one's stance with regard to the mind-body problem − that is to say, by one's beliefs concerning the relationship between the body and the mind. According to Brennan, "The most pronounced differences in the national intellectual traditions relate to the concept of the mind. At one extreme, the mind is viewed as essentially active; at the opposite pole, the mind is a superfluous concept. In between is the position that the mind concept is needed, but its role is confined to a passive receptor of ideas and memories" (1985, pp. 127 - 128). Coan (1968), having factor analyzed psychological theories, found the first factor to be subjectivism versus objectivism. Buss (1978) has expressed the underlying assumptions in psychology in terms of the efficacy of the individual in constructing reality. In each case, there is a polarization between a materialist position that would be compatible with the traditional scientific view as discussed in Section 2 and a transcendentalist view whereby one does not believe that all of reality is the result of material processes.

The predominant presupposition about the nature of reality, at least within science, is materialism, which is taken for granted by most scientists. For example: Natsoulas

> I shall frame the discussion to follow on the assumption of the truth of physical monism, or physicalism as regards the relation of mind to body. According to this thesis, the perceiving organism, including all of its psychological attributes (e.g., its perceptual awarenesses) is nothing over and above its body, with all its physical attributes. . . .
> I may be accused, therefore, of prejudicing my conclusions; however, I find dualistic ontologies totally unconvincing, on groups additional to phenomenal objects, and prefer to spend my time trying to improve our understanding of a single, continuous reality. (Natsoulas, 1980, p. 103)

As a result of this, there is an emphasis on approaches to consciousness which favor that presupposition (Osborne, 1981) and which begrudge consciousness its "metaphysical charms" (Toulmin, 1982, p. 56). Dualists, those who believe that there is a mind, ontologically distinct from the body, are left defending their beliefs rather than giving a theoretical exposition of consciousness (Battista, 1978). These differences in perspective have led to preferred beliefs about conscious experience which cannot be resolved by argument (White, 1982). Because some of these presuppositions are mutually exclusive, they have led necessarily to notions of consciousness which are incompatible with one another (Strange, 1978). In order to arrive at an understanding of the notions of consciousness, therefore, one cannot disengage them from the context of beliefs within which they occur, particularly beliefs regarding the resolution of the mind-body problem and beliefs about the exclusivity of science as a means of generating knowledge.

In fact, knowing a specific context of beliefs, should enable one to derive the concept of consciousness that follows from it:[14]

> Given a sufficiently accurate and comprehensive description of the role of innate, cultural, sub-cultural and personal determinants of

---

[14]This assumption was used in Chapter 1 to surmise that Llinas' and Pellionisz' theory of consciousness would resemble their theory of mind.

memory for some individual, it should be possible to predict from that information alone that individual's beliefs about conscious experience. This does nothing to encourage the supposition that such beliefs are either valid or sufficient. (White, 1982, p. 23)

The purpose of this research is to determine the extent to which such relationships can be found empirically.

In Chapter 1, the volatility of the subject area was mentioned with regard to attitudes towards this work itself. More generally, the beliefs that people hold about reality appear to be held with a certain sense of commitment that involves not only the intellectual elements of a person's personality, but emotional and motivational elements as well. As a result, a certain position may be maintained as a correct position with a certain amount of emotional volatility if that position is questioned. Although in a slightly different context, Stevens has incisively illustrated this point:

Each person had *one* view, and that was the way that I was supposed to see it. When I said (experimentally) that my sickness was organic, some people got mad. When I said that it was psychosomatic, others got mad. When I said that it was both, everyone got mad. (Rogers & Stevens, 1967, p. 138; emphasis in original)

Now one could, in arguing against a position, advance an argument not against the rational basis of the position, but against the motivations of the person who holds such a position. One can charge a person with holding a given intellectual position, not because that position is incorrect, but because the person has an emotional investment in that position, and cannot, for that reason, abandon it. This kind of strategy has been called the "psychoanalytic method of argumentation" by Walter (1974). Thus, one could argue that a materialist has a vested interest in professing a materialistic position because it is politically expedient to do so within the current academic climate. Alternatively, a transcendentalist can be accused of being unable to cope with the hard facts of a finite reality and of succumbing to wishful fantasies concerning the existence of a transcendental dimension.

Belief systems, once they are held, are irrefutable, as Dilley has pointed out:

Belief-systems are sets of propositions about how reality is to be interpreted, based upon viewing the world from the angle of vision which is believed to yield the true story about the world. In the final analysis the justification of a belief-system is in terms of an appeal to the facts, but this appeal cannot be made in any simple way because 'the facts' are always interpreted by our way of experiencing them. Rules for evaluating truth claims as well are . . . themselves metaphysically predisposed.

It is in these senses that both belief-systems, religious and naturalistic, are irrefutable. Religions and naturalisms both have within themselves resources to handle any of the kinds of occurrences which anyone expects to see happen as well as all events which adherents of those systems believe have already happened. If this were not so, by the way, these belief systems [sic] would not be taken seriously by intelligent people. Those belief-systems which cannot be developed comprehensively are discarded or become the cults of small groups of devotees. (Dilley, 1975, pp. 222 – 223)

The purpose of this book is not to refute or endorse specific belief systems, but to show their relationship to notions of consciousness. Thus, it is to be seen to what extent notions of consciousness can be organized according to the beliefs of the one holding a certain notion and perhaps to find clues to those events that may have led to changes in one's beliefs. That is another way of stating the purpose of the empirical research described in this book.

The first two chapters, in addition to having provided evidence from the literature for the thesis, have also contained some of the material concerning personal beliefs and purported experiences which is used later in the development of the research instrument. Before embarking on the empirical investigation itself, two things need to be done. Thus far in the book, the term consciousness has been used without definition. The first thing that needs to be done is to seek clarification concerning the use of the term consciousness and that is done in the next chapter, Chapter 3. Second, the diversity of views concerning consciousness has been alluded to many times in the preceding pages. While it is not possible here to give a complete overview of the various versions of consciousness or to develop them in all their intricate details, the range of notions of consciousness is presented in Chapter 4 and a few of the perspectives concerning consciousness are discussed in more detail. Thus, these next two chapters bring together some of the additional material that is necessary for the development of a questionnaire concerning consciousness.

CHAPTER 3

METANALYSIS OF DEFINITIONS OF CONSCIOUSNESS

The reader will find no discussion of consciousness and no reference to such terms as sensation, perception, attention, will, image and the like. These terms are in good repute, but I have found that I can get along without them both in carrying out investigations and in presenting psychology as a system to my students. I frankly do not know what they mean, nor do I believe that anyone else can use them consistently. (Watson, 1919, p. viii)

In Chapter 1, some examples were given of the variety of ways in which consciousness is understood. Section 2 contained a discussion of the problem of consciousness arising from the apparent discrepancy between the private, subjective nature of consciousness and the public, objective methods that are used to study it. Some suggestions for expanding the enterprise of science to allow for an adequate study of consciousness were reviewed. The chapter ended by considering the importance of beliefs in determining notions of consciousness. However, through all of this, consciousness itself was not defined.

The purpose of this chapter is to focus on the referents of the term consciousness as they have appeared in the academic literature. In particular, the strategy here is to carry out a metanalysis. Thus, 29 definitions of consciousness by 11 authors are examined, 26 of which are organized into a set ordered by their apparent relationship to one another. In addition, these definitions are grouped as either phenomenological or behavioral and passive or active. It is suggested that five meanings of the term consciousness be distinguished: $consciousness_1$ is the characteristic of an organism in a running state which entails the registration and processing of, and acting upon information; $behavioral\ consciousness_2$ refers to the explicit knowledge of one's situation, mental states or actions, as demonstrated by one's behavior; $subjective\ consciousness_2$ refers to subjective awareness characterized by intentionality; $consciousness_3$ refers to the sense of existence of the subject of mental acts and $conscientia$ refers to participation in a shared plan.

In order to adequately examine the question of the referent of the term consciousness, one can turn to the study of concepts and concept formation. However, the work done in psychology in this area has been done primarily with natural concepts rather than abstract concepts (Medin

39

& Smith, 1984), so that in this case,   one is left in the metatheory of psychology. If the discussion were about stones, rather than consciousness, one could point to a stone and say, "this is an example of what I am talking about." Nonetheless, an effort will be made to indicate the phenomena that are at issue here.

A number of authors have tried to find the referent of the term consciousness, and some have looked at this work and noticed that there are a number of phenomena to which the term consciousness refers. The purpose of this chapter is to look at these analyses of the meanings of the term consciousness and to reorganize them so that they can then be used in further discussions of consciousness. It should be pointed out that, except for the inclusion of one of the distinctions made by James, the analyses of the term consciousness discussed here are all contemporary. For a metanalysis from a historical point of view one can consult Strange (1978).

Before going ahead with the task, it should be remarked that a distinction is being made here between definitions and explanations of consciousness. That is to say, a distinction is being made between the phenomena which are referred to by the term consciousness and explanations of these phenomena. In the literature, this distinction is usually not made, with consciousness often implicitly defined in terms of an explanation for it.[15] Ultimately, of course, any definition already rests upon an understanding of the world, so that it is somewhat artificial to try to extricate definitions from the theoretical context within which they arise. "Making sense of a working definition requires mastery of nearly an entire, unfamiliar, conceptual framework" (Natsoulas, 1978a, p. 908). Nonetheless, to facilitate the discussion of the understanding of consciousness and a comparison of theories about consciousness, it is worthwhile seeking to clarify the referent of the term consciousness.

3.1 Metanalysis

Historically, the term consciousness originates from the Latin *conscientia* which refers to the mutual understanding or joint knowledge of a number of agents in a shared plan (Natsoulas, 1978a; Toulmin, 1982). The meaning of the term has shifted, however, from referring to something in the public domain, to referring, often, to that which is most private and difficult to define (Toulmin, 1982). In fact, the term consciousness has become an   "umbrella term" that refers not only to private mental events, but also to a number of topics in psychology and on the fringe of psychology (Helminiak, 1984). Since the original meaning of the term consciousness has been lost, it is suggested that the original term *con-*

---

[15]For   example,   Klein's   (1984)   definition   of   consciousness   as information, mentioned in Chapter 1, Section 1 and, again, later in this chapter.

scientia be used to refer to the mutual understanding or joint knowledge of a number of agents in a shared plan. It is further suggested that the current meanings which refer to cognitive experience be catalogued into three groups as discussed below, and that frivolous uses of the term consciousness be abandoned in the academic literature.

A number of definitions of consciousness are included in Figure 3.1 organized into a partially ordered set where apparent ontological necessity is the order on the set of definitions. What is meant by that is that the condition alluded to at the tail of an arrow is necessary for the condition alluded to at the head of the arrow to be possible. It should be noted that this scheme is not meant to reflect the nature of consciousness, but is simply a heuristic for organizing the referents of the term consciousness.

A second dimension along which definitions of consciousness can be

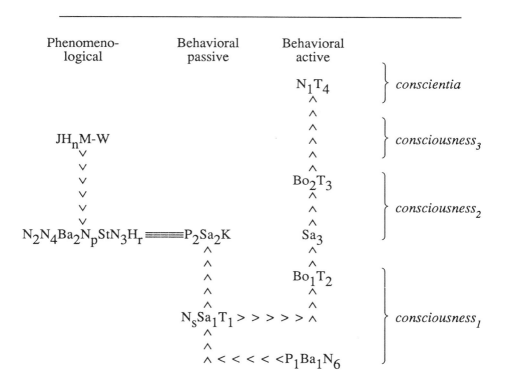

Figure 3.1 Partially ordered set of definitions of consciousness (where the order is apparent ontological necessity). A key to symbols is given in Table 3.1 on the next page.

Table 3.1

Symbols and Their Meanings, with References, for Figure 3.1

Symbol	Meaning and Reference
Ba_1	Battista's "theoretical construct" (1978)
Ba_2	Battista's "awareness of being aware" (1978)
Bo_1	Bowers' "first order consciousness" (1987)
Bo_2	Bowers' "second order consciousness" (1987)
H_r	Helminiak's "reflexive consciousness" (1984)
H_n	Helminiak's "non-reflexive consciousness" (1984)
J	James's "I" (1890/1983)
K	Klein's "consciousness as information" (1984)
M-W	Merrell-Wolff's "consciousness without an object" (1973b)
N_1	Natsoulas' "joint or mutual knowledge" (1978a)
N_2^1	Natsoulas' "internal knowledge or conviction" (1978a)
N_3^2	Natsoulas' "awareness" (1978a)
N_4^3	Natsoulas' "direct awareness" (1978a)
N_6^4	Natsoulas' "normal waking state" (1978a)
N_s^6	Natsoulas' "sensory consciousness" (1981)
N^s	Natsoulas' "perceptual consciousness" (1981)
P_1^p	Pribram's "cuddleness criterion" (1976)
P_2^1	Pribram's "self-consciousness" (1976)
Sa_1	Savage's "consciousness$_1$" (1976)
Sa_2	Savage's "consciousness$_2$" (1976)
Sa_3	Savage's "consciousness$_3$" (1976)
St	Strange's "state of being aware" (1978)
T_1	Toulmin's "sensibility" (1982)
T_2^1	Toulmin's "attentiveness" (1982)
T_3^2	Toulmin's "articulateness" (1982)
T_4^3	Toulmin's "*conscientia*" (1982)

organized is a phenomenological-behavioral dimension. Sometimes it is inferred or stated that the referent of the term consciousness is an event within one's private experience, and sometimes that it is to be described in terms of observable behavior. Often, one has to infer from the context on which side of the line a definition is meant to fall. Heated debates have taken place, not only over the issue of whether or not subjective experiences of consciousness exist and, if so, whether or not they can be explained in objective terms, but whether or not phenomenological descriptions of the referent of consciousness can be entirely replaced by behavioral ones. For example, Savage has given a definition of consciousness: "Consciousness$_3$ is consciousness of what one is doing and what one's situation is. It is self-consciousness, in the ordinary sense of that term" (Savage, 1976, p. 140), which some, such as Eccles, would understand as a phenomenon accessible, subjectively, to oneself (Eccles, 1975). Savage, however, has gone on to say, "if a dog is brought home from a long stay in the hospital, and immediately proceeds to search for familiar objects and places, then he knows what his situation is, and is conscious$_3$" (Savage, 1976, p. 141), indicating thus, that self-consciousness is not to be defined phenomenologically but behaviorally.

A third dimension along which some of the definitions of consciousness range is that of passivity versus activity. This dimension is relevant for behavioral definitions in which consciousness is used to refer to awareness[16] or the ability to make discriminations, theorize and carry out a planned course of activity. Phenomenologically, activity ascribed to the referent of consciousness implies that the capacity for volition can be ascribed to mental processes, and involves the issue of the free will of a self.

3.2 *Consciousness$_1$*

Figure 3.1 includes three groups of definitions which are termed *consciousness$_1$*, *consciousness$_2$* and *consciousness$_3$*. At the bottom of the figure is a group of definitions in which consciousness is understood simply as the functioning or range of potential cognitive functioning of organisms that are "alive." Thus, Pribram would infer consciousness where there is "growth and replication in some asymmetrical mass showing varied parts . . . [and] movement in space" (1976, p. 298), and because he would restrict the use of the term to furry animals, has called this the "cuddleness criterion" for consciousness. This use of the term consciousness further implies, usually, that the furry animal is not comatose, but is "up and about." Battista has understood the term consciousness to be used as a "theoretical construct referring to the system by which an individual becomes aware" (1978, p. 57). That is to say, consciousness is that which gives rise to awareness. The term consciousness also refers to the result of this process, namely the normal waking state, "a *general* state or condition of the person" (Natsoulas, 1978a, p. 912; emphasis in original), which is Natsoulas' *consciousness$_6$*. It may be that this sense of consciousness can be considered as a variable – something that there can be more or less of (Natsoulas, 1981). It should be noted that in these definitions, the implication is that consciousness is ascribed to sufficiently humanlike biological systems. Computers that are up and running are not usually considered conscious by virtue of that fact alone.

The next group of definitions, considered here as part of *consciousness$_1$*, is concerned with the registration of sense impressions. Thus, Natsoulas' "sensory consciousness," culled from a number of authors, refers to events such as seeing red or feeling pain without implying that

---

[16]Whereby the awareness itself may have to be revealed behaviorally.

one is aware of such sensory experiences. Similarly, "he is conscious in the sense that he sees: we may call this consciousness$_1$" (Savage, 1976, p. 138). Toulmin seems to have had the same phenomenon in mind with his first definition of consciousness as a "basic sensory responsiveness to, and awareness of, our situations" (1982, p. 57) although, in his discussion of this definition, he has talked about the loss and regaining of consciousness, bringing his definition closer to that of Pribram's cuddleness criterion and Battista's theoretical construct. Going a small step further, Bowers' "first order consciousness" consists of "noticing events and the contingencies between them" (1987, p. 95) where such noticing conditions one's behavior. Toulmin's attentiveness entails "knowing what we are doing, acting with due attention, and/or readiness to monitor some sequence of events in which we are involved" (1982, p. 57), where there need not be any awareness of such knowledge.

In summary, it is suggested that *consciousness$_1$* refer to the characteristic of an organism in a running state which entails the registration, processing and acting upon information. There is no reason why this definition needs to be restricted to furry animals, although, as Pribram has pointed out, this is the context in which the presence or absence of this characteristic is of practical importance (1976). It should be noted that the organism need not be aware of these processes.

3.3 *Consciousness$_2$*

In trying to define *consciousness$_2$* it is easy to stray from the task of looking for the referent of consciousness and instead to try to explain it in terms of *consciousness$_1$*, by saying, as MacKay does for example, that there can be cognition of cognitive processes (1966), with the implication that this exhausts all other uses of the term consciousness. Within the domain of subjective experience, this explanation translates into the phenomenon of one's being a witness to one's own acts, and hence is a referent of the term consciousness which can be, presumably, identified within experience, rather than being a theoretical construct accounting for that experience. This referent of consciousness is Natsoulas' "consciousness$_2$", the "inner witness" (1978), and his "perceptual consciousness", which is the awareness of "sensory consciousness" (Natsoulas, 1981). For Strange, "consciousness is the state of being aware" (1978, p. 27). Natsoulas, with "consciousness$_3$", "awareness", has brought in explicitly the issue of intentionality: "one's being conscious, whatever more it might mean, must include one's being aware of something" (1978a, p. 910). Helminiak (1984) has called this "reflexive consciousness" although the term "reflexive" is a misleading one because it implies a relationship of a subject to itself, rather than to an object, possibly separate from itself. A better term may be "relational consciousness" that implies an object of awareness which may be one's own awareness, "an awareness of being aware" (Battista, 1978, p. 57). Awareness of one's own awareness is Natsoulas' "consciousness$_4$", "direct awareness" (Natsoulas, 1978a).

In Figure 3.1 an equivalence is indicated between this phenomenological sense of awareness, and a passive, behavioral group of definitions. This latter group is difficult to characterize because, although the authors of these definitions would not deny subjective experience, their discussion of consciousness is given in computational, behavioral or physiological, rather than phenomenological terms. For example, Pribram has said that "subjective awareness is the reciprocal of smooth control of input-output relationships in the central nervous system" (1976, p. 306) and that "self-consciousness is a construction" (1976, p. 310). Savage has said that "consciousness$_2$ is a sort of *self*-consciousness: consciousness of the actions and perceptions of oneself" (1976, p. 138; emphasis in original), which is evidenced by the apparent monitoring of one's activities. (In substance, this referent is similar also to Toulmin's "attentiveness"). Klein has obliquely defined consciousness by saying: "As a process, consciousness constitutes a transitive relation. One is conscious *of* objects and bodily conditions" (1984, p. 174; emphasis in original) and "Equating consciousness with information dissipates the mystery associated with consciousness seen as an entity" (1984, p. 175), although he has not clarified elsewhere either of these contentions. Summarizing the thrust of these definitions, it may be said that the referent of consciousness is to be found neither within a subjective domain, nor a purely biological one, but somehow in an informational domain which lies at the interface of these two, as discussed by Pribram (1986).

Active behavioral definitions are easier to understand than those of the preceding group. Savage's consciousness$_3$ has been discussed earlier. Bowers' "second order consciousness" involves the mounting of theories and beliefs to account for behavior (1987), and Toulmin's third definition, "articulateness", focuses on the "ability to give an explicit account of the character of our actions, the point of view and perceptions in the light of which they are performed, and the intentions associated with them" (1982, p. 57). *Conscientia* is an extension of this cognizance and articulation of one's situation and planned activities.

It is suggested here that *consciousness$_2$* refer to all subjective awareness characterized by intentionality, and to the explicit knowledge of one's situation, mental states or actions evidenced behaviorally. For certain purposes, it may be necessary to distinguish between the subjective aspect of this definition and its behavioral characterizations.

3.4 *Consciousness$_3$*

The final referent of the term consciousness is the most elusive. James is credited with having made a distinction between the object of thought and the knower, which itself can never be one of the ideas that can be known (Miller and Buckhout, 1973). Although that is accurate, it should be remarked that for James, the "I" was not a self but was whatever thought was present at any given time (James, 1890/1983). In essence, this entails the "direct awareness" of Natsoulas' "consciousness$_4$". However, Natsoulas (1986) has specifically argued against a non-intentional definition of consciousness$_4$. Consciousness$_3$ is, however, what Helminiak (1984) has called "non-reflexive consciousness". It is the subjectivity inherent in any intentional mental act. It entails the sense of existence, not as information which occurs as the object of one's thought, but as knowledge of one's existence as a concomitant of one's experience. By its nature, such knowledge is self-validating. It has been claimed, furthermore, that certain processes of psychological training can result in the presence of subjective consciousness without there being an object of consciousness. This is Merrell-Wolff's "consciousness without an object" (Merrell-Wolff, 1973b). It is suggested here that consciousness$_3$ be defined as the "sense of existence of the subject of mental acts".

It should be noted that the notion of "self" is tied to this consciousness of the subject. A number of definitions, not included in Figure 3.1, allude to the self. For example, Natsoulas' "consciousness$_5$", "personal unity", refers to the fact that, for each person, consciousness manifests in a cohesive way. Disruptions of the unity of self characterize multiple personality disorder, which entails Natsoulas' "double consciousness" (Natsoulas, 1978a). It is with the introduction of the self that the issue of the free will of the self arises, and brings into question the volitional capacity of consciousness.

3.5 Conclusions

There are still definitions left over that have not been catalogued, although most of them would fit somewhere into the foregoing scheme. It has been intimated that such schemes are not necessary. For example, Battista has said that "consciousness is best utilized as a general term referring to all forms of experience or awareness" (1978, p. 57). Although this definition seems simple to use, it can lead to confusion. For example, from the point of view of consciousness$_2$, consciousness$_1$ is unconsciousness. If both were called "consciousness", discussions could proceed at cross-purposes. As another example, from an information-processing point of view, consciousness$_2$ is an extension of consciousness$_1$ and consciousness$_3$ does not exist, so the use of the term consciousness in the sense of consciousness$_3$ would be interpreted as consciousness$_2$ and again, arguments could result from confusion concerning the term consciousness. It is hoped that the present scheme can avoid some of that confusion.

This concludes an explicit discussion of the referents of the term consciousness. It is apparent, also from such a seemingly straightforward discussion of a definition of consciousness, how diverse are the positions regarding consciousness from which one selects a referent for the term. This becomes even more apparent as the discussion is widened to consider more generally the notions of consciousness that have been important in psychology, and in the western academic community more generally.

CHAPTER 4

NOTIONS OF CONSCIOUSNESS *only partly read*

The empiricist universe [is] like one of those dried human heads with which the Dyaks of Borneo deck their lodges. The skull forms a solid nucleus; but innumerable feathers, leaves, strings, beads, and loose appendices of every description float and dangle from it, and save that they terminate in it, seem to have nothing to do with one another. Even so my experiences and yours float and dangle, terminating, it is true, in a nucleus of common perception, but for the most part out of sight and irrelevant and unimaginable to one another. (James, 1904b, pp. 535 – 536)

Chapter 1 presented the disparity of views concerning consciousness. Some of the issues surrounding the subjective nature of consciousness and the implications of this for the methods used for studying consciousness were discussed in Chapter 2. In addition, the potential importance of one's personal experience and beliefs about reality were discussed with respect to the understanding of consciousness. An examination of all of this material led to a recognition of the importance of carrying out an empirical study, to seek to verify and make more precise the relationships among personal beliefs, purported experiences and notions of consciousness. Before proceeding with an empirical study, however, it was thought to be necessary to define the term consciousness and to describe in more detail the variety of ways of understanding consciousness. The referents of the term consciousness were organized in Chapter 3; the notions of consciousness are discussed in the present chapter. Thus, these two chapters contribute material necessary for the development of a survey instrument to be used in exploring the role of the personal in the understanding of notions of consciousness, as well as providing a framework for understanding the findings from the empirical study.

In this chapter, there is no effort made to give an exhaustive survey of the variety of perspectives and issues that concern consciousness, nor are any specific versions of consciousness developed in particular detail. There is greater emphasis placed on some notions of consciousness than on others, according to the following rationale. Serious discussions concerning consciousness in the academic literature usually start by considering the philosophy of James, so that it is, in a

47

sense, unavoidable that he be mentioned. Section 1 gives a short account of, and commentary on, his ideas about consciousness. Because the emphasis in this book has been on the diversity of views concerning consciousness, two extreme notions of consciousness are subsequently discussed in some detail: that of eliminative materialism which would dispense with the concept of consciousness altogether and talk only about neurophysiology, and an extreme transcendentalism that views consciousness as a primary reality to be fully understood and experienced only after prolonged, intensive spiritual training. The former position is discussed in Section 2 as it is given by Churchland and Churchland, while the latter is introduced in Section 4 as propounded by Merrell-Wolff and Walsh. One prominent version of consciousness, that lies somewhere between the previous extremes, is that of cognitive science. Dennett's discussion of consciousness is given in Section 3 as an example of this perspective. Finally, some remarks are made about the recent explosion of interest in the study of consciousness in Section 5, for example, Sperry's ideas about causality, which he says have led to a consciousness revolution.

The study of consciousness today resembles the many-feathered skull mentioned by James in the opening quotation of this chapter. The structure of this chapter is the same as that skull. The versions of consciousness discussed in greater detail are situated amidst versions of consciousness that are given in less detail, all of which arise from a general background discussion of the contexts, issues and perspectives concerning consciousness.

4.1 James's notion of consciousness

It is difficult to know what to say about James. Perhaps the best policy is to proceed in a loosely organized and unplanned manner, a criticism that has been levelled against James's work (Hilgard, 1987).

It is difficult to decide, often, what James really wanted to say. This is due, in part, to the fact that he contradicted himself frequently. For example, in one part of his book *The principles of psychology* (1890/1983), he advocated an interactionist position with regard to the mind-brain duality. A chapter later he advocated a form of psychophysical parallelism (Hilgard, 1987).[17] Similarly, his insistence on the efficacy of the will and his manifestly phenomenalist stance are contradicted by both his statement at the beginning of the *Principles* whereby he claims to adopt a positivist philosophy, and his reification of experience in terms of physiological events. The modern student of psychology has little patience

---

[17]James's psychophysical parallelism was similar to that of Wundt's.

with such contradictions[18] (Hilgard, 1987), which may be one reason why the details of James's theories have not survived him or his fame in psychology. The misrepresentation of James's work[19] and the trend on the part of many psychologists to trace the origins of their own thought back to James (Natsoulas, 1986 - 87) may be due, in large part, to the plethora of contradictory statements that James made.

How is one to understand these contradictions? Three possible explanations are considered here. First, one could argue that James did not really mean what he said – that he was speaking metaphorically. Such an argument could be levelled against the quotations given in Chapter 1 in which James reified thought as the movement of the breath and which Lyons has called "vintage James tongue-in-cheek" (1986, p. 22). This raises the problem of deciding which of James's positions are the metaphorical ones and which are legitimate. One could just as easily argue that James's denial of the existence of the soul is "vintage James tongue-in-cheek" especially since James maintained in 1910 that one had to come to terms with Fechner's "Earth-Soul" if one were to evolve (Taylor, 1981). While it could in fact be the case that some of these seemingly straightforward statements by James were meant to be metaphors, assigning some of his statements to that status without sufficient evidence that they, in fact, were such, leads one to the dangerous position of selecting from James's writing that which one finds palatable, and relegating the remainder to metaphorical status.

A second explanation could be constructed from Lyons' observation that James himself identified description and explanation as two aspects of psychology. The subject matter of psychology was obtained through the introspection of one's mental events. "On the other hand, the explanation of these events was to be found only at the physiological and neurological level" (1986, p. 8). But what does that mean? It means that James could spend pages discussing mental events and then in the end say: Oh, by the way, let me explain these complex mental processes: they are just the breath! In other words, this is not an explanation, but another contradiction in James.

---

[18]The author admits that he is one such student. This is not due to the lack of sensitivity to constructive contradictions such as those entailed in Sartre's notion of dialectical reasoning (1960). There are contradictions that can be used in the dynamics of an argument, to clarify understanding. The contradictions in James, however, do not appear to be of this nature although Rychlak (1978) has argued that they are.

[19]For example, by Hebb, who has claimed that James himself did not introspect (Natsoulas, 1986 – 87).

A third explanation, which may be closer to the truth, has been stated by Barrett (1978). He has maintained that, while James was interested in the functioning of the human being, he was only secondarily interested in the metaphysical problems that that entailed. Whether or not that was the case, James incorporated conflicting philosophical views in his writing without resolving them. This third explanation can be better understood by considering some of the influences on James's thinking.

James was sensitive to the climate of his time, in that he associated with many leading intellectuals and was familiar with the directions of thought in the academic world. In particular, he was aware of the positivist school of thought, and the work of other psychologists, especially in England and Germany. In addition, he was trained as a physician, and began his career by teaching anatomy and physiology (Hilgard, 1987).

There was a second strong influence on James, however. His father was a follower of the philosophy of Swedenborg, the prolific eighteenth century Swedish mystic. The Swedenborgian philosophy which James inherited from his father was supplemented in his adult years through his contacts with mental healers (Morrow, 1984) and practitioners of Eastern religions (E. Taylor, personal communication, 1986). It is possible then, that James struggled to reconcile the positivist and transcendentalist influences on his thought. The result was not so much a psychological account as a battleground for these two seemingly irreducible positions. It is within this probable turmoil, that James's notions of consciousness were developed.

James enjoyed his period of productivity from 1865 to 1910 (E. Taylor, personal communication, 1989). He started by looking at the volitional as well as exceptionally healthy aspects of human functioning. Then, at the time of the *Principles*, his focus was on ordinary people and normal waking consciousness. From there he moved into deviations of consciousness and its pathological manifestations. Finally, his interest left the domain of the conscious for the subconscious, religious experiences and the possibilities of concurrent alternate realities (Taylor, 1981).

In 1868, consciousness for James was associated with moral awareness and one's volitional capacity (Taylor, 1981). It has been remarked already, that, in 1870, James had written that he had chosen to accept the doctrine of free will for himself. Thus, his concern was with the active role that one could play in the betterment of one's own life. In 1874, James countered the claims of materialist interpretations of Darwin's theories in which it was maintained that "human beings were automata and that consciousness was a mere epiphenomenon in the process of natural selection" (E. Taylor, 1981, p. 41). This was not the case, according to James, because of the role that consciousness itself played in guiding the course of human culture. In 1880 he wrote about the personal consciousness of the genius and of those moments when ordinary persons have deep insights into life (Taylor, 1981).

The most popular version of James's understanding of consciousness has appeared in *The principles of psychology* (1890/1983). At that point he was concerned with normal human consciousness:

> *The first fact for us, then, as psychologists, is that thinking of some sort goes on. . . .*
> How does it go on? We notice immediately five important characters in the process, of which it shall be the duty of the present chapter to treat in a general way:
> 1) Every thought tends to be part of a personal consciousness.
> 2) Within each personal consciousness thought is always changing.
> 3) Within each personal consciousness thought is sensibly continuous.
> 4) It always appears to deal with objects independent of itself.
> 5) It is interested in some parts of these objects to the exclusion of others, and welcomes or rejects – *chooses* from among them, in a word – all the while. (James, 1890/1983, pp. 219 - 220; emphases in original)

How does one know this? One knows this by introspection, by examining one's own mental events. But, as indicated previously, introspection has had a difficult history, and some comments about it would be appropriate here.

Brentano[20] made a distinction between "inner perception" and "inner observation." Inner perception consisted of discretely noticing what was happening to mental events as they occurred, without interfering with them. Inner observation, on the other hand, involved a direct focus on mental events which led to the destruction of what it was that one was attempting to introspect. This destruction occurred because the direct focus had become a significant aspect of the ongoing thought (Lyons, 1986). Brentano advocated the former method of introspection. This was also the method that the German psychologist Wundt had used for collecting data. In order to make the approach rigorous and "scientific," Wundt constrained the situation in which a subject was to perceive inner events by controlling the external situation and the stimuli presented to the subject, often with the use of tachistoscopes or metronomes. The result was to so confine the scope of the experiments that they were simply experiments in perception and did not merit the designation of being introspective reports (Lyons, 1986).

It was James who advocated Brentano's second version of introspection, that of inner observation. But he had to present an argument

---

[20]Brentano's notion of intentional inexistence is introduced in Chapter 4.

against the positivist Comte's objection to introspection. Comte claimed that introspection was not possible because it involved a splitting of consciousness into a part that observes and a part that is observed (Lyons, 1986). James agreed that consciousness could not be split. However, he felt that introspection was in fact "retrospection" whereby one could observe the residue, or deposit, of one's stream of thought in one's memory. In this manner, one could make earlier portions of the stream of thought, that which could be known, the content of a present mental event. In this way, one has not interfered with the previous event, so that it remains, in fact, observed as it was (Lyons, 1986).

But there is a problem with this also, as Lyons has pointed out. The memory of the stream is not the stream. To resurrect it as a full-blooded entity would land one in the same difficulty that one had started from. To leave it as a lifeless memory is to strip it of its character, which is fine as far as that goes, but does not distinguish retrospection from memory more generally.

There are a few comments that can be made concerning the foregoing. First, just because Lyons can identify retrospection with memory does not, of itself, invalidate retrospection as a means of gaining information about mental events. Second, it is not clear that the method of introspection that James advocated necessarily validated James's five characters of thought. How does one know that consciousness is a stream, for example, if one has no awareness of a present, but only of a past? Third, which brings this discussion back to the point made in Chapter 2, introspection may be a personal matter that can only ultimately be understood by each person for herself.

Comte's second objection to introspection spelled the end of consciousness as an object of study in North American psychology. He maintained that introspection did not yield consistent results. This was perhaps most evident with Titchener's form of introspection, in which the external constraints of Wundt were internalized and elaborate rules devised for introspecting (Lyons, 1986). Although Titchener was an influential figure in early North American psychology, after the turn of the century, he was isolated from its main stream, which went on without him and without introspection (Boring, 1929).

This discussion concerning introspection may help to clarify the first and fourth characters of James's stream of thought. "Every thought tends to be part of a personal consciousness," said James. It is not clear what "I" ended up being. In the *Principles* he has said: "No psychology . . . can question the *existence* of personal selves" (1890/1983, p. 221; emphasis in original). Yet when James went on to discuss the self, he ended up with a "me" that was made up of an aggregate of feelings and thoughts that were to be found in the residue of past mental events. In addition, he offered the following comment:

This me is an empirical aggregate of things objectively known. The *I* which knows them cannot itself be an aggregate; neither for psychological purposes need it be considered to be an unchanging metaphysical entity like the Soul, or a principle like the pure Ego, viewed as 'out of time.' It is a *Thought*, at each moment different from that of the last moment, but *appropriative* of the latter, together with all that the latter called its own. . . .

If the passing thought be the directly verifiable existent which no school has hitherto doubted it to be, then that thought is itself the thinker, and psychology need not look beyond. (James, 1890/1983, p. 379; emphases in original)

Natsoulas has summarized the relationship that held between introspection and the self for James:

In making his case against a subject, James emphasized what is introspectively 'verifiable,' and argued one finds no unifying principle inhering in individual awarenesses, as opposed to their sensibly continuous succession and the personal appropriation of one by the next, and so on. (Natsoulas, 1986 - 87, p. 311)

Thus, for James, the self that we usually refer to is an aggregate of material in memory; there is a "thinker" but that "thinker" is just the "passing thought" itself.

There are some problems with such a development. First, given that one has knowledge only in retrospect, how would one directly verify the existence of a passing thought? Second, just because James wanted to stay with that which was present in experience, does not mean that those items were necessarily the ontologically correct building blocks. Third, is not the understanding of "thought" changed as much as "I" in the case of such identification? Thought, then, is not just thought, but is inherently constituted of self as well. In other words, the term "thought" may have subsumed more for James than it ordinarily would – enough to include some form of "I". But then, it is not at all clear what James meant by the first character, since the terms "thought" and "personal" depend on one another for definition.

The fourth character of thought in the *Principles*[21] is an interesting one, in that it was missing from James's 1892 briefer version of the *Principles*. Taylor has maintained that this was an indication of his movement towards a position James called "radical empiricism," one in which physical reality no longer necessarily existed independently of thought (Taylor, 1981). This is an extreme empiricist position, whereby all

---

[21]"It always appears to deal with objects independent of itself" (James, 1890/1983, p. 220).

that one has access to is one's own experience, certain portions of which are interpreted as an objectively existent world.

One of James's statements concerning radical empiricism also further elaborates the previous discussion concerning the self:

> My thesis is that if we start with the supposition that there is only one primal stuff or material in the world, a stuff of which everything is composed, and if we call that stuff 'pure experience,' then knowing can easily be explained as a particular sort of relation towards one another into which portions of pure experience may enter. The relation itself is a part of pure experience; one of its 'terms' becomes the subject or bearer of the knowledge, the knower, the other becomes the object known. (James, 1904a, p. 478)

Relations themselves were to be found directly in experience. As James has explained:

> To be radical, an empiricism must neither admit into its constructions any element that is not directly experienced, nor exclude from them any element that is directly experienced. For such a philosophy, *the relations that connect experiences must themselves be experienced relations, and any kind of relation experienced must be accounted as 'real' as anything else in the system.* (James, 1904b, p. 534; emphasis in the original)

This position is a phenomenalist position and, as such, belongs in the context of phenomenology.[22] This, despite James's insistence in the *Principles* that he was a positivist.

Starting from this position of pure experience, James has attempted to wade out of solipsism:

> To me the decisive reason in favor of our minds meeting in *some* common objects at least is that, unless I make that supposition, I have no motive for assuming that your mind exists at all. Why do I postulate your mind? Because I see your body acting in a certain way. Its gestures, facial movements, words and conduct generally, are 'expressive,' so I deem it actuated as my own is, by an inner life like mine. (James, 1904c, p. 565; emphasis in the original)

---

[22]One has to be careful here. The use of the term phenomenology is sometimes strictly tied to the details of a theory in philosophy that centres around Husserl. In this book, the term phenomenological is used more generally to refer to those aspects of any theory which are concerned with phenomena as experienced by a person.

Practically, then, our minds meet in a world of objects which they share in common, which would still be there, if one or several of the minds were destroyed. I can see no formal objection to this supposition's being literally true. On the principles which I am defending, a 'mind' or 'personal consciousness' is the name for a series of experiences run together by certain definite transitions, and an objective reality is a series of similar experiences knit by different transitions. (James, 1904c, p. 566)

The first quotation poses, of course, the problem of zombies, discussed in Chapter 2. The second quotation is vintage James. One is left wondering what the ontological status of the physical world was supposed to be and, hence, how to make sense of his later definitions of consciousness.

Taylor has reconstructed James's 1896 Lowell Lectures concerning exceptional mental states (E. Taylor, 1982) making available the under-standing of James's thought between the time of his *Principles* and his later interest in religious experience. There are a number of important features about this work, which consisted of eight lectures: "Dreams and hypnotism", "Automatism", "Hysteria", "Multiple personality", "Demoniacal possession", "Witchcraft", "Degeneration", and "Genius" (E. Taylor, 1982). In this series of lectures, James stressed the importance of the "margin" of consciousness and argued for the presence of "a subconscious, dynamic substrate to waking awareness" (E. Taylor, personal communication, 1989). He maintained that there was a number of streams of intelligence of varying quality, some demoniacal, some spiritual, to which a person could gain access. It was the prerogative of a person to make choices between the streams, thereby determining their experience (Taylor, 1981).

This line of thought was further developed in James's 1901 - 1902 Gifford Lectures, the *Varieties of religious experience* (1902/1958), in which he explicitly stated that normal waking consciousness was only one type of consciousness, and that one could gain access to other types of consciousness through one's own subconscious processes. These ideas were taken further to include, as mentioned at the beginning of this section, the idea of developing "earth-soul" consciousness and states of conscious-ness normally termed mystical. Before his death, James cited four ex-amples from his own experience, along with corroborating cases of mysticism, in support of his hypotheses (Taylor, 1981).

To complete this discussion of James, it is necessary to address the quotation from James given in Chapter 1, in which James has maintained that consciousness does not exist, that thoughts exist, but that these thoughts are just the breath. It would appear that James wanted to deny that consciousness could exist as a metaphysical entity. Rather, it was to be found directly in experience. But when James looked to his experience, he did not find consciousness, but thoughts. Thus far, there is no prob-lem. But now James goes further and explains thoughts in terms of physical events. This was a strategy that James had used previously. In papers published in 1880 and 1884, James had postulated that the feelings of effort as well as those of emotion were complexes of afferent sensations in the body, and that there were no "intermediary entities" (E. Taylor, personal communication, 1986).

Now the question is, given that James was a physician and that he made reference to the brain and brain processes in his writings, why did he not define thoughts as brain processes? In the quotation from James, given above, in which radical empiricism is defined, James maintained that only those relationships can be established which *can be found in experience*. James presumably could not find neural processes in his experience.[23] James knew that he was thinking. What else was there that he could find upon introspection? The only thing moving in his body was the breathing apparatus and so, perhaps taking a cue from Swedenborgian or Eastern philosophies,[24] James found a relationship between one's thoughts and one's breathing. Is that relationship itself given in experience? Perhaps for James it was. It is unlikely that most people would find revealed upon introspection that their thoughts are the breath. Whatever the case, however, it allowed James to discharge the existence of mystical entities. Consciousness did not exist. Thoughts existed, but thoughts were the breath.[25]

It is perhaps fitting that the figure regarded as one of the first major discussants of consciousness in North American experimental psychology, should offer such a variety of versions of what it is that consciousness is.

4.2 The matter of consciousness

The purpose of this section is to consider the relationship between the material nature of the world and consciousness in a more specific way than done thus far in this book. In pursuing this purpose, this section begins by reviewing the possible positions with regard to the mind-body problem and making the distinction between behavioral and physiological

---

[23]James was thereby to circumvent a problem that was to plague later theories of introspection. If consciousness is brain events, why does one not see neurons upon introspection (Lyons, 1986)?

[24]In the case of both Swedenborg's thought and Eastern philosophies there is discussion concerning the relationship between thinking and breathing (E. Taylor, personal communications, 1986 & 1989).

[25]This kind of explanation of consciousness has resurfaced with Fischer (1986b), who has maintained that mental activities can be thought of as muscular acts.

explanations of consciousness. This is followed by a critical discussion of the eliminative materialist version of consciousness as an example of an extreme materialist position. The section concludes by discussing more generally some of the physiological mechanisms that appear to have some bearing on human consciousness.

Traditionally, the understanding of the relationship of consciousness to the material world has followed the possible resolutions of the mind-body problem. At one end of the spectrum, the only things that really exist are matter and energy as they are usually understood, so that mind is just matter and energy. Such is the position of Llinas and Pellionisz, for example, as indicated in the discussion of Chapter 1. It is a position known as physical monism or simply materialism.[26] This was the position taken by the various versions of behaviorism. If, in addition to holding such a position, one advocates that any concepts which do not directly refer to physical events be removed from the language, then such a position is known as eliminative materialism.

A variation of the materialist position is one in which mental events are deemed to occur, but are deemed to be wholly explicable in terms of physical events with types of mental events being identified with types of physical states of an organism. This type-identity version of materialism has not survived (e.g., Fodor, 1981) but has been replaced by various versions of functionalism, whereby mental activity of a given kind is not necessarily identified with the same state of the organism. The functionalist stance is that generally taken in cognitive science and is further discussed in Section 3.

Dualism is the position in which it is maintained that both the physical and mental are real. Parallelism is a dualist position similar to the type-identity version of materialism, except that mental events are deemed to exist in their own right. Wundt's and James's versions of this position, called "psychophysical parallelism," were discussed in Chapter 2 and in Section 1 of this chapter.

Interactionism is a position in which matter and mind are both deemed to be real, and to have causal effects on one another. A problem with this position has been the inability to identify the mechanisms of such an interaction. It has been argued that such a mechanism is *a priori* not possible, because of the impossibility of a purely mental agency exerting an effect on a physical substance. In turn, a problem with this *a*

---

[26]Flanagan (1984) has distinguished between materialism and naturalism. Naturalism is a form of materialism in which explanations of events are to be given at appropriate levels of organization. Llinas' and Pellionisz's position is a materialist but not a naturalist position.

priori objection is that it is based on an unexamined notion of matter.[27]

Finally, at the other end of the spectrum, one could argue that only that which is mental exists, and that the material world, for all its seeming immediacy, is a byproduct of mental activity. This position is known as Berkleyan monism. This particular version of monism is less popular in the literature than a position in which both the mental and physical are real, but are seen to emanate from a common source. For Bohm (1980), the common source has been the "implicate order" which "explicates" or gives rise to the material and mental domains. This position may in essence be close to Berkleyan monism. For James, the common source was "pure experience"; the difficulty of determining the ontological status of that position was discussed in Section 1. For Pribram (1986) the common ground was made up of information and appeared to need a physical medium for its expression.

Because consciousness has traditionally been conceived of as allied with the mental domain, a person's stance with regard to the mind-body problem would likely affect the way in which they understood consciousness. In addition, because of the sway of materialism in twentieth-century thought, attempts have been made to explain consciousness in material terms. One of the most facile ways of doing that has been to deny the existence of consciousness or at least to assert its causal impotence, *a priori*, without having examined it. Such has been the case historically. Generally, however, in contradistinction to Watson's statements given in Chapters 1 and 2, a physicalist account of consciousness is seen as necessary (e.g., Lycan, 1987).

It is important to make the distinction between behavioral and physiological explanations of mental events. Just as James did not resort to explanations of thoughts in terms of brain events, but in terms of breath, so too behaviorists, such as Lashley and Skinner, understood inner events not in terms of brain processes but as behavior that never quite made it to the status of overt, observable behavior. Lashley, for example, in 1923, postulated building a machine that was physically like a human being, and claimed that such a machine would be conscious, where consciousness was identified with the mechanisms of speech and gesture. For Skinner, while such covert behavior provided one source of explana-

---

[27]It is curious that consciousness is thought to be problematical but not matter. That should be a warning signal that perhaps unwarranted assumptions are being made about the nature of material reality. An attempt to understand matter reveals the same kinds of problems that one faces when studying consciousness – that is to say, it is not at all clear what matter is (Hanson, 1963), although in contradistinction to consciousness, there is no disagreement about the notion of matter in the academic literature.

tion for inner events, another way of explaining them away was to say that one had kept track of one's overt behavior and then, on the basis of those environmental conditions, had accurately predicted one's behavior. Sometimes, for Skinner, explanations of inner events would require a combination of covert and overt explanation (Lyons, 1986). Just as James had taken pure experience as the substratum of reality and built everything else up out of it, so the behaviorists fastened on observable behavior and used it to explain everything in the objective and subjective domains. The behaviorist program failed, precisely because of its inability to deal with the matter of private events:

> It was behaviorism's failure to cope with the so-called problem of privacy that was most influential in subsequent theorizing about the mind, for it is now notorious that behaviorism cannot give an analysis of covert acts of, say, thinking or imagining except in terms of the discredited postulation of internal miniature behavior. (Lyons, 1986, p. 52)

A second materialist thrust has been to give an account of consciousness in terms of brain processes. For example, Place's paper, "Is consciousness a brain process?" (1962) was "one of the classics of modern physicalism" (Lyons, 1986, p. 49). In that paper, Place argued that it is not logically impossible that consciousness be identified as a brain process. His argument hinges on a naive acceptance of science as the provider of "explanations" for phenomena. Thus he has said:

> We treat . . . two sets of observations as observations of the same event in those cases where the technical scientific observations set in the context of the appropriate body of scientific theory provide an immediate explanation of the observations made by the man in the street. (Place, 1962, p. 106)

Having assumed the hegemony of science, it was a simple matter to conclude that:

> There is nothing that the introspecting subject says about his conscious experience which is inconsistent with anything the physiologist might want to say about the brain processes which cause him to describe the environment and consciousness of that environment in the way he does. (Place, 1962, p. 108)

While Place's arguments are flawed, his conclusions are tenable from the point of view of an ordinary understanding of physical reality.

The explanations of consciousness given by the behaviorist position are not discussed further in this book. Some of the possible physiological correlates of consciousness are discussed in the last subsection of this section, but before doing that, the eliminative materialist position with regard to consciousness is examined as an extreme example of a physiological version of consciousness.

4.2.1 The eliminative materialist explanation of consciousness

Eliminative materialism is a position in philosophy which is based on the assumption that only neuroscience can give a proper account of human cognition, and that current descriptions of mental events that rely upon a common-sense psychological framework are unlikely to reduce smoothly to descriptions in terms of brain events. It is the purpose here to examine some of the ingredients of the eliminative materialist notion of consciousness and to point out a few of the problems with such an account.

It is worthwhile to consider, at the outset, why an extreme position such as eliminative materialism should be entertained at all. To begin with, Place's contention should be considered carefully in any open-minded investigation of consciousness, and the eliminative materialist position is one example of such consideration. Secondly, if eliminative materialism were to be the correct theory of human cognition then the impact upon human culture would be devastating. In particular, much, if not all, of the disciplines of jurisprudence, literary criticism and philosophy, would simply disappear (Stich, 1983). Thirdly, eliminative materialism is in some ways a caricature of a more general materialist position. Not only has it tempted other materialists by offering quick solutions to long-standing problems with materialism (Foss, 1985), but it reflects the intuitive notion that the general populace has of the scientific view of human cognition, which notion itself already conditions social processes as Bohm, for example, has suggested (Factor, 1985). Fourthly, even if eliminative materialism is not the correct theory of human cognition, it may argue convincingly to reveal problems with other theories that may be difficult to see from other perspectives (Foss, 1986, commenting on Stich, 1983). Finally, because of their arguments in favor of a neurophysiological explanation of mental events, eliminative materialists use recent results in neuroscience to demonstrate the potential capabilities of such explanations (Churchland, 1980). These results are given in technical, neurophysiological terms and often, in mathematical terms as well (e.g., Llinas & Pellionisz, 1984), so that it becomes difficult to assess the implications of such work for an understanding of human nature. The continued advances in neuroscience and the mathematical modelling of brain activity will appear to strengthen an eliminativist account of human cognition. For these reasons, it is important to consider eliminative materialism as a position in philosophy.

Foss (1985) has provided an overview of some of the proponents of the eliminative materialist position, as well as arguments against such a position from a more moderate materialist point of view. The purpose here is to examine specifically the work of Churchland (1983) and parts of Churchland's monograph (1984) in order to explicate the eliminative materialist notion of consciousness.[28]

According to the eliminative materialist, the concept of conscious-ness has lost its usefulness and should be replaced by statements about neurological events (Churchland, 1983). Thus, the eliminativist thesis compounds the problem of explicating the referent of the term conscious-ness. Having decided that consciousness is a vacuous concept, the elimi-native materialist has seemingly decided also that the term consciousness need not be defined.

A distinction needs to be made here, between the concept of consciousness and the existence of a referent for the term consciousness. While the eliminativists may think that the concept of consciousness has lost its explanatory value, it is not clear that they would go so far as to say that the term consciousness has never had a referent. In fact, in her paper, P. S. Churchland has used the term consciousness in a manner that has called upon an implicit understanding of the use of that term. For example:

> The imagination may wonder whether, from the point of view of the brain, the difference between states which are conscious and those which are not, is in fact very significant. (Churchland, 1983, p. 92)

Her argument has been against the utility of the concept of consciousness rather than against the existence of a referent for the term, although that referent is never delineated.

P. M. Churchland also does not define the term "consciousness" but does indicate the sense in which he uses the term "self-conscious":

> To be self-conscious is to have, at a minimum, *knowledge* of oneself. But this is not all. Self-consciousness involves knowledge not just of one's physical states, but knowledge of one's *mental states* speci-fically. Additionally, self-consciousness involves the same kind of *continuously updated* knowledge that one enjoys in one's continuous perception of the external world. Self-consciousness, it seems, is a kind of continuous apprehension of an inner reality, the reality of one's mental states and activities. (Churchland, 1984, p. 73; emphases in original)

This definition falls generally into the category of *consciousness$_2$* whereby the term consciousness is taken to refer to the explicit knowledge of one's situation, mental states or actions.

---

[28]Churchland and Churchland are, according to Flanagan, "the most able and articulate contemporary defenders of eliminativism" (Flanagan, 1984, p. 219).

As done in Chapter 3, it is useful also to make the distinction between the referent of the term consciousness and an explanation of what consciousness is. That is to say, once the referent of the term consciousness has been fixed, one would like to know the nature of that to which reference is made. In practice, of course, any definition of consciousness already presupposes a framework within which such definition takes place, so that, to the extent that the choice of a referent depends upon such a framework, it will also already suggest the direction that an explanation is to take.[29]

P. S. Churchland, who has maintained that the concept of consciousness has lost its utility, has depended upon an implicitly understood referent for the term, and explained consciousness as a monitoring system or interactivity of monitoring systems of the brain (Churchland, 1983). Taken as a whole, her explanation of consciousness has apparently vitiated the need for carefully specifying a referent for the term consciousness. For her, the concept of consciousness has been a misattribution of conceptual unity to phenomena which themselves are not coherent, but given, as it were, as products of neural activity.

This is not, however, a satisfactory resolution of this matter. If Churchland has chosen to argue against a notion of consciousness, then she cannot depend upon an implicit understanding of what it is that she has promised to replace with monitoring systems of the brain. The phenomena of consciousness have not disappeared; rather, they are to be explained in a radically different way. One needs to know exactly what it is that is being explained. And this Churchland has failed to point out.

For P. M. Churchland, the definition of self-consciousness has relied heavily on an explanatory scheme for consciousness, as shown by the quotation given above. Further in his monograph, Churchland has gone on to summarize his notion of self-consciousness:

> In summary, self-consciousness, on this view, is just a species of perception: *self-perception.* It is not perception of one's foot with one's eyes, for example, but is rather the perception of one's internal states with what we may call (largely in ignorance) one's faculty of introspection. Self-consciousness is thus no more (and no less) mysterious than perception generally. It is just directed internally rather than externally. (1984, p. 74; emphasis in original)

This seemingly subjectivist account has been immediately reduced, howe-

---

[29]This distinction between the referent of the term consciousness and an explanation for it is rarely made in the literature, although such a distinction could help to explicate the world-view within which discussions of consciousness take place.

ver, to an explanation of introspection in terms of objective, neural events. Introspection, then, has been understood in terms of self-monitoring, made possible by rich connections between parts of the brain, some of which receive signals from others. "Who will express surprise that one kind of brain activity enjoys rich causal connections with other kinds of brain activity?" (Churchland, 1984, p. 74).

The preceding argument is an interesting one for the eliminativist to make, because it is an example of an instance in which folk psychology is expected to reduce smoothly to brain events. Self-consciousness has been defined as the continuously updated knowledge of one's mental states and activities. This is certainly one aspect of the experience of self-consciousness that one can have for oneself, an experience that, because it involves knowledge of something, is intentional and hence well within the domain of folk psychology. P. M. Churchland has maintained that this same structure is carried over into the neural realm – that self-perception *is* one part of the brain richly causally connected to another. Folk psychology, then, cannot be entirely incorrect. It is correct in that knowledge of one's own mental states is possible.

One does not, however, have to let folk psychology in through the back door if one maintains a sufficiently rigorous eliminativist position. One need not grant structural parallels between self-perception and brain events. Self-perception may be some pattern of neural firing that need not entail the discrete interaction of two different parts of the brain. This seems to have been the position taken by P. S. Churchland who has stated that "the naturalness of our self-appraisal and our explanations 'from the inside' can easily be mistaken for privileged access" (1983, p. 83). She appears to have been saying that self-appraisal, which is only a variant of appraisal more generally and which occurs naturally, does not give one greater access to one's own condition than it does to others, and that one is mistaken in believing that such privileged access is possible.

But what happens to subjectivity and the notion of self by either of these accounts? One could ask of P. M. Churchland how the part of the brain that is to be the knower becomes circumscribed. Is it a single cell, a nucleus of cells or groups of nuclei of cells that act as selves to "perceive" the electrochemical activity of other groups of cells? There are many "rich connections" in the brain. On what bases do specific parts of the brain determine whether they are the observer or the observed, a distinction necessary if one part of the brain is to be the knower that corresponds to the experience of the self of folk psychology and another part the repository of those neural events that correspond to the mental activity that is to be known? One expects Churchland to provide an account that solves this problem of the knower and the known.

For P. S. Churchland, the knower is the brain, and references to subjective or private events are actually references to events in the brain, events that a given brain has no more access to than anyone else. What happens to the self? As a result of questioning the unity of consciousness, the self has been described as being potentially "a disconnected collection of wants, needs, and whatnots, flying in loose formation" (Churchland, 1983, p. 85). As a result of discussions concerning the role of language in self-representation, it has been intimated that the self is a construct, a brain's model of itself, misinterpreted by the brain as a self (Churchland, 1983).

It is not clear how either of these versions of the self are to be understood. In the first case, P. S. Churchland seems to have had an implicit notion of self in mind, which may correspond to the notion of self as it is usually understood. In that case, one wants to know how her disconnected collection adds up to what is normally understood to be the self. In the case of the second version, no explanation has been given as to what it means to assert that the brain can model itself. In either case, the admission of the existence of a self that is to be explained or the postulation of a brain's model of itself, takes the discussion of the self out of the realm of neurophysiology back into that of folk psychology, so that Churchland would have to give a further explication of the nature of the self.

Finally, from the foregoing discussion, it can be surmised what would happen to the sense of existence of the self. Whatever the self may or may not be, there is the further issue of *consciousness*$_3$ – the recognition of self-existence or the recognition of existence more generally. That is to say, one can meaningfully assert that being "is". Not so, the eliminativist would say. Apparent givens, raw feels or qualia, all depend upon a theoretical framework (Churchland, 1984) so that, in fact, if one were to adopt an eliminativist position, one could account for the sense of existence in terms of neural processes.

One can ask, at this point, whether there is anything special about explanations given in terms of neural processes, at least insofar as the definition and explanation of consciousness, subjective events and the sense of existence are concerned. It would seem that any sufficiently restrictive explanatory scheme would work equally well.

To illustrate this last contention, suppose that one held the following manifestly absurd theoretical position that, in fact, the electrochemical activity of the brain was a concept that has been long overdue for the rubbish heap and that electrochemical cerebral events could best be described using a revitalized, completed alchemical theory. Thus, one could refuse to define what one meant by electrochemical events, since they would go the way of the celestial spheres and intentionality anyway. One could rely, rather, upon an implicit, common sense understanding of neural events and then explain them away in terms of the qualities of *phlogiston x* and *phlogiston y*. When asked to account for the cellular composition of the brain, one could argue that it is not composition but constitution that one is talking about and that constitution is nothing but the qualities of *phlogiston x* and *phlogiston y*. In fact, one could say that the brain is unlikely to be a unit or a natural kind, but that it is rather a loose collection of flying whatnots or perhaps a construct, *phlogiston* modelling the *sacred vapours*, opaque to its own true nature. When asked how one could conceivably refuse to acknowledge the existence of the brain, which is seemingly so given, one could trundle out all the qualia literature and wonder how anyone could still possibly fall for that old raw observation argument for the existence of the brain, especially since the publication of the paper entitled "Why the brain is not" as an accompaniment for that classic "Why I do not exist". One could point out that insisting upon neurophysiological explanations is as absurd as ancient insistence upon meaning and truth, and that one need not acquit oneself using the erroneous, outdated fallacies of folk neuroscience. In addition, the charge that an alchemical theory is pragmatically incoherent, would be a red herring. The thesis of alchemy would be expressed without incoherence: "the principles of folk neuroscience are substantially false and its ontology nonexistent". Needless to say, a completed alchemical theory would be highly mathematical, using more recent categorical constructions rather than the outdated, cumbersome tensorial models of folk neuroscience.

Such a position is quite simple to defend, not because it is correct, but because it has an algorithm for invalidating all counterarguments, namely, by insisting that they be reinterpreted into alchemical terms, by which act, of course, alchemy is vindicated. This same strategy is the one used by eliminative materialism to give the account of consciousness given above.

At the basis of the eliminativist world-view is a single contention – that psychological events are neural events. All arguments against an eliminativist position are swept with the same broad brush – the advocation of an entirely neurophysiological explanation of all human mental events. As such it is a rigid position, whose strength depends upon discrediting any descriptions of explanations of phenomena in terms of mental events, and the apparent replacement of "folk psychology" with neurophysiology.

It is easy to see, in fact, that acceptance of the eliminativist assumptions undermines the eliminativist position. To understand this, one needs to notice the consequences of the rigor with which the eliminativist position must be maintained if it is to succeed at all. One must, indeed, reinterpret all mental events in terms of neurophysiological processes, including those which occur within the person of an eliminativist at the time when such a person is maintaining their eliminativist position. When a person is thinking that eliminativism is the correct theory, what is really happening is that *telodendrion x* releases *Substance P* which is taken up by *receptor site y*, and so on. But thereby, the meaning of the eliminativist's contentions has been lost. *Telodendrion x* releasing *Substance P*, and so on, is not apparently a statement about the correctness of the eliminativist position, nor can such neural events be identified with the correctness of the eliminativist contention because such contentions are, in fact, only brain events not requiring the invocation of intentionalist language for their understanding.

P. M. Churchland would concede the above argument, but has made the following remark:

> If eliminative materialism is true, then meaningfulness must have some different source. To insist on the 'old' source is to insist on the validity of the very framework at issue. (Churchland, 1984, p. 48)

That leaves one, however, in an untenable position. The "old" source of meaningfulness is gone, but there is no replacement. One does not know what meaningfulness will be by the eliminativist account; indeed, one does not know that meaningfulness can ever be established by this account and if it is, what relationship it will bear to the "old" notion of meaningfulness. Until such time as an adequate exposition of meaning is given in terms of neural events, an eliminative materialist's assertion of the eliminativist thesis is technically meaningless and hence neither correct nor incorrect.

The eliminative materialist position is not a new one. It is a position that has shown up over and over again in stronger or weaker versions and will likely show up in various versions as future thinkers attempt to come to grips with the problem of consciousness. It appears initially to be a tenable position but, as one examines it more carefully, it becomes clear that it invalidates itself and fails to resolve the problem of meaning.[30] It is more reasonable to seek to determine the relationship between physiological events and consciousness.

4.2.2 The physiological bases of consciousness

A number of collections of papers have appeared that have specifically addressed the relationship between the physiological processes of the brain and the experience of consciousness (e.g., Davidson & Davidson, 1983; Eccles, 1966; 1982; Globus, Maxwell & Savodnik, 1976). The understanding of consciousness that the different contributors have demonstrated ranges along the spectrum of notions from consciousness understood

---

[30]Eliminative materialism also fails to adequately address its own foundations, e.g., the nature of matter.

strictly in behavioral terms (e.g., Savage, 1976) to consciousness understood as a transpersonal reality (e.g., Eccles, 1976a). The purpose here is
not to unravel the specific notions of such contributors, but to look at
some of the concerns in physiology that may help to constrain the
understanding of consciousness.

For example, the patient H. M. had had bilateral removal of the
medial temporal lobes with subsequent anterograde amnesia, so that he
seemingly could not encode information from short-term into long-term
memory. Sidman, Stoddard and Mohr (1968) utilized an apparatus consisting of a three by three matrix of translucent plastic squares upon which
stimuli could be projected from the rear. H. M. was seated in front of
this apparatus, and without verbal instructions, had to learn to press the
square upon which a circle was projected, the other squares being
initially dark and in later trials, showing ellipses. Whenever H. M. correctly pressed the square upon which a circle was projected, chimes
would sound and a penny would be dispensed. He learned correctly the
criterion for the task and would press the circle when the array consisted of a single circle, seven ellipses and a dark centre square. Immediately after the last trial in a series, he was asked what he had been
doing, to which he correctly responded that he had been trying to get
the circles. Then he was given the distraction task of counting the
pennies, which was followed by asking him what he had done to earn the
pennies. This time he confabulated about what it was that had taken
place. However, when he began the task again after this report, there
was no loss of accuracy. Thus, learning in the sense of animal learning
had been taking place, even though the patient had lost his ability to
recall task-related events. This suggests that one's patterns of behavior
and one's awareness of one's own experience are mediated by anatomically
separate brain mechanisms. H. M. certainly exhibited *behavioral consciousness*$_2$ in the course of the learning task. He was unable to retrospect,
however. Although he appeared not to be a zombie, but to be *subjectively
conscious*$_2$ and *conscious*$_3$, he did not have conscious recall of events
that occurred more than a few minutes before. At the least, this case
shows that associative learning is not the same as learning which is
consciously mediated.

It would seem that this case could be a rich source of counter-
examples for those who discuss consciousness, yet no references to this
case, or the results of the work of Sidman, Siddard and Mohr were found
to be cited outside the context of the physiology of memory. Similarly,
the results of Mark, Ervin and Yakovlev (1962) have failed to appear in
the literature in the philosophy of mind, despite the fact that pain, the
subject of their study, is the prototypical qualium in that subject area.
These researchers showed that lesions to the dorsomedial thalamic nuclei
resulted, not in the loss of the sensation of pain, but of the person's
concern over the pain. In other words, a person would be aware of the
pain which still, presumably was mapped to the appropriate projection

areas of the brain, but the person no longer cared about being in pain. What is interesting here, is that the dorsomedial thalamus is critically involved in both anterograde amnesia and the loss of the affective component of pain.

The ideas of Penfield seem to bear on these two cases as well. While it is difficult to locate precisely the brain mechanisms that he was referring to, Penfield (1969a, 1969b, 1975) has indicated the thalamic area of the brain as the site of two separate mechanisms. As a result of his clinical and surgical studies of epileptic patients, he has claimed that he could isolate a "computer's mechanism" and a "mind's mechanism". When working smoothly together these systems were to constitute the "centrencephalon" or "central integrating system" (Penfield, 1975, p. 44). It was the responsibility of the "computer's mechanism" to coordinate sensory input from the environment and to act on the basis of that information. The mind's mechanism, on the other hand "is essential to the existence of consciousness" (1975, p. 44).

Penfield has suggested that in some cases *petit mal* epileptic seizures selectively inhibit the operation of the mind's mechanism without interfering with the computer's mechanism. In such cases, the person becomes a zombie:

> [The] attacks of epileptic automatism show clearly the automatic, complex performance of which man's computer is capable. In an attack of automatism the patient becomes suddenly unconscious, but, since other mechanisms in the brain continue to function, he changes into an automaton. He may wander about, confused and aimless. Or he may continue to carry out whatever purpose his mind was in the act of handing on to his automatic sensory-motor mechanism when the highest brain-mechanism went out of action. Or he follows a stereotyped, habitual pattern of behavior. In every case, however, the automaton can make few, if any, decisions for which there has been no precedent. He makes no record of a stream of consciousness. Thus, he will have complete amnesia for the period of epileptic discharge and during the period of cellular exhaustion that follows. (1975, pp. 38 - 39)

Thus, according to Penfield, human beings consist of two elements: a computational element which regulates and controls bodily functioning and behavior, and a mind element capable of the stream of consciousness and of ideas for creative actions that are conveyed to the computer's mechanism.

For Penfield, the capacities of the mind element transcend those of the computer element:

> For my own part, after years of striving to explain the mind on the

basis of brain-action alone, I have come to the conclusion that it is simpler (and far easier to be logical) if one adopts the hypothesis that our being does consist of two fundamental elements. (1975, p. 80)

If one chooses . . . the dualistic alternative, the mind must be viewed as a basic *element* in itself. One might, then, call it a *medium* or *essence*, a *soma*. That is to say, it has a *continuing existence*. On this basis, one must assume that although the mind is silent when it no longer has its special connection to the brain, it exists in the silent intervals and takes over control when the highest brain-mechanism does go into action (1975, p. 81; emphases in original)

The findings of Sidman *et al.* could be explained by saying that H. M. learned the task through the process of associative learning by the computer's mechanism; the mind's mechanism, although connected, was not capable of laying down a stream of consciousness in memory. The work of Mark *et al.* could be interpreted in a macabre way by saying that the mind had been disconnected from the brain through destroying the mind's mechanism, and that the reason the subjects no longer cared about the pain was that there was no conscious person left to care.

It is difficult to know what conclusions to draw from these three cases of pathology involving disturbances of consciousness. In addition, the question still remains, of discerning the relationship between the medial diencephalic nuclei[31] and a possible incorporeal mind, and how such a relationship could result in a stream of consciousness.[32] It is worth pondering what implications these studies have for the understanding of consciousness.

A better known series of case studies that concern consciousness has resulted from the surgical separation of the cerebral hemispheres. Although it is not the purpose here to review the literature that has resulted from the observation of commissurotomized patients, a great deal has been written about the *lateralization of consciousness* (e.g., Beaumont, 1981; Galin, 1976; Marks, 1981). It has been suggested, for example, that the stream of human consciousness consists of two streams, one from each of the two hemispheres (Bakan, 1978) or that human cognition and behavior, normal and abnormal, can be understood as the result of the interaction of a two-element system (Flor-Henry, 1983). One is often presented with the metaphor of two homunculi (one verbal, the other

---

[31]Penfield appears to include areas of the brainstem inferior to the thalamus (1969a; 1969b; 1975).

[32]Incidentally, Penfield had read James's *Principles*.

nonverbal, one assertive, the other receptive, and so on) struggling for control of a person or in some manner co-operating to produce any given behavior. There is some evidence from studies done with subjects with commissurotomized brains, and subjects with intact brains, that seriously undermines this contention (Ellenberg & Sperry, 1980). Yates (1980) has suggested that this metaphor be laid to rest for a while. It is more realistic to look at the interplay of asymmetric, bilateral control systems in the intact brain, as described by Tucker and Williamson (1984) in order to understand the phenomena currently being explained by lateralization arguments.

What does all of this have to say about the notion of consciousness? Although these studies circumscribe in some ways the understanding of consciousness, the definition of what consciousness is remains implicit and seems to be thought of as James's stream of thought. The notion of consciousness is radically altered however, if Penfield's contention that the mind is an entity separate from the brain is to be taken seriously. There is a critical test for any would be integrator of physicalist and transcendentalist positions. Do they believe that consciousness survives physical death? Consciousness can be as mental and causal as one pleases, but if it disappears once the brain from which it emerged ceases to function, then such a position is a materialist one. The dualist would maintain that the body dies but the mind survives. It is premature to speculate about the implications for consciousness of such possible survival, although Tart (1985) has made a beginning in that regard.

This section has raised some of the issues concerning materiality and consciousness. Materialist explanations of consciousness often take the form of denying its existence or importance. If forced, consciousness has been explained historically in terms of behavior. Both historically and more recently, neurophysiological explanations of consciousness have been attempted. Eliminative materialism is a modern movement that seeks to discard the concept of consciousness and to use only neurophysiological explanations for human phenomena. While this position invalidates itself, much can be gained perhaps from a consideration of the implications of brain pathology. Finally, the question of the relationship between materiality and consciousness comes to a head with the question of death.

4.3 The notion of consciousness in cognitive science

The main impetus today for dealing with the mental has not been in the direction of finding behavioral or neurophysiological substrates for mental events, but of finding causal computational chains to explain them. This change of direction coincides with the recognition that a computer could be used to model human cognitive functioning. The idea is simple. One does not have to refer to a computer's internal mechanical states in order to make sense of its computational behavior. One needs only to know the composition of the programs that process information in the computer.

Metaphysical functionalism is the philosophical position that justifies explanations of mental events in their own terms without reference to physical events.[33] This effort to understand human cognition is interdisciplinary in nature, bridging the disciplines of cognitive psychology, psycholinguistics, philosophy of mind and artificial intelligence.

A great deal of enthusiasm has been exhibited for this position (e.g., Hilgard, 1987; Lycan, 1987). At the same time, some of the computationalists have been aware of the limitations of their program (Fodor, 1981).

What have functionalists had to say about consciousness? Perhaps the best approach would be to look first at the criteria that a functionalist would be willing to adopt for the presence of intelligence. Then, Dennett's notion of consciousness will be presented and some of the problems with it discussed. A more general overview of the understanding of consciousness in cognitive psychology has been given by Mandler (1985).

As computers exhibit increasingly greater information-processing powers, the question can be asked at what point one ascribes intelligence to a machine. Turing answered this question in 1950 by proposing what he called the "imitation game," which has since become known as the "Turing test." The game was to be played as follows: There is a computer, a person who is called the "witness" and a person called the "interrogator." The computer and witness are isolated from the interrogator, who does not know which is which. The object of the game is for the interrogator to ask questions of the computer and the human being in order to determine which of the two is the human being. The computer's purpose in the game is to cause the interrogator to make an incorrect identification. The "witness" attempts to help the interrogator make the correct identification. If the interrogator makes the incorrect identification, the computer has passed the test for intelligence (Turing, 1950).

What makes the Turing test attractive is that the notion of intelligence has been operationalized. With the same stroke, however, *consciousness$_3$* has been removed as a criterion for intelligence. Turing anticipated this objection, but thought it unimportant. He maintained that one used procedures of interrogation whenever one sought to find out

---

[33]Empirical functionalism as opposed to metaphysical functionalism refers to an epistemological position, to a view of how mental states are picked out and on how psychological explanations are most appropriately framed. According to epistemological functionalism, mental states are identified in terms of the characteristic causal relations which hold among environmental events, other mental states, and action (Flanagan, 1984).

whether or not someone else understood a subject matter, or whether they were simply repeating something that they had learned by rote. One would be using, according to Turing, the same criteria for making a judgement about machines that one used for making judgements about other people (Turing, 1950).

Harnad, who has stated a similar position more recently, has explicitly addressed the issue of subjectivity:

> What I have called Methodological Epiphenomenalism is the research strategy of attempting to account only for our performance capacity − the ability to discriminate, manipulate, identify and describe objects and states of affairs, and to produce and respond appropriately to names and descriptions − not the subjective phenomenology that accompanies the exercise of these performance capacities (except indirectly insmuch [sic] as it enters into the contents of the descriptions). No attempt is made to interpret the performance of the underlying processes mentalistically until one succeeds in producing a candidate that can pass the Total Turing Test, i.e., display ALL of our generic performance capacities in a way that is indistinguishable from the way a real person does. At that point we give the candidate the same benefit of the doubt (about "other minds") that we do to one another every day − AND ON EXACTLY THE SAME BASIS.
>
> That's all there is to it. Methodological Epiphenomenalism is just the acknowledgment that observable behavior is all that psychologists will ever have by way of objective data, that the only case in which one can know there are subjective experiences going on for sure is one's own, and that the only ground for imputing them to anyone else is behavior indistinguishable from one's own. (Harnad, 1987; emphases in original)

One does not know, and cannot know, using the usual sensory processes, whether a machine, or another person can be conscious in the sense of *subjective consciousness_2* or *consciousness_3*. The Turing test is just a statement of *behavioral consciousness_2*. What happens in the case of functionalism, is that *subjective consciousness_2* and *consciousness_3* are identified with *behavioral consciousness_2*.

Dennett has claimed that functionalist theories can adequately explain the subjective aspects of consciousness, although he has not been able to give a conclusive argument for that contention. Part of his theory is presented here, because he has been one of the few functionalists who has explicitly attempted to give an account of consciousness. In doing so, Dennett has had the sense of *consciousness_3* when he said that consciousness was characterized by a sense of being something.

The question, "Is it like something to be an *X*?" may in the end be the wrong question to ask, but it excellently captures the intuitions that constitute the challenge to a theory of consciousness. Until one's psychological or physiological or cybernetic theory explains how it can be like something to be something (or explains *in detail* what is wrong with this demand), one's theory will be *seriously* incomplete. It is open to the theorist, of course, to reject the challenge out of hand. One can emulate those behaviorists who (it has been charged) 'feign anesthesia' and categorically deny that anyone *has* an inner life. This course has little or nothing to recommend it. (Dennett, 1978, p. 150; emphases in original)

How has Dennett explained this phenomenon? He has explained it by maintaining that this sense of being is a characteristic of information-processing at subpersonal levels. He has changed the question from one of consciousness to one of describing the mechanism whereby parts of an information-processing system have access to other parts. This explanation of consciousness in terms of mechanism is consistent with the usual strategies in cognitive psychology of talking about consciousness in terms of mechanisms or in terms of mental processes that have crossed some sort of threshold (Mandler, 1985).[34]

Dennett described a system that was *behaviorally conscious₂* and wanted it also to be *subjectively conscious₂* and *conscious₃*. His argument that he had not merely described a zombie was by appeal to personal experience (Dennett, 1978). A few years after his paper giving an information-processing account of consciousness, Dennett (1982) had become impatient with those who would have charged him with having created a zombie with no inner life. Subsequently, he has been willing to dispense with immediate experience altogether (Dennett, 1988).

It should be remarked that Dennett was aware of the accusations that he had spirited away consciousness by a sleight of hand:

Does the heterophenomenological enterprise, whatever its utility to science, simply leave the *real* problems of consciousness untouched? John Searle, in rebutting my commentary on his attack on 'strong' artificial intelligence, explicitly warns you not to let me hoodwink you with this *hetero* approach. . . . Now have I tricked you? Why would I want to do a thing like that? (Dennett, 1982, p. 177; emphases in original)[35]

---

[34]As Dennett (1978) and Mandler (1985) have pointed out, discussions of consciousness in cognitive psychology have generally been either avoided or incidental to a more technical discussion concerning mental events.

[35]Dennett's heterophenomenology and Searle's arguments are considered later. The philosophical position of strong artificial intelligence is

Dennett would have one believe that the transition from *subjective consciousness₂* to *consciousness₃* has been carried through successfully.

It is time to turn to a more detailed examination of Dennett's notion of consciousness. Dennett has discussed consciousness in terms of that which one is conscious of. Because of his assumption that there are mental processes going on analogous to those of a computer, Dennett has explained consciousness in terms of access to mental processes. Thus, "That of which I am conscious is that to which I have *access*, or (to put the emphasis where it belongs), that to which *I* have access" (1978, p. 150; emphases in original). But now, access has a computer analogue. Dennett has made the distinction between computational access, the access of a computer to the results of procedures for use in further procedures; and public access, the availability of the results of procedures for a mechanism that can provide a printout. Dennett's answer has been straightforward. Consciousness involves "the *print-out faculty's* computational access to the information it publishes" (Dennett, 1978, p. 152; emphasis in original).

The print-out faculty, however, is not the "I" but a subpersonal component. Dennett has admitted that, according to his view, a human being resembles an organization with various components. Since the functionalist's claim is that it is the processing of information that is important and not the substrate within which that processing takes place for the presence of mental faculties, Dennett has had to allow for the possibility that other kinds of organizations have conscious experiences. In 1978, Dennett agreed that there was a problem there:[36]

> Davis [in an unpublished paper] has raised a graphic version of this objection with regard to functionalist theories of pain. Let a functionalist theory of pain (whatever its details) be instantiated by a system the subassemblies of which are not such things as *C*-fibers and reticular systems but telephone lines and offices staffed by people. Perhaps it is a giant robot controlled by an army of human beings that inhabit it. When the theory's functionally characterized conditions for pain are now met we must say, if the theory is true, that the robot is in pain. That is, real pain, as real as our own, would exist in virtue of the perhaps disinterested and businesslike activities of these bureaucratic teams, executing their proper functions. It does *seem* that there must be more to pain than that. (Dennett, 1978, p. 153; emphasis in original)

---

that a properly programmed computer really is a mind (Flanagan, 1984).

[36]The problem that Dennett identified is, in essence, the same as Searle's argument provided later.

Dennett left this problem aside at that point and remarked instead that the explanation of the subjective "I" in subpersonal terms is common practice in cognitive psychology. He went into some detail then to produce a flow-chart and to account for some conscious phenomena using this flow-chart. "Having an inner life – being something it is like something to be – is on this account a matter of having a certain sort of functional organization, but the only natural entities that could be expected to have such functional organizations would be highly evolved and *socialized* creatures" (Dennett, 1978, p. 171; emphasis in original).

Having given such an account of consciousness, what justification could Dennett offer that such a scheme could work?

> There is no *proving* that something that seems to have an inner life does in fact have one – if by 'proving' we understand, as we often do, the evincing of evidence that can be seen to establish by principles already agreed upon that something is the case. In this paper I set myself the task of constructing an 'I', a something it was like something to be, out of sub-personal parts of the sort encountered in cognitivistic theories. I do not now wish to claim that I have *demonstrably* succeeded in this. (Dennett, 1978, p. 172; emphases in original)

Rather, Dennett has claimed that, having examined his own experience, he has found it to be compatible with a functionalist explanation and that his effort has been one of attempting to elicit the same realization in others (1978).

In 1982, Dennett introduced the idea of "heterophenomenology" whereby he claimed to provide a method for adequately taking into account a person's conscious phenomenal contents. In essence, this method is the Turing test. Dennett suggested that a person or zombie be given the opportunity to explain, at any length she wishes, her beliefs, feelings, and so on. These verbalizations would be recorded as a text which would then be used as a basis for an interpretation. This interpretation would yield a world-view which could be examined and understood in the same way that a fictional world encountered through a novel, is understood.[37] In particular, a work of fiction may have a narrator who may or may not bear any resemblance to the author. This narrator Dennett has called the "heterophenomenological subject":

> The particular *point of view* of the subject is an objectively extrapolatable abstraction about which much can be said independently of whether or not that point of view is, as we might say, *inhabited*.

---

[37]One could, of course, do this with Dennett's own account of reality.

If our subject is a zombie, the point of view we define and describe by the heterophenomenological method is vacant, not occupied – there's nobody home, you might say – but curiously enough this dire prospect (well, isn't it a dire prospect?) has no apparent bearing on the utility for theory of the construct. It will be perspicuous, no doubt, to describe much of what goes on in and with the experimental subject (the *thing* we are investigating) from the subject's point of view (from the heterophenomenological subject's point of view), whether or not there really is – or there appears to be – something it is like to be the subject in question. (Dennett, 1982, pp. 166 - 167; emphases in original)

In particular, Dennett has said, descriptions of mental imagery can be legitimately considered in this heterophenomenological manner. Such descriptions do not, thereby, necessarily have any serious implications for the actual cognitive processes that take place in a person or a zombie. To support this argument, Dennett has cited recent research in artificial intelligence in which machines have been able to successfully manipulate the environment or account for their own actions. These machines could potentially give an account of their recognition of the objects in their environment in imagistic terms, even though the machines did not process information in this way.

What about zombies? Dennett has accepted the Turing test. If a machine can produce a heterophenomenological text that is indistinguishable from that produced by a human being, then it has the same ontological status as a human being:

I have been playing along with this zombie idea – for tactical reasons that should now be obvious – but in fact I think (in case you have not already guessed) that the concept is just incoherent. The idea of a being that could pass all the heterophenomenological tests but still be a merely unconscious automaton strikes me as simply bizarre. I don't know how to argue against it, however, beyond presenting the case I have just presented for heterophenomenology. This leaves a symmetrical standoff, however, for those who think the secret light of consciousness is untouched by my reflections are equally unforthcoming in support of their creed. (Dennett, 1982, p. 179)

Dennett's concluding sentence of his 1982 paper is illuminating: "Consciousness is not a *process* that *makes things*; it is a state of being informed – or misinformed – about what is actually happening" (Dennett, 1982, p. 179; emphases in original). It seems that Dennett has said that consciousness does not concern itself with existent subjective phenomena, but is fallible information about a state of affairs. Thus, as Lyons (1986) has recognized, Dennett's version of consciousness is derivative on his version of introspection, namely, the speech mechanism's access to inner processes. Full blooded consciousness has been replaced with information.

This has not only been the thrust made by Dennett to account for consciousness, but represents the position in cognitive psychology more generally. Just as, for James, all of existence was made up of the building blocks of pure experience, and for the materialist, matter is the ontological cornerstone, so for the functionalist, it is information from which all else is made.[38] This was most evident with Klein's definition of consciousness as information, given in Chapter 1. Similarly Lowenhard (1981) has considered consciousness to be further information in an information-processing system whose purpose is to make the system more efficient. Other explanations in terms of mechanisms and properties of information-processing have been reviewed by Mandler (1985).

One question that arises, given such accounts of consciousness, is the question of why, if consciousness is an aspect of information-processing, is consciousness conscious? Eccles has expressed this well:

I would like to invert the present discussion by asking as a neuro-physiologist, why do we have to be conscious at all? We can in principle, explain all our input-output performance in terms of activity of neuronal circuits; and, consequently, consciousness seems to be absolutely unnecessary. I don't believe this story of course; but at the same time I do not know the logical answer to it. In attempting to answer the question, why do we have to be conscious? it [sic] surely cannot be claimed as self-evident that consciousness is a necessary requisite for such performances as logical argument or reasoning, or even for initiative and creative activities. (1966, p. 248)

An analogous way of phrasing this may be to ask whether information about something is the same as understanding that something. This difference between information and understanding has been pointed out by Searle with his, now famous, Chinese room.

Suppose that one has been placed in a room. While in that room, one has been given pieces of paper with Chinese symbols on them as well as other pieces of paper written in English giving other Chinese symbols that one is to produce whenever one has a first set. Now, knowing no Chinese, an English speaker could use the rules given in the second set to produce a response to the first set and give it to those outside the

---

[38]This last position is an oversimplification of the position in some respects. However, Pribram (1986) has explicitly stated that matter is energy and energy and information are the same thing, so that one can say that information is the material out of which all else in the universe is built.

room. From the point of view of someone who speaks Chinese, these answers would be indistinguishable from the writing of a Chinese-speaking person. In other words, the Chinese room passes the Turing test. But there is no way that the person in the Chinese room could be said to "understand" what they have said (Searle, 1981).

It does not help, Searle has said, to insist that it is the system as a whole and not just the person inside the room to whom understanding should be attributed, because one could, in principle, memorize the code for translating one set of symbols into another, so that the room becomes internalized with respect to the person. Furthermore, one has to recognize that the functionalist is not merely seeking to anthropomorphize mechanical systems, but would maintain that the machine's understanding is ontically the same as a human's (Searle, 1981).

It would appear that there is still something left over after the best attempts to characterize consciousness functionally, a point conceded by Fodor:

> Having qualitative content is supposed to be a critical factor in what makes a mental state conscious. Many psychologists who are inclined to accept the functionalist framework, are nonetheless worried about the failure of functionalism to reveal much about the nature of consciousness. Functionalists have made a few ingenious attempts to talk themselves and their colleagues out of this worry, but they have not, in my view, done so with much success. . . . As matters stand, the problem of qualitative content poses a serious threat to the assertion that functionalism can provide a general theory of the mental. (Fodor, 1981, p. 122)

A second problem, according to Fodor, that functionalists have to deal with, is the problem of intentionality. Intentionality has been hiding just below the surface throughout this book. It is time to bring it into the open.

4.4 Phenomenological notions of consciousness

In Section 2, the attempt to discount consciousness from a position of extreme objectivity, that of eliminative materialism, was discussed. A more moderate, computationalist version of consciousness was introduced in Section 3. In this section, some of the issues concerning consciousness from a subjective point of view are examined. Intentionality is considered in the first subsection and extreme transcendentalist versions of consciousness in the second subsection.

4.4.1 Intentionality

What is intentionality? In seeking to find a common feature of mental phenomena, Brentano in 1874 gave the following characterization of mental events:

> Every mental phenomenon is characterized by what the scholastics of the Middle Ages called the intentional (and also mental) inexistence . . . of an object . . . and what we could call, although in not entirely unambiguous terms, the reference to a content, a direction upon an object (by which we are not to understand a reality in this case), or an immanent objectivity. Each one includes something as object within itself, although not always in the same way. In presentation something is presented, in judgment something is affirmed or denied, in love loved, in hate hated, in desire desired, etc.
> This intentional inexistence is exclusively characteristic of mental phenomena. No physical phenomenon manifests anything similar. Consequently, we can define mental phenomena by saying that they are such phenomena as include an object intentionally within themselves. (Brentano, 1874/1960, pp. 50 - 51)

This sense of intentionality has been characterized as "aboutness" – that feature of mental events whereby they are about something. For Brentano, this was precisely the quality of mental events that physical phenomena could not have.

The discussion of intentionality was taken up by Brentano's student, Husserl, who developed a theory of conscious mental acts. Because of Husserl's prominence as the founding father of the philosophical position of phenomenology as well as, ironically, being touted as the father of cognitive psychology by Dreyfus (1982), some of the features of his theory are summarized here from Smith and McIntyre (1982).

Husserl called acts of consciousness, those events which consist in "(a conscious subject's) intending . . . or being directed . . . to, or being related . . . to, an object" (Smith & McIntyre, 1982, p. 5). One approach used in trying to understand intentionality, was to examine the nature of the objects towards which acts of consciousness are directed. While it is possible to interpret Husserl's work as also belonging to this genre, Smith and McIntyre have explained how Husserl's account can be seen as one which seeks to understand intentionality by looking at the relationship between the subject and the object.

Each conscious act, for Husserl, consisted of three components – a *noesis*, a *noema* and an object. The *noesis* was that real part of a conscious act which made the experience intentional. The *noema*, on the other hand, was not "real" but an atemporal kind of meaning or *Sinn*. The ontological status of the object was unimportant on this account. Thus, "an act *intends* (is directed toward or is intentionally related to) an object if and only if the act (or its noesis) entertains a certain noematic

Sinn and that Sinn prescribes that object" (Smith & McIntyre, 1982, p. 143; emphasis in original).

Objects of natural experience were transcendent objects in the sense that they could never be fully conceptually captured in a single act. This was due to the fact that the perceptual evidence for the existence of such objects was always incomplete from the point of view of a single act. In fact, perceptual experiences were more complicated than other intentional experiences such as, for example, judging, remembering and imagining, because they entailed a sensory aspect. The barrage of sensations or *hyle* was a phase of the noesis and required a *Sinn* to give it shape so that it could be experienced as a perception of something. For Husserl, perception formed the basis of one's understanding of the world and hence received much of his attention. In keeping with Husserl's emphasis, the discussion here uses an example from perception.

This problem of the perception of transcendent objects highlights the fact that no act of consciousness exists in isolation from other acts. Something about the object is always left open in an act with a particular *Sinn*. In order to explicate the way in which further determinations of an object are possible, Husserl introduced the notion of an act-horizon – a collection of possible acts whose *Sinne* are compatible with the *Sinn* of the original act, that can further determine a given object. Parallel to this act-horizon was an object-horizon which was the collection of further determined objects that these further acts of consciousness were directed towards.

In order to recognize that the notion of further determinations has been made precise by Husserl, one needs to see that, for Husserl, each *Sinn* could be broken down into two components: the predicate senses which prescribed the properties that an object was to have, and an X which specified the object to which the properties were ascribed. Further determination, then, consisted of further conditions that were to be met by an object, given in acts with the same X.

Following an examination of Husserl's notions of horizon and manifold, however, Smith and McIntyre relaxed the constraints on the definition of an act-horizon, so that the *Sinne* of the acts in the horizon did not need to be strictly compatible with the *Sinn* of the original act,[39] allowing for further perceptions of an object that could have revealed it to have been different from what had been originally perceived, and so that these further acts need not necessarily have further determined the object, in the sense of including further information about it.

For Husserl, each act-horizon was predelineated in an act of con-

---

[39]That is to say, the predicate senses need not be compatible.

sciousness so that some possible acts were understood to further determine the object of the original act, and others were seen as not doing so. These further possible acts could not be merely logically possible, but needed to have been motivated by what the subject believed to be possible. This brings to light the importance of relevant background beliefs and items of knowledge that determined which *Sinne* were to be included in an act-horizon.

The act-horizon had a temporal structure. In the case of perception, for example, one could have a series of possible future perceptions that further determined an object. Thus, if one were to see a tree on a hillside, walking closer to the tree may reveal that it is a maple tree with red leaves, and so on. These further possible perceptions would be acts in the horizon of the original act in which the tree would have been first noticed. Now, if the tree were a maple tree with red leaves on a hillside, then there are a number of possible combinations of further perceptions that would have revealed this. Thus, Smith and McIntyre have called continuous series of possible further perceptions, "possible verification chains," and collections of series of further perceptions, which revealed the same object, they called "a family of possible verification chains." The collection of all families of possible verification chains made up the act-horizon.

To summarize, for Husserl there were two major characteristics of any conscious mental act, the *Sinn* and the horizon. The first of these encapsulated the intentional nature of one's mental acts, and the second revealed mental acts to be dynamic in nature. Thus, Husserl presented a specific analysis of conscious acts as they appeared to be experienced.[40]

The term intentionality, however, has taken on a fairly loose meaning, as Barwise has indicated:

> Fodor often says that 'intentionality' is just fancy talk for 'aboutness'. . . . But all too often talk of intentionality is talk of a mixed bag, where properties, concepts and meanings get identified, with aboutness lost in the shuffle. (Barwise, 1986, p. 327)

In particular, it is not clear what the relationship of intentionality is to consciousness. Searle has brought this matter up explicitly. He has defined intentionality as "that property of many mental states and events by which they are directed at or about or of objects and states of affairs in the world" (Searle, 1983, p. 1). According to Searle, there are intentional states that are not conscious. There may be, for example, unconscious

---

[40]His "phenomenological reduction" whereby mental acts are themselves the objects of mental acts, has raised considerable controversy (Dreyfus, 1982).

beliefs that one holds. Alternatively, there may be conscious states that are not intentional. Undirected anxiety or depression are not intentional. Searle has pointed out that the apparently intentional feature of anxiety suggested by the linguistic formulation "experience of anxiety" results from the conflation of two different formulations of the supposed object of intentionality.

> The experience of anxiety and the anxiety are identical; but the fear of snakes is not identical with snakes. It is characteristic of Intentional states, as I use the notion, that there is a distinction between the state and what the state is directed at or about or of (though this does not exclude the possibility of self-referential forms of Intentionality. . . .) (Searle, 1983, p. 2)

Thus, in general, it is not clear that conscious mental acts are necessarily characterized by intentionality.

In spite of these problems of clarifying intentionality, as mentioned in Section 3 of this chapter, Fodor has admitted that intentionality poses a problem for the functionalist program. One way around that problem is to replace intentional occurrences with linguistic occurrences that have certain characteristics, and then to show that such intentional sentences can be replaced with extensional sentences that do not have these characteristics. This attempt has involved considerable effort on the part of philosophers (Arbib, 1972).

Fodor does not think that the problem of intentionality is as intractable as the problem of qualitative contents or qualia. It does involve, however, postulating a mental language, sometimes referred to as "mentalese" (e.g., Dennett, 1978), in which these sentences with intentional properties are to be written.

> To think of a system (such as the nervous system) as a computer is to raise questions about the nature of the code in which it computes and the semantic properties of the symbols in the code. In fact, the analogy between minds and computers actually implies the postulation of mental symbols. There is no computation without representation. (Fodor, 1981, p. 122)

In other words, according to Fodor, human cognitive activity is the formal manipulation of formal symbols in the manner of generating a proof in an elementary language in mathematics.

> What has captured Fodor's imagination is that we logicians have developed formal proof procedures for certain formal languages, procedures that can be used to build inference engines, machines that can carry out formal proofs, even if not very well. Here, Fodor thinks, is hope for a mechanism underlying thinking. Posit an

internal, formal language of thought. (Barwise, 1986, p. 331)

Barwise has been skeptical of the view that a person is necessarily endowed with an inner mentalese or that such logical constructions would work. His arguments have been based on the contention that embedding circumstances have to be taken into account whenever considering human cognitive functioning – circumstances which do not have to be taken into account in formal operations.

But the whole project of reducing intentionality to syntactic properties is based on the assumption of the omnipotence of language. Intentionality is in essence, a feature of mental activity. It is lived as part of experience, and it is an article of faith that it can ever be adequately characterized syntactically. For example, as Van Dusen has said: "I would have no quarrel with anyone who asserted the [sic] language of the novelist, poet, or musician is closer to the quality of human experience than the language of psychologists" (1967, p. 214).

4.4.2 Subjectivist accounts of consciousness

Whether explicitly characterized by intentionality or not, the work of those who followed Husserl reflected his phenomenalist stance. Heidegger, one of Husserl's students, replaced the notion of consciousness with that of being as the central notion of his philosophy (Tapper, 1986). But his emphasis on experience as the ground for all understanding strengthened the mentalist tradition adopted by Brentano, James and Husserl. There was a more general movement, existentialism, represented in Germany by Heidegger and in France by Sartre (1960) and Marcel (1976) which in turn has influenced the third force movement in psychology spearheaded in part by Maslow (1968), that sought to place human concerns at the centre of psychology.[41] Although humanistic psychology has not been accepted into the mainstream of psychology, it has acted, in part, as a conscience to remind psychologists of the deeper issues with which psychology is concerned (Hilgard, 1987). One of the tenets of humanistic psychology is that a person is motivated to always grow beyond their present limitations (Maslow, 1968). Furthermore, each person can supposedly only know for themselves what direction they should take.

The psychoanalysts had given control of the person over to the unconscious with which one was to make a pact so as to avoid conflicts. The behaviorists had denied consciousness in any meaningful form, viewing the personality as a product of environmental contingencies. The humanists granted full consciousness to the person and provided her with the opportunity of coming to grips with her own life. It became evident

---

[41]The first force in psychology was considered to be Freud's psychoanalysis, and the second force, Watson's behaviorism.

to some that certain disciplines would be required to adequately deal with existential issues and personality growth. These techniques for self-transformation have sometimes been called the "consciousness disciplines".[42]

There are at least two reasons why the organized procedures used for understanding the purpose of one's life have been called the "consciousness disciplines". To begin with, the consciousness disciplines involve an attempt to increase one's awareness, understanding, and knowledgeability of oneself, one's mental processes and reality more generally. Secondly, consciousness itself is understood to be the key that enables personal growth to take place. The development of latent understanding with regard to the existential issues does not occur automatically. It is thought to be something that requires considerable conscious effort. Paradoxically, as one's understanding of reality changes, one may go through a period of being uncertain about what consciousness is:

> I don't know whether I'm right or wrong or how correct my currently cherished set of beliefs, assumptions, and world views are. I don't know how my mind works, how deeply it extends, how to control it, how to escape from the all-encompassing realities it appears to create. I don't know what consciousness is, what its limits are, don't even know if the concept of limits applies to consciousness or to us. I don't know how unaware I am or how aware I can become, what the limits to knowledge are, what our capacities and potentials may be, or whether I can accurately assess the wisdom and well-being of anyone significantly wiser than myself. (Walsh, 1984a, p. 31)

Having made a sustained effort to practice the exercises outlined in the consciousness disciplines, one may find one's understanding of reality dramatically changing:

> I do feel that I know that I've been wrong, that I've underestimated the mind, consciousness, us, the extent to which we are asleep, sleepwalking, and trapped in our individual and shared cultural illusions. I've also underestimated the vastness of human suffering,

---

[42]It would be a mistake to say that the humanistic movement gave rise to the consciousness disciplines. These have always been present, in religious or philosophical literature. Merrell-Wolff, in the quotation of Chapter 2, referred to "manuals" which he used in order to guide him in his search for understanding of himself and the reason for his existence. The humanistic movement provided a framework, at least on the periphery of academia, within which the consciousness disciplines could take root; but it was, itself, only one of the factors contributing to the growth of interest in such subjects.

especially the extent of unnecessary, well-intended suffering. I am clear that I've totally misunderstood the nature of the great religions, the practices such as meditation and yoga, and that I've underestimated the potential sensitivity of perception and introspection and the extent of wisdom that lies within us all.

How did this come about? Very simply, by starting to examine my own mind and to pay attention to what was formerly unrecognized subliminal experience. (Walsh, 1984a, p. 32)

Normal consciousness is viewed as a state of being asleep and altered states of consciousness attained through consistent practice seen as states of that consciousness in which one can see reality more clearly (Chang, 1978; Merrell-Wolff, 1973a, 1973b; Walsh, 1976, 1980, 1984a, 1984b, 1988). One's consciousness is seen to change with one's transformation so that, in particular, one's notion of consciousness may change so that one comes to see it as pivotal in one's own growth – unbounded, potent, in consonance with transcendent beliefs more generally.

Walsh (1980) has discussed the dependence of the validity of the consciousness disciplines on the beliefs and experiential background of the person who is investigating them. Because of the ineffable nature of many of the experiences of altered states of consciousness, they must be experienced in order to be adequately understood and judged. As Merrell-Wolff has pointed out in the quotation given in Chapter 2, one cannot just stand back passively as an observer. If one is to gain access to these experiences, one must commit oneself to the process.

Thus, the subjective aspects of consciousness have been historically understood from a number of perspectives. The issue of intentionality has focussed attention upon the subjective aspect of conscious mental acts. Existentialism and humanistic psychology have emphasized the importance of personal experience. Within the "consciousness disciplines" self-transformation is understood to be an important ingredient of understanding consciousness. Such self-transformation involves sustained participation in self-observation and introspection. Consciousness itself, on such an account, is understood as a reality that gives rise to the physical world.

4.5 Miscellaneous notions of consciousness

A number of specific issues have been examined in this chapter which have been important in shaping notions of consciousness. In this section, the point is made that there has been an increase of interest in the subject area of consciousness and some of the forms that the revitalized activity in consciousness is taking are mentioned.

4.5.1 The consciousness revolution

A number of authors have pointed to the resurgence of interest in the subject area of consciousness (e.g., Osborne, 1981; Pelletier, 1985b; Sperry, 1987; Webb, 1981). Natsoulas (1978a) has pointed out that discussions of the problem of consciousness have been appearing in respectable locations in the academic literature. Helminiak (1984) has argued for an adequate treatment of the issue of consciousness without concern for disciplinary restrictions.

Sperry (1987) has called the resurgence of interest in human mental functioning the "consciousness revolution" in order to emphasize the importance of consciousness. Although Sperry could be labelled a functionalist, he has brought attention to the importance of subjective, conscious experience. He has advocated a theory of downward causation, which is similar to that of Hofstadter, given in Chapter 1:

> The physical and chemical forces in the brain, though still present and operating, are enveloped and programmed by the higher laws and dynamics of conscious and subconscious mental processes. The more highly evolved 'emergent' mental properties of brain action determine when, where, and how the brain's molecular events will occur but without interfering with the laws of physics and chemistry at the molecule level. . . . Brain cell excitation no longer waits solely on biophysical forces but also obeys a higher command involving feelings, wants, choice, reasoning, moral values, and all other 'things of the mind.' The subjective dynamics of mind and consciousness transcend and control brain physiology at the same time that they are determined by it. (Sperry, 1986, p. 418)

Sperry has suggested that mental activity has primacy over physical activity for the control of behavior. Thus:

> According to the new mentalist view, by contrast, things are controlled not only from below upward by atomic and molecular action but also from above downward by mental, social, political and other macro properties. Primacy is given to the higher level controls rather than to the lowest. The higher, emergent, molar or macro phenomena and their properties throughout nature supersede the less evolved controls of the components. (Sperry, 1987, p. 45)

Sperry has suggested that it is the possibility of understanding consciousness as a causal agent within a materialist framework as a solution to the problem of free will that has made the widespread acceptance of cognitivism possible.

> To topple behaviorism and its base required . . . that the conventional reductive microdeterminist reasoning of science itself must be toppled also. Only the principle of emergent or molar determinism . . . appears to qualify. Whereas the basic behaviorist paradigm was not jeopardized by computer science nor by other cogni-

tive developments of the 1960s, it could not cope with this causal concept of consciousness. If the new interactionist view of consciousness were correct, the opposed behaviorist philosophy of science had to be wrong. (Sperry, 1987, p. 45)

It is not the purpose here to support or refute Sperry's claims. Certainly there has been a cognitive revolution, but has there been, as well, a consciousness revolution? Natsoulas has remarked:

I surely do not need to demonstrate here the curious fact that, after years of revival, the topic of consciousness still awaits to be fully admitted into mainstream psychology. It is as though American psychology were working through, over numerous sessions of a protracted self-therapy, some very strong defenses against consciousness. Insight into 'the problem' occurred some time ago. The existence of the repressed and its relevance to comprehending human mental function have been acknowledged. But the patient struggles on to give to the phenomena of consciousness an enlightened form of expression. (Natsoulas, 1983a, p. 13)[43]

Osborne has noted that, although consciousness has been studied, this has been done only within specified contexts:

A plea for greater interest and activity in the psychology of consciousness and the closely related field of transpersonal psychology is often met with irritation. We are told that there is no need to continue flogging a 'dead horse.' Of course, consciousness is important! Consciousness, we are told, has long been acknowledged as an important aspect of human functioning. There is no need to fuss. However, the point overlooked by exponents of this view is that consciousness is usually dealt with incidentally within specialized fields of psychology. (Osborne, 1979, p. 92)

Thus, while there has been a revolution towards cognitivism in psychology, the subject area of consciousness itself has yet to be adequately addressed.

4.5.2 Miscellaneous issues concerning consciousness

The remainder of this chapter is devoted to mentioning some of the specific areas of research within which the subject of consciousness has come up, in an effort to bring them together in one place.

------

[43]Natsoulas' formulation of this problem is the same as Harman's third reason for the failure of sufficient research in the area of consciousness, mentioned in Chapter 2.

Perhaps the first problem on any research agenda is to clarify the definition and concept of consciousness. As seen from Chapter 3, there are a number of referents for the term consciousness. *What is being argued in this book is that the ontological status of the referents is a function of one's beliefs about reality and purported personal experiences.* This leads to the more general problem of determining the ways in which consciousness is conceptualized and explained.

Along with the problems of definition and conceptualization, is the problem of determining under what circumstances an organism is conscious. This is the question of zombies raised in Chapters 2 and 4 for machines and the problem of other minds. This includes the more practical problem of deciding whether or not animals are conscious (e.g., Appleton, 1976). In addition, there is the issue of the status of the consciousness of any given individual following brain trauma (e.g., Pribram, 1976). Clearly, whether or not something or someone is conscious will depend not only on the definition one is willing to accept, but also on one's notion of consciousness more generally, as discussed in previous sections of this chapter.

There is also the topographical problem of measuring cognitive activity in terms of its relationship to consciousness. Thus, the tradition of the unconscious, which fell into disrepute with the cognitive revolution, needs to be re-established as an important aspect of human functioning (Bowers, 1987). The term "unconscious" usually carries meanings derived from the psychoanalytic tradition. That which is not conscious can be further elaborated into the preconscious, the subconscious and the superconscious. The preconscious consists of material that one could be conscious of if one were to pay attention to it. The subconscious itself has two recognized meanings: on the one hand, the term refers to cognitive processes that one is not, and may not be able to be, aware of; on the other hand, the term can assume the most prevalent meaning of the term "unconscious" – namely cognitive material that is actively repressed from awareness. Lastly, one can talk about a superconscious which is more knowledgeable than the conscious, preconscious or subconscious realms and from which can purportedly emerge insights as well as inspiration and a deep sense of well-being (Assagioli, 1965). It is not always clear how consciousness is related to these not-conscious domains. In addition, the term co-conscious has been used to refer to two or more seemingly separate personalities within a person that are aware of one another.[44]

The problem of epistemology has been discussed in Chapter 2. How is one to understand consciousness when understanding is an activity that

---

[44]This was mentioned also in connection with the definitions of Chapter 3.

itself involves that which is understood? Perhaps consciousness is mysterious, and ultimately unknowable.[45]

Aside from the general issues concerning consciousness, the discussion of consciousness comes up naturally in the context of human cognition. The topics of perception, visual imagery, memory, attention, problem-solving and language production all require some discussion of consciousness. In fact, consciousness itself is often discussed peripherally within those subject areas without being tied to the wider body of literature concerning consciousness. Most of these discussions are, furthermore, within the context of cognitive psychology which uses a restricted notion of consciousness, as discussed in Chapter 4.

The usual way of introducing the subject of consciousness is not, however, by examining the subject as such, nor does it occur in the context of human cognition; rather the topic of consciousness arises in the context of the discussion of altered states of consciousness (e.g., Wolman & Ullman, 1986). This is also the way that the subject of consciousness is typically introduced in introductory psychology courses (Webb, 1981). While consciousness was not itself the object of study for a long time in North American psychology, its various states were being examined. Webb, for example, who worked in the area of sleep research for 20 years, came to wonder what it was that altered with the onset and termination of sleep (Webb, 1981). Similarly, Hilgard (1987), working in the area of hypnosis, has turned his attention to the question of consciousness more generally (Hilgard, 1980). Roberts (1983; 1984; 1985) has argued that the notion "state-of-consciousness" is a central one in psychology and that discussions of cognitive events necessitate reference to the states of consciousness to which such discussions apply.

The recurrence of interest in consciousness can, to a large extent, be attributed to the effects of the use of hallucinogenic drugs in the 1960s (Blewett, personal communication, 1984). The use of psychedelic drugs can lead to drug-induced altered states in which personal experience changes with changes in consciousness (Jarvik, 1979; Grinspoon & Bakalar, 1979; Leary, 1983; Tart, 1969). Mandell (1980) has sought to determine the brain mechanisms whereby such changes are possible.

But alterations in the state of consciousness can be induced in a number of ways. For example, this can be done through biofeedback (Green & Green, 1986), meditation (Carrington, 1986), hypnosis (Hilgard, 1979), psychotherapy (Walsh, 1976), mathematics (Muses, 1970) and walking on hot coals (Farrell, 1985 - 86). There are more spontaneous alterations of consciousness that take place during the waking hours

---

[45]Although no more so than matter itself, as suggested, for example, by Gregory (1980).

(Rossi, 1986), with the onset of sleep (Broughton, 1986) and with death (Moody, 1979; O'Regan, 1985; Tart, 1985). One of the longstanding problems that researchers have been faced with is the problem of deciding when an "altered" state is really an altered state, and when the phenomena under observation are really influenced by the alterations in the state of consciousness (Hilgard, 1980). At any rate, there remains the problem of determining what it is that is being altered with alterations of states of consciousness.

The most visible growth of interest in consciousness has not been within the academic community at all but in the population at large. Within popular psychology and the "wellness industry" there has been an explosion of interest and writing concerning the quality of one's personal experience and one's life. The term consciousness appears to be used in this context in a non-specific way simply to indicate this as the area of discourse. This phenomenon could bear more careful investigation to determine its importance, if any, to the understanding of consciousness. Such an effort has been made, for example, by Roberts (1986) in examining the emergence of a hero archetype, "the hero as consciousness explorer," in popular movies and books.

Associated in part with popular interest in consciousness is the term "group consciousness" which is used to refer to a person's awareness of her position within her social environment. This use of the term consciousness is an example of *behavioral consciousness*$_2$. Toulmin (1982) has argued that the notion of consciousness properly refers to events in the public domain, so that consciousness takes on the meaning of the original Latin term *conscientia* as discussed in Chapter 3. Often, however, when talking about group consciousness, it is not that of which one is aware as a group member that one is talking about but, more generally, group-appropriate thoughts, feelings and experiences (Roberts, 1984) that may not be conscious. This is an important phenomenon, and one central to the thesis of this book. Heidegger (1926/1962) sought to demonstrate how each person naturally appropriates an understanding of reality from the culture within which she finds herself, and lives her life in accordance with the expectations of society. For Walsh (1984b), the understanding and behavior consistent with today's social expectations are destructive, not only to the individual, but to all of civilization, and therefore, pathological. A change in attitudes and beliefs was seen as necessary in order to resolve the present-day world situation.

The notion of consciousness shows up in the context of parapsychology, which has been caught in an argument concerning its validity (e.g., Child, 1986; Clemmer, 1986; Tyler, 1981). Gregory (1980) has suggested that consciousness itself is a paranormal phenomenon, in that it cannot be explained by science, although it is not clear that this is not just a renaming of the phenomenon. Some of the recent work in contemporary physics has suggested that consciousness may play a role in anomalous events (Jahn, 1981; Jahn & Dunne, 1986, 1987; Walker, 1974). This is suggested also by Alexander, who has maintained that mental activity has been exploited for military purposes: "There are weapons systems that operate on the power of the mind and whose lethal capacity has already been demonstrated" (Alexander, 1980, p. 47).

What is the relation between consciousness and time, space and matter? Miller and Buckhout (1973) have maintained that the limitations of consciousness determine the extension of time and space. When is now (Fischer, 1986a)? Heidegger (1926/1962) has argued against the conceptualization of time as beads on a string. In a similar vein, is it possible, because of consciousness, to transcend three or four-dimensional space (McLaughlin, 1986)? The problem of the relationship between consciousness and matter also arose in Section 2.

Interpretations of the principles and results of modern physics have been made which argue that consciousness plays a critical role directly in the determination of reality (Baruss, 1986; Bohm, 1980; Briggs & Peat, 1984; Jahn & Dunne, 1986, 1987; Stapp, 1985, 1986; Walker, 1970, 1974, 1977; Wigner, 1972; Wolf, 1984; Ziemelis, 1986), although such a position has not been generally accepted in contemporary physics (Ballentine, 1986; Wasserman, 1983). The problem is compounded by the difficulty of the subject area (e.g., Wheeler & Zurek, 1983) and by differing implicit notions of consciousness ranging from that of unconscious information processing to subjective, intentional awareness. In addition, there has been an enthusiastic but often uncritical effort to demonstrate parallels between modern theoretical physics and Eastern mysticism (Restivo, 1978) in part, perhaps, motivated by a desire to improve the acceptability and status of mysticism (Restivo, 1982).

While James's notion of a stream of consciousness was to make little impact on a psychology that was to deny the importance of mental events, it did make an impact in art and literature. Pope and Singer (1978) have argued that, although consciousness has emerged as a legitimate area for scientific investigation, because of the nature of the techniques employed in studying consciousness, it appears to possess a quality of organization and rationality that is inconsistent with one's experience of the flow of consciousness or with its portrayal by artists. This flowlike aspect of the nature of consciousness must be kept in mind when trying to understand it.

One of the interesting things about the concept of consciousness that makes it difficult to study, is that the notion of consciousness tends to function as a Rorschach blot, giving various authors an opportunity, not to address the problem of consciousness, but to tell their favorite stories or vent their philosophy of life (e.g., Klein, 1984; Ornstein, 1972; Wolf, 1984). Furthermore, taking up the subject of consciousness has not been confined to those with a background in philosophy, psychology, psychiatry, neuroscience or computer science, but appears to have been undertaken by the intelligentsia at large. Thus, for example, Arkle (1974) trained as an engineer, but renovating houses for a living, has described consciousness in terms of vectors.[46] Oxley (1982), who appears to be allied with the humanities more generally, has given a philosophical discourse about consciousness in which he argues for the philosophical necessity of divinity. Jaynes is a psychologist, but has an anomalous theory of consciousness. He has maintained that consciousness arose within the last 3000 years as a result of the disappearance of hallucinated voices. Thus, human cognition and language developed without consciousness but gave a person the capacity for metaphorical thinking. Metaphorical thought is the basis of consciousness according to Jaynes (Hilgard, 1987; Jaynes, 1976; 1986).

Consciousness has always been part of the subject matter of psychiatry and clinical psychology. Psychoanalysis consists of making the unconscious, conscious; and Rogerian therapy, by placing initiative within the client, has recognized consciousness as causal within its own domain (Rogers, 1961; Rogers & Stevens, 1967). It is often thought that clinicians have little to say about consciousness, but Globus, Maxwell and Savodnik (1976) have pointed out that the understanding that comes from participation in a therapeutic relationship cannot be ignored. Beck (1976) has argued that the only model of the mind-brain relationship that is able to account for clinical observations is an interactive one. Czikszentmihalyi has reviewed evidence to show that "*the inability to focus attention voluntarily leads to psychic disruption, and eventually to psychopathology*," (1978, p. 348; emphasis in original). Frith (1981) has maintained that aberrations of one's conscious functioning can lead to psychopathology, while O'Regan (1983) and Zweig (1985) have pointed to the possibility that such aberrations can result in organic damage. Sometimes the roots of pathology are understood to be on the fringe of consciousness (e.g., E. Taylor, 1981, 1982; Wolman, 1986). The possible role of consciousness in pathology has suggested to some that alterations of consciousness can be effective in psychotherapy (e.g., Assagioli, 1965; Beck, 1976; Budzynski, 1986; Ujhely, 1982).

The question of meaning comes up in the context of consciousness. Here one has to distinguish between the use of the term meaning to refer to the referent of a thought or symbolic expression and the use of the term meaning to refer to the purposiveness of life. The former can be understood without invoking the notion of consciousness, while the latter seems to depend upon it. Perhaps one way of getting at a connection between consciousness and meaning is to notice that the mainstream of

---

[46]As such, Arkle's system bears a superficial resemblance to that of Llinas and Pellionisz mentioned in Chapter 1. However, whereas Llinas and Pellionisz are materialists, Arkle is a transcendentalist.

the intelligentsia of the past few centuries has seen the world as a mechanistic, meaningless system, and that the re-endowment of the world with meaning is associated with notions of consciousness (Berman, 1986).

For any given person, self-consciousness arises gradually in childhood as part of a process of personal growth, so that consciousness can be understood in the context of human development (Pattison & Kahan, 1986). This is an important point of view, because it suggests that consciousness as it is normally experienced may not be the end-point of development, but that other states of being may succeed these. This is, in fact, a contention that is frequently made (e.g., Assagioli, 1965; Wilber, 1979, 1980). It may be that those who have experienced developmentally later stages of conscious functioning, which they may describe as transcendent or mystical experiences, would be less inclined to accept notions of consciousness in terms of material systems, and to advocate transcendent notions of consciousness. In addition, it has been argued that a person's moral sense is also developmentally determined and can be influenced by experiences of "higher" states of consciousness (e.g., Roberts, 1983; Merrell-Wolff, 1973b).

The contention has been made that Eastern religions and philosophical systems have described the developmentally higher aspects of consciousness (e.g., Taylor, 1978) and, sometimes, that they have a generally more comprehensive account of human nature. One has to be careful, however, not to attribute too much knowledgeability to the Eastern philosophies. In particular, the understanding of the unconscious may not be as comprehensive as it is in the Western culture (Russell, 1986), although this may be difficult to judge because of the heterogeneity of viewpoints concerning consciousness in the Eastern traditions (Izutsu, 1984). An attitude appears to be developing that Eastern philosophies may contribute to our understanding of human nature, and that they should be carefully examined without *a priori* accepting or rejecting them (Sheikh, 1988).

Discussions concerning the unity of consciousness bring up the notion of a self. There is certainly the appearance of an existent self for oneself as argued in Chapter 2, but what the nature is of such a self is not clear. The most prevalent view is that the unity of consciousness is a construct and the self a matter of failed reference (e.g., Lycan, 1987; Natsoulas, 1983b, 1986; Pribram, 1976). Others (e.g., Assagioli, 1965; Merrell-Wolff, 1973a, 1973b) have maintained that there is something that can be called a self and that that follows a developmental sequence resulting in a process of self-transformation, although the self that one is may change in the process. The suggestion has also been made that self-transformation is not something that occurs spontaneously[47] but some-

---

[47]There can, however, be critical situations in one's life such as

thing that is the result of long and continual effort. Part of this process may involve the need to resolve the validity and role of introspection in the self-transformation process. The point is made however, that one can deliberately undertake to change one's experience and one's understanding of consciousness through self-transformation (Assagioli, 1965; Chang, 1978; Walsh, 1984a).

This chapter has consisted of reviews of James's notion of consciousness, the eliminative materialist position, Dennett's computational account, the phenomenological and transcendentalist positions and Sperry's notion of a consciousness revolution. Finally, this last subsection has been a catalogue of some of the contexts, issues and perspectives concerning consciousness that had not been mentioned, thus far, in this chapter. This survey of the notions of consciousness, together with the theoretical discussion of Chapter 2, and the metanalysis of definitions of consciousness of Chapter 3, provides some of the material for the development of a survey instrument, as well as an interpretive framework, for the findings of the empirical study which follows.

---

mystical experiences (Merrell-Wolff, 1973a, 1973b; Roberts, 1983) or near-death experiences (Grosso, 1981) that can radically change one's understanding of reality.

CHAPTER 5

AN EMPIRICAL EXAMINATION OF THE ROLE OF THE PERSONAL

IN THE UNDERSTANDING OF CONSCIOUSNESS

It is important that what is tacit should be made fully explicit. What is untested should be tested, otherwise it should not be used as an assumption on which to erect scientific theory. (White, 1988, p. 40)

In Chapter 1, the confusion surrounding the notion of consciousness was introduced. In Chapter 2, the problem of consciousness was discussed in terms of the disparity between the apparently subjective nature of consciousness and the objective methods of science by which consciousness is to be studied. It was suggested in Chapter 2, Section 3 that much of the confusion concerning consciousness could be attributed to firmly held, differing beliefs about the nature of reality and how it is to be understood. Having clarified the referents of the term consciousness in Chapter 3 and elaborated on the notions of consciousness in Chapter 4, it is possible to proceed with an empirical study. The development, implementation and analysis of a questionnaire which was designed to examine empirically the relationship between notions of consciousness and demographic variables, personal experiences, attitudes towards life and beliefs about reality is described in this chapter. The implications of the results of this study are discussed in Chapter 6.

5.1 Introduction

That a system of beliefs or a world-view informs and guides human activity is not a new idea. Heidegger (1926/1962) gave an incisive, if somewhat inaccessible, account of this phenomenon by describing a person's everyday existence as one in which the events that constitute a person's experience are interpreted by the person in an inauthentic manner according to the dictates of unseen social norms. Although similar statements concerning the efficacy of beliefs for human activity have appeared with apparently increasing frequency in the psychological literature, there have been few systematic studies carried out with regard to this contention, and none that have looked at the way in which notions of consciousness are situated within belief systems. This section briefly introduces the literature which has some relevance to the issue at hand.

Harvey, Hunt and Schroder (1961) perceived conceptual systems as experiential filters that serve to evaluate sensed events of the external world. They have maintained that "the difference in how various people react in the same situation reflects the operation of different conceptual systems" (p. 204) and have discussed the structure and dynamics of such systems. Similarly, Rokeach (1960; 1976) has developed a theory of the structure of belief systems within a person-centered framework.

Straker (1985) has maintained that the paradigms that one uses for understanding the world are historically created and sustained and that scientific reality, more specifically, is essentially an historical construction arising from collective perceptions of the self.

The salient dimension of belief systems in the western intellectual tradition appears to be a physicalist-transcendentalist dimension. As remarked in Chapter 2, according to Osborne (1981), it is this dimension that is reflected in approaches to consciousness. Although the scientific world-view, as normally understood, corresponds to the physicalist pole of this dimension, the transcendentalist dimension is variously characterized.

Frank (1977) has discussed this dimension as that of scientific-humanism *versus* transcendentalism and has noted that, although these belief systems differ in terms of their metaphysical contents, they both embody the same altruistic ethic. He has pointed out that the scientific-humanistic belief system, because of its avowed interest in truth, is more tolerant of other belief systems than transcendental belief systems which can be more dogmatic. Frank seems to be considering an idealized form of scientific-humanism since, in practice, it appears that the scientific-humanistic world-view is as closed to alternatives as some of the transcendental world-views.

More generally, in the psychological literature, there has been a growing awareness of the vulnerability of beliefs about reality. Hill (1986), for example, has admonished psychologists to be sensitive to some of the results in theoretical physics which call for a re-examination of realism, physicalistic monism and the locality assumption. "We in psychology cannot afford to ignore these fundamental changes in assumptions as we attempt to plumb the depths of human consciousness" (p. 1172).

Coan (1968) has examined the writings of various theorists in the history of psychology and, upon factor analysis of their major tenets, has found, as a first factor, subjectivism *versus* objectivism. The positive pole of this factor he has described as "subjectivistic, mentalistic, phenomenological, or psychological" (p. 717); and the negative pole as "objectivistic, physicalistic, positivistic, materialistic, or behavioral" (p. 717). One outcome of this work has been the development of a survey instrument which could be used for assessing the theoretical orientations of psychologists (Coan, 1979).

Krasner and Houts (1984) have used Coan's Theoretical Orientation Survey as well as two instruments that they had developed, the Epistemological Style Questionnaire and Values Survey, in order to study the differences in assumptions about psychology and scientific epistemology between a group of behavioral psychologists and a group of non-behavioral psychologists. They have found that psychologists could be conceptualized as constituting "communities of scholars who share different assumptions," (p. 847) but warned that these differences did not appear to extend beyond discipline-specific assumptions to the social domain.

Kimble (1984) has found two subcultures within psychology using an instrument that he had developed, the Epistemic Differential. The values of psychologists tend collectively towards one or the other end of five dimensions: scientific *versus* humanistic scholarly values; observation *versus* intuition as the basic source of knowledge; laboratory *versus* field study/case history as the appropriate setting for discovery; nomothetic *versus* idiographic laws; and elementism *versus* holism as the appropriate level of analysis.

Interested in a more general population, Unger, Draper and Pendergrass (1986) have developed the Attitudes About Reality Scale in order to measure the extent to which a person believes in either social constructionism or logical positivism. They have found that a person's "personal epistemology", as given by scores on the Attitudes About Reality Scale, was correlated with the respondents' personal experiences. Using a sample of college students, Unger *et al.* have found that a social constructionist position was associated with a feminist ideology, political liberalism, lack of religious affiliation, a higher grade point average, age and higher birth order. They concluded that:

> People do not often appear aware of the extent to which they create the reality with which they deal. An important area for exploration remains. We need to learn more about the extent to which covert ideology impedes the acquisition of information that is seen as self-evident by others with a different epistemological perspective. (p. 76)

This paragraph is also applicable to the area of consciousness studies, and summarizes the broader purpose of the research that follows.

Through the use of an original questionnaire administered to intellectuals who could potentially write about consciousness in the academic literature, in the course of the present study relationships were sought among a person's conceptualization of consciousness and demographic variables, personal experiences, attitudes towards life and beliefs about reality. Cluster and factor analyses were used to find the dimensions of these relationships, and bivariate statistical analyses were used to determine the relationships between specific variables and factor scores.

It was hypothesized that the physical-transcendental dimension would be salient and that it would include items concerned with consciousness. It was hypothesized that science, objectivism and materialism would be positively correlated with consciousness understood as an emergent property, or with consciousness understood in terms of information processing, and, that these notions would be negatively correlated with notions of consciousness in which it is conceptualized as important and meaningful in its own right. As this research was meant to be exploratory, it was fully expected that additional dimensions or correlations would appear as well.

5.2 Development and implementation of the Consciousness Questionnaire

The purpose of this research was to develop, administer, and analyze the results of a questionnaire designed to obtain demographic data and information about a person's experiences, attitudes towards life, notions of consciousness and beliefs about reality. The project began with numerous casual discussions and informal interviews with undergraduate and graduate students, faculty and members of the professional community. These discussions gave rise to two precursory questionnaires which were subsequently evaluated by psychology graduate students and faculty. Out of this work emerged a questionnaire that was used to determine the kinds of questions an academically-experienced, non-specialist in consciousness could respond to. On the basis of this preliminary study, a consciousness questionnaire was developed, pretested in a pilot study, and after a detailed revision, administered in a wide-scale survey. The three major stages in the evolution and implementation of the questionnaire are discussed below.

5.2.1 The Preliminary Questionnaire

What is consciousness? What are its properties and characteristics? What relationship does it bear to meaning and reality? How is consciousness to be properly investigated? These were the kinds of questions that arose in trying to establish how consciousness was understood. In seeking answers to these questions, more than 150 academic papers and books were read that involved discussions of consciousness.[48] Since each particular notion reviewed clearly could not be fully articulated in a questionnaire, representative statements were extracted from the source material in order to present an essential understanding of a given version of consciousness, without including all its details and qualifications. This process resulted in a Preliminary Questionnaire consisting of 158 items.

---

[48]Some of these are included in the References.

A number of examples will help clarify the process of how items for the Preliminary Questionnaire were generated from the source material. To facilitate this discussion, Table 5.1 presents items from the Preliminary Questionnaire and Table 5.2 a number of source quotations.[49] In some instances, items were obtained by summarizing a position held by a number of authors. For example, Item 24 would be consistent with the writings of Chang (1978), Walsh (1984a) and Merrell-Wolff (1973a; 1973b). Other items were obtained by summarizing a single author's ideas, as in the case of Items 3 and 126 which were derived from Alexander (1980) and Items 44 and 67 which were discussed at length by Merrell-Wolff (1973a, 1973b respectively). In some cases, an author's statement was reproduced verbatim or with small changes of wording. This is illustrated by comparing the quotations in Table 5.2 with the relevant entries of Table 5.1. Item 77 arose from a discussion by Gregory (1980) which he himself did not endorse. Items 78, 79 and 83 give Hofstadter's (1979) emergentist position. Item 80 is a modification of Item 78 which takes into account the fact that there may be something distinctive about the kind of information-processing systems that humans enjoy. This is an argument that has been made by Searle (1981) and Lowenhard (1981). Item 81 is one of three beliefs about conscious experience listed by White (1982). Items 84, 85, 87 and 88 follow in a straightforward manner from the source material.

Following its development, a survey was carried out using the Preliminary Questionnaire in order to discover the extent to which participants could respond to such items as well as to give some indication of the direction of their responses. Thus, respondents were given the opportunity to indicate whether or not a given item made sense to them, whether or not it was relevant to their understanding of consciousness, and whether they agreed, disagreed or did not know whether to agree or disagree with a particular statement. The Preliminary Questionnaire is included in Appendix A.

Eighty copies of the preliminary questionnaire were circulated, with over 30 being sent to members of the faculty in a number of disciplines at the University of Regina, 15 being given to graduate students in psychology, at least 23 given to undergraduate students taking courses in psychology and a few others being distributed to members of the intellectual community at large. A total of 30 questionnaires was returned: 16 from faculty, 6 from graduate students and 8 from undergraduate students.

---

[49]Table 5.1 includes not only items that pertain to the present discussion but also items that will be referred to later in the section. The entire Preliminary Questionnaire as well as the sources for the items are given in Appendix A.

Table 5.1

Examples of Items from Preliminary Questionnaire

3. The notion of consciousness is useful in military settings.

24. Ultimately, the only way to understand human consciousness is through meditation or a religious way of life.

44. Consciousness is more real than physical reality.

67. It is possible for there to be consciousness in which there is awareness but no contents of awareness.

77. Consciousness is an accidental property of complex neural tissue.

78. Consciousness is an emergent property of information-processing systems.

79. Consciousness entails an interaction between levels of an information-processing system in which higher levels reach back down towards lower levels, influencing them, while at the same time being themselves determined by the lower levels.

80. Human consciousness is an emergent property of cellular interaction.

81. Conscious experience is associated with control processes of the brain.

83. A reductionistic explanation of consciousness, in order to be comprehensible, must bring in soft concepts such as levels, mappings and meanings.

84. Consciousness represents a principle of economy that makes information-processing more efficient and reduces the number of elements necessary to perform a task.

85. Consciousness sets goals and activates behavioral action systems appropriate to accomplishing these goals.

87. Consciousness is a limited capacity mechanism of attention.

88. Attention refers to processes that organize the contents of consciousness into one or another conscious state.

(table continues)

91. The understanding we have of our own conscious experience is self-evident.

124. Our culture can be viewed as a vast conspiracy against self-knowledge and awakening in which we collude together to reinforce one another's defenses and insanity.

126. A greater understanding of consciousness can lead to military applications.

127. The subject of consciousness is a legitimate subject of study.

Some of the respondents indicated that the task was too difficult and that they had become confused about what it was that they really thought about consciousness by the time they had reached the end of the questionnaire. This, plus the high frequency of "no sense", "not relevant" and "don't know" responses led to the conclusion that the questionnaire items concerning consciousness to be included for further study should be general, rather than particular and detailed. For example, Items 3 and 79[50] were not included in the final version of the questionnaire.

At the end of the Preliminary Questionnaire, respondents had been asked to rank, in descending order of importance, the ten items that they believed best characterized their understanding of consciousness. These items were weighted with descending values, the first choice receiving a weight of 10 and the tenth choice a weight of 1. The weights for each item were summed across respondents and a rank attached to each questionnaire item, with the lowest numerical ranks corresponding to the highest weights. The ten most important questionnaire items – that is, the ten items with the lowest rank – were chosen for inclusion in the Pilot Questionnaire.

In addition, in order to index the amount of support for research in the area of consciousness, items on which there was a high rate of agreement or disagreement, and which were statements about the status of consciousness or consciousness studies, were included. An example of this type of item is Item 127. The respondents were asked to indicate their academic discipline and this variable was recoded as a dichotomous variable: a respondent belonged to either a physical or non-physical discipline group. Items that had a good number of agree or disagree scores and that showed a substantial difference in the response bias for those of physical *versus* non-physical discipline were also included in the

---

[50]The items referred to in the remainder of this subsection are included in Table 5.1.

Table 5.2

Examples of Quotations Which Gave Rise to Preliminary Questionnaire Items

77. "A way out from [the dilemma of supposing that consciousness is the result of evolutionary processes but has no causal value] is to suppose that consciousness is a biological fluke. . . . A further way out may be to say that consciousness is an *accidental* property (or, similarly, an emergent property) of complex neural tissue or function – or of whatever increases physically at the top end of evolution." (Gregory, 1980, pp. 33 - 34; emphasis in original)

78-79. "My belief is that the explanations of 'emergent' phenomena in our brains – for instance, ideas, hopes, images, analogies, and finally consciousness and free will – are based on a kind of Strange Loop, an interaction between levels in which the top level reaches back down towards the bottom level and influences it, while at the same time being itself determined by the bottom level." (Hofstadter, 1979, p. 709)

81. "The general beliefs that we hold about conscious experience are:
"1. Conscious experience is associated with higher-order activities and control.
"2. All and only conscious events enter verbal reports of the non-mechanical type (with minor qualifications).
"3. Conscious events become memories, at least in the short term." (White, 1982, p. 24)

83. "A reductionistic explanation of a mind, *in order to be comprehensible*, must bring in 'soft' concepts such as levels, mappings, and meanings." (Hofstadter, 1979. p. 709; emphasis in original)

84. "One may . . . ask why consciousness arises at all? A suggestion is, that consciousness represents a principle of economy that makes information processing more efficient and reduces the amount of elements, necessary to perform this task." (Lowenhard, 1981, p. 25)

85. "Other investigators see consciousness as an internal programmer or executive decision maker that plans and co-ordinates mental activity. . . . The best worked out example is Shallice's (1972) proposal that consciousness sets goals and activates behavioural action systems appropriate to accomplishing those goals." (Carr, 1979, p. 124)

(table continues)

87. "Current positions generally subscribe to an active view of conscious states and processes. One of the early versions of these views is the theoretical account of automatic activation and conscious processing contributed by Posner and his associates. The conscious processing discussed by Posner and Snyder is 'a mechanism of limited capacity which may be directed toward different types of activity.' Consciousness is 'directed toward' an unconscious structure or process which then becomes 'conscious.'" (Mandler, 1985, p. 54)

88. "'Consciousness' refers to states which have contents; 'attention' refers to processes which organize these contents into one or another conscious state." (Pribram, 1980, p. 49)

---

next version of the questionnaire. An example of such an item is Item 91. Finally, items were included if they were statements that were about issues that were judged to be central in the literature about consciousness, or if they would shed light on the relationship between personal experience and consciousness. An example of the former is an item concerning intentionality, Item 67, and of the latter, Item 24.

The breakdown of responses by educational level was also examined, but, although there were differences among the groups, these differences were thought not to be sufficiently great to discard respondents from lower educational levels. It is also possible that these differences resulted from changes in the disciplinary variable rather than level of education since the students were all associated with the discipline of psychology, and the faculty were from a variety of disciplines.

The foregoing process resulted in the selection of 32 items from the Preliminary Questionnaire for further consideration: 30 of these items were explicitly concerned with consciousness and 2 reflected beliefs thought likely to be correlated with concepts of consciousness, such as Item 124. Some of these items were rephrased a number of times as a result of comments by those who responded to the preliminary questionnaire, in order to clarify the wording as much as possible.[51] Finally, a number of the items and tasks of later questionnaires used the material from the Preliminary Questionnaire in more general ways.

---

[51]In addition to clarifications of wording resulting from an examination of the items by the author and his supervisor, and from the comments of the respondents to the preliminary as well as pilot questionnaires, they were read also by a teaching assistant in English before being included in the final version of the questionnaire.

5.2.2 The Pilot Questionnaire

On the basis of the foregoing analysis of the Preliminary Questionnaire and additional information concerning personal belief systems, a questionnaire was developed to be employed in a pilot study.

For the Pilot Questionnaire, the 30 items from the Preliminary Questionnaire concerned with consciousness were supplemented by 2 additional tasks concerning the respondents' notions of consciousness. On page 1 of the Pilot Questionnaire, the respondents were asked to provide a written description of their understanding of consciousness, while on page 3, the respondents ranked 13 statements about consciousness in the order of greatest to least agreement. These statements had been obtained from a larger collection in which an attempt had been made to catalogue major notions of consciousness.

A difficulty arose in the construction of the Pilot Questionnaire when trying to find items to assess a person's belief system. It was thought that an adequate instrument should include items or tasks from the following categories:
1. Epistemological beliefs: the extent to which a person felt that consciousness could be understood through a process of scientific investigation and whether they would be willing to consider alternative methodologies.
2. Ontological beliefs: the material-transcendental dimension, mind-body problem, determinism vs free will and the status of reality.
3. Religious and parapsychological beliefs.
4. The importance of meaning.
5. Values: values and attitudes toward life and death, the role of values in scientific investigation, ethical concerns in general.
6. Extraordinary experiences: whether or not a person believes that they have had inexplicable, mystical or out-of-body experiences.
7. Intolerance of ambiguity.

The intention had been to put together this part of the questionnaire using existing clinical and research instruments. An exhaustive search revealed, however, that, although theories of the structure and dynamics of belief systems have been advanced, not only were there no instruments to assess a person's belief system along the dimensions described above, but that there were no instruments that could adequately form part of a questionnaire for the intended target population of academics and professionals.

Nonetheless, 17 items, often in reworded form, were selected from five instruments. Two items were taken from Krasner and Houts' Epistemological Style Questionnaire and two from their Values Survey (L. Krasner, personal communication, 1986; Krasner & Houts, 1984). Five items from Reker and Peacock's Life Attitude Profile were used (Peacock &

Reker, 1982; G. Reker, personal communications, 1985,1986; Reker & Peacock, 1981), along with four items from Kirton's revision of the Budner Intolerance of Ambiguity Scale (M. Kirton, 1981; personal communication, 1986). The Intrinsic/Extrinsic Scale of religious orientation developed by Feagin (1964) and the Extraordinary Belief Inventory (L. Otis, personal communication, 1986; Otis & Kuo, 1984) each yielded two items. In addition, three items for the Pilot Questionnaire were obtained as variations of items from the following three instruments: the Theoretical Orientation Survey (Coan, 1979; L. Krasner, personal communication, 1986), Extraordinary Belief Inventory (L. Otis, personal communication, 1986; Otis & Kuo, 1984), and the Epistemic Differential (G. Kimble, 1984; personal communication, 1985).

In an attempt to reveal possible inconsistencies between a person's personal and academic beliefs, it was decided that some questionnaire items should be worded in a personal manner, referring to a person's experience, and others in a more objective, neutral manner.

Two-hundred and forty-one copies of the Pilot Questionnaire and a cover letter were mailed out: 100 to faculty across disciplines at the University of Regina; 60 to the mental health care workers at Regina Child and Youth Services, Regina Mental Health Care Clinic and the Crisis Centre associated with the Regina Mental Health Care Clinic; 53 to graduate students across disciplines at the University of Regina; 16 to the respondents of the Preliminary Questionnaire who had given their names and addresses; and 12 to people across Canada who were believed to have an interest in research concerning consciousness.

Seventy-two questionnaires were returned. Written responses were read carefully and many of them encoded. In addition, the ranking task and all dichotomous and Likert-type items were encoded. The data were extensively analyzed using bivariate, cluster and factor analyses. The general, overriding conclusion drawn from these analyses was that there appeared to exist strong relationships between a person's notions of consciousness and a number of the demographic variables and items assessing personal experiences, values and attitudes towards life and beliefs about reality.

5.2.3 The Survey Questionnaire

A number of minor changes and additions were made to the Pilot Questionnaire in developing the instrument to be employed as the Survey Questionnaire. Additional information concerning religious affiliation and practice was requested from respondents. The written statement of the respondent's understanding of consciousness was made optional. The ranking task was simplified by shortening some of the statements about consciousness and asking respondents to indicate which statements most accurately reflected their understanding of the notion of consciousness rather than rank ordering the statements. Although some of the dichotomous and Likert-type items were reworded, all were retained for the final version of the questionnaire, with the dichotomous items changed to four point Likert-type items. In addition, six items were added to the questionnaire: one to the personal experiences list and five to the main body of the questionnaire. Two of these six items were reworded items from Reker and Peacock's Life Attitude Profile. This process resulted in a total of 89 Likert-type items.

With these modifications, the Survey Questionnaire took on the following structure[52]:
1. Demographic Data.
2. Personal Beliefs: Likert-type, personal beliefs and experiences items, referred to using the prefix "B".
3. Notions of Consciousness: endorsement and writing task, notions of consciousness, referred to using the prefix "C".
4. Consciousness and Reality: Likert-type items concerning consciousness, epistemological, ontological, religious and parapsychological beliefs, meaning and values, referred to using the prefix "Q".
5. Written Comments.
A copy of the final version of the questionnaire, as well as a list of the sources for the items, are included in Appendix A under the titles "Survey Questionnaire" and "Sources for items of Survey Questionnaire."

A number of respondents to the pilot survey had commented on the ambiguity of many of the key words in the questionnaire, such as the words, "consciousness", "science" and "reality". This ambiguity is, however, inherent in the literature itself, where the meaning that a person invests these terms with can sometimes be understood from the context. For the purposes of the present research, the remainder of the items in the questionnaire constituted the context for each item from which the meaning of a term for the respondent could be derived. In addition, it was brought to the attention of respondents, both before and throughout the questionnaire that they might find many of the items ambiguous, but to interpret them in terms of their own beliefs. What is surprising is the extent to which patterns of response emerged in the pilot questionnaire, given the frequent complaints about ambiguity by the respondents. The approach described here is consistent with that of Unger, Draper and Pendergrass (1986) who used ambiguous phrasing for their Attitudes About Reality Scale in an effort to elicit differences in response that would reflect differences in epistemological frameworks.

On the other hand, not all items were ambiguous. Some could be assumed to have good content validity (e.g., "Reincarnation actually does

---

[52]These are the names of the sections of the Survey Questionnaire that will be used in the discussion of the results.

occur") while concurrent validity could subsequently be claimed for other items given their pattern of intercorrelations with the remaining items (e.g., "Consciousness transcends time.")

In general, for the purposes of this research, concepts and beliefs are operationally defined in terms of the endorsement of specific items on the questionnaire, without attempting to infer what a respondent may really believe or what an item really means to them. Those issues are outside the scope of this study and require a separate investigation. Since this work employed statements concerning consciousness from the literature, it is enough for the purposes of this study to look at the patterns in the statements that people endorse.

5.2.4 Respondents

The target population for the Survey Questionnaire was that body of individuals who would be in a position to make statements about consciousness in the academic literature. Some effort was made to stratify the sample so that those possibly more likely to be interested in consciousness were represented in larger numbers. An effort was also made to include a substantial number of women in the study.

Thus, over 1491 copies of the Survey Questionnaire were sent out to academics and professionals, mostly in Canada and the United States (Table 5.3). Of these, 1043 copies of the questionnaire were mailed out and over 448 were sent as electronic files. The breakdown of the distribution within the Canadian Psychological Association is given in Table

---

Table 5.3

Distribution of Survey Questionnaire

Affiliation	No.
Society for the History and Philosophy of Science	143
Canadian Association of Physicists	
− Division of Theoretical Physics	132
Canadian Psychological Association	264
Canadian Psychiatric Association	79
Jesuits and instructors of Religious Studies	58
University of Saskatchewan faculty	171
California Institute of Integral Studies	100
Special mailing to those interested in consciousness research	66
Psychnet Newsletter	448+
Total	1491+

5.4. An electronic file of the questionnaire was initially sent to the editor of the *Psychnet Newsletter*, a psychology newsletter originating at the University of Houston and distributed electronically around the world. It was sent to the regular recipients of the newsletter as well as being made accessible to other callers. From there, the questionnaire was circulated to an unknown extent around the world. One respondent found a copy in the *AI Digest*, and completed copies of the questionnaire were received from the Netherlands and Ireland.

5.3 Results

The results of this study are discussed in the following order. First, a brief commentary is made concerning the response pattern to the items in the various sections of the Survey Questionnaire. Then, the findings from more complex statistical analyses are described. These began with a cluster analysis of all items of the questionnaire. Then each cluster was factor analyzed and factor scores were calculated to be used for bivariate analyses with the demographic data and endorsed notions of consciousness.

5.3.1 Item analyses

Three-hundred and forty-six Survey Questionnaires were returned in time for the data analysis, of which 288 had been sent out as hard copies and 58 as electronic copies. Many of the respondents had included extensive comments or copies of their academic papers. Of the 346 who undertook to answer the questionnaire and returned it, 334 completed it. Thus, the response rate for hard copies was 27 percent and for all copies, it was less than 23 percent. In addition, a few respondents sent back letters or academic papers rather than completing the questionnaire.

In general, the process for the selection of respondents resulted in a sample that mirrored the spectrum of opinions found in the literature. This was reflected both in the respondents' written definitions and comments, which were often more extreme than those found in the literature, as well as from the frequencies of responses to the questionnaire items. The written responses for Sections 3 and 5 appear in Appendix B. The frequency of endorsement of each of the response alternatives to all of the items in the various sections of the Survey Questionnaire appears in Appendix C. For the purpose of presenting these results, a sampling of the items is presented to draw attention to particular findings and to enable the reader to appreciate the diversity of response. The items from each section of the Survey Questionnaire are discussed separately.

5.3.1.1 Demographic Data

Some of the demographic characteristics of the population of respondents

Table 5.4

Distribution of Survey Questionnaire within Canadian Psychological Association: Field of Interest and Section Affiliation

Field of interest	No.
Clinical psychology and counselling	52
Cognition or cognitive/social psychology	106
Psychophysiology	8
Psychopharmacology	8
Developmental psychology	21
Psychology of women	21
Social psychology	7
Neuropsychology or neurophysiological dysfunction	30
Existentialism	8
Information processing	39
Brain and behaviour	16
Philosophical psychology	19

Section affiliation	No.
Brain and behaviour	40
Community psychology	7
Developmental psychology	54
Social psychology	21
Women and psychology	62

are given in Tables 5.5 and 5.6 as well as Table C.1 of Appendix C. It can be noted from Table 5.5 that one-quarter of the sample was made up of women; that two-thirds held a doctorate (only 11.1% had a Bachelor's degree or lower level of education); and that the distribution across religious orientations was varied. From Table 5.6 it can be seen that disciplinary affiliation reflects the stratification of the distribution of the Survey Questionnaire, as given in Table 5.3. In general, disciplines subsumed under the natural or applied sciences are included in the category "hard sciences" and those under social or medical sciences under "human sciences."

5.3.1.2 Personal Beliefs

Examination of the frequency of responses to the items of this section reflects a wide variety of beliefs and experiences amongst the respondents (Table 5.7). For example, the percentage of respondents claiming to have had unusual experiences is quite high (Items B9, B13 and B20: 53, 47 and 23% respectively). As well, the belief that one's consciousness is located

Table 5.5

Demographic Characteristics of Subject Population

Item	Frequency	%	Valid %[a]
Age			
Up to 29 years	38	11.4	11.4
30 to 44 years	149	44.6	44.7
45 to 59 years	115	34.4	34.5
60 to 99 years	31	9.3	9.3
Missing	1	0.3	--
Sex			
Female	89	26.6	26.7
Male	244	73.1	73.3
Missing	1	.3	--
Doctorate			
No doctorate	110	32.9	32.9
Doctorate	223	66.8	67.0
Missing	1	0.3	--
General area of discipline			
Hard sciences	109	32.6	32.7
Human sciences	149	44.6	44.7
Humanities	75	22.5	22.5
Missing	1	0.3	--
Religious affiliation			
None	82	24.6	26.3
Traditional	141	42.2	45.2
Own beliefs	89	26.6	28.5
Other or missing	22	6.6	--
Frequency of religious practice			
Daily	84	25.1	27.8
Occasionally	82	24.6	27.2
Never	136	40.7	45.0
Missing	32	9.6	--

Note. Further information concerning education and disciplinary affiliation is given in Table C.1, Appendix C.

[a]"Valid percent" refers to the percentage of respondents within a given category for a given item corrected for the number of respondents who could not be classified for that item.

Table 5.6

Response Frequencies of Disciplinary Affiliation of Subject Population

General distribution of subject population

Discipline	Frequency	Valid %
Psychology	140	42.0
Physics	40	12.0
Philosophy	21	6.3
Computer Science	17	5.1
Psychiatry	16	4.8
Religion/spirituality	10	3.0
Other	90	26.9

Distribution of psychologists

Discipline	Frequency	Valid %
Clinical/applied	53	37.9
Experimental/physiological	26	18.6
Cognitive	19	13.6
Social/personality/community/developmental	19	13.6
Transpersonal	16	11.4
Not specified or other	7	5.0

in the center of one's head is split almost half and half between those who believe that that is the case, and those who do not.

5.3.1.3 Notions of Consciousness

Table 5.8 shows the frequency with which each of the notions of consciousness presented to the respondents was endorsed. Again, the range of responses reflects the diversity of statements made in the literature. The most popular notions were those that gave consciousness as a stream of thought (C6) or explicit knowledge or awareness (C7). Consciousness understood as an emergent property and as a non-physical reality were also strongly supported.

Seventy-one respondents wrote their own definitions of consciousness or included written comments in this section of the questionnaire. A few of these are presented in Appendix B under the title "Respondents' written definitions of consciousness." There was a wide range of responses that included both definitions of consciousness and more general comments. A number of these definitions of consciousness referred to

Table 5.7

Response Frequencies to Selected Questions from Personal Beliefs Section

Item	Frequency	%	Valid %
1. I think about the ultimate meaning of life.			
No	56	16.8	16.8
Yes	278	83.2	83.2
3. My accomplishments in life are largely determined by my own efforts.			
No	52	15.6	15.7
Yes	280	83.8	84.3
Missing	2	0.6	--
5. My ideas about life have changed dramatically in the past.			
No	144	43.1	43.2
Yes	189	56.6	56.8
Missing	1	0.3	--
8. My spiritual beliefs determine my approach to life.			
No	136	40.7	41.3
Yes	193	57.8	58.7
Missing	5	1.5	--
9. I have had experiences which science would have difficulty explaining.			
No	153	45.8	46.4
Yes	177	53.0	53.6
Missing	4	1.2	--
13. I have had an experience which could best be described as a transcendent or mystical experience.			
No	174	52.1	52.6
Yes	157	47.0	47.4
Missing	3	0.9	--
16. It seems to me that my consciousness is located in the center of my head.			
No	175	52.4	54.5
Yes	146	43.7	45.5
Missing	13	3.9	--

(*table continues*)

Item	Frequency	%	Valid %
18. It is important for me to spend periods of time in contemplation or meditation.			
No	89	26.6	26.7
Yes	244	73.1	73.3
Missing	1	0.3	--
20. I have had an experience which could best be described as an out-of-body experience.			
No	254	76.0	76.7
Yes	77	23.1	23.3
Missing	3	0.9	--

specific theoretical orientations (e.g., Marxism or eliminative materialism) that were not part of the list presented in this section of the Survey Questionnaire. Others composed their own versions of consciousness, for example, "Consciousness is one of those things you either know for yourself or you don't. If you do, we can talk about it; if not, I may as well talk to the wall." Finally, some participants provided comments concerning specific notions of consciousness given in this section of the questionnaire. For example, one respondent had written "bullshit" beside the twelfth version of consciousness. In some cases the comments were only indirectly related to a respondent's understanding of consciousness: for example, "I have been trying to publish my own physical theory of consciousness for ten years without success, and hope some day to work on it full time when I retire." Altogether, the written notions of consciousness reflected, in a pronounced way, the diversity of views held in the literature.

5.3.1.4 Consciousness and Reality

The diversity of ideas about consciousness and reality is reflected again in Table 5.9, which details the response frequencies of a number of Likert-type, impersonally-worded items presented to the respondents in the fourth section of the Survey Questionnaire. For example, the contradictory positions with regard to a materialist-transcendentalist dimension are evidenced by the fact that 25 percent of the respondents maintained that there is no reality other than the physical universe (Q5), and 30 percent maintained that physical reality is an extension of mental reality (Q29).

5.3.1.5 Written Comments

One hundred and twenty respondents gave comments at the end of the questionnaire, some of which appear in, "Respondents' written comments"

Table 5.8

Frequencies of Endorsement of Notions of Consciousness

Definition	Frequency	%	Valid %
1. The concept of consciousness is neither desirable nor useful.			
Not endorsed	326	97.6	97.6
Endorsed	8	2.4	2.4
2. Consciousness is an emergent property of sufficiently complex neural systems.			
Not endorsed	171	51.2	51.2
Endorsed	163	48.8	48.8
3. Consciousness is further information in certain information-processing systems.			
Not endorsed	270	80.8	80.8
Endorsed	64	19.2	19.2
4. What is meant by consciousness changes with changes in the state of consciousness. Thus, the term consciousness only has meaning with reference to a particular state of consciousness.			
Not endorsed	245	73.4	73.4
Endorsed	89	26.6	26.6
5. Consciousness is the end product of unconscious and preconscious mental events.			
Not endorsed	267	79.9	79.9
Endorsed	67	20.1	20.1
6. Consciousness is a stream of thoughts, feelings and sensations, some of which are more directly the focus of attention than others.			
Not endorsed	124	37.1	37.1
Endorsed	210	62.9	62.9
7. Consciousness is the explicit knowledge of one's situation, mental states or actions as opposed to lack of such awareness. It is the opposite of automatic functioning.			
Not endorsed	132	39.5	39.5
Endorsed	202	60.5	60.5

(*table continues*)

Definition	Frequency	%	Valid %

8. Consciousness is characterized by reference to an object of thought, inherent in every conscious act. That is to say, consciousness is always consciousness of something.

Not endorsed	210	62.9	62.9
Endorsed	124	37.1	37.1

9. Consciousness is the subjective component of a mental act which allows one to be subject to an object of thought.

Not endorsed	249	74.6	74.6
Endorsed	85	25.4	25.4

10. Consciousness is a subjective experience, not accessible to outside observers, that attests to our existence.

Not endorsed	208	62.3	62.3
Endorsed	126	37.7	37.7

11. Consciousness is a personal experience that requires a process of self-transformation to be adequately understood.

Not endorsed	266	79.6	79.6
Endorsed	68	20.4	20.4

12. Consciousness is a non-physical reality that can have causal effects on physical systems.

Not endorsed	225	67.4	67.4
Endorsed	109	32.6	32.6

Comments concerning definitions of consciousness

Comments not provided	263	78.7	78.7
Comments provided	71	21.3	21.3

---

in Appendix B. Thirty-nine of these were concerned with methodological issues, including 32 which stated that the questionnaire items were ambiguous. Twenty-five comments were positive about the questionnaire, for example, "Excellent! We need more research in this area." There was further discussion concerning consciousness by 19 respondents. Ten statements indicated that the questionnaire was a waste of time or were otherwise antagonistic. The following is an example of the latter:

As well as the results, I would like an explanation of *how* this questionare [*sic*] is supposed to be useful for research into a supposed phenomena [*sic*]. Does heart research make use of questionaires [*sic*] that ask about Cupid? Neither should brain research (consciousness is certainly a brain phenomena [*sic*]) need questionaires [*sic*] about ill-defined quasi-spiritualistic ideas.

Table 5.9

Response Frequencies to Selected Questions from Consciousness and Reality Section

Item	Frequency	%	Valid %
2. Science can legitimately concern itself with subjective events only to the extent that these events have objectively observable correlates.			
Disagree	127	38.0	39.8
Agree	192	57.5	60.2
Other response	15	4.5	--
3. Free will is an illusion.			
Disagree	212	63.5	69.5
Agree	93	27.8	30.5
Other response	29	8.7	--
5. There is no reality other than the physical universe.			
Disagree	211	63.2	71.8
Agree	83	24.9	28.2
Other response	40	12.0	--
7. Extrasensory perception is possible.			
Disagree	99	29.6	36.5
Agree	172	51.5	63.5
Other response	63	18.9	--
9. The existence of human consciousness is evidence of a spiritual dimension within each person.			
Disagree	137	41.0	46.8
Agree	156	46.7	53.2
Other response	41	12.3	--
12. One's personal experience is ultimately the test of any contention about reality.			
Disagree	168	50.3	55.6
Agree	134	40.1	44.4
Other response	32	9.6	--
13. Awareness is a term equivalent to consciousness.			
Disagree	107	32.0	34.1
Agree	207	62.0	65.9
Other response	20	6.0	--

(table continues)

Item	Frequency	%	Valid %

17. Introspection is a necessary element in the investigation of consciousness.

Disagree	36	10.8	11.4
Agree	281	84.1	88.6
Other response	17	5.1	--

21. Reincarnation actually does occur.

Disagree	192	57.5	82.1
Agree	42	12.6	17.9
Other	100	29.9	--

24. In trying to understand consciousness one must take into account evidence from subjective experience as well as objective observation.

Disagree	15	4.5	4.7
Agree	304	91.0	95.3
Other response	15	4.5	--

26. It does not make sense to ascribe a location to consciousness.

Disagree	88	26.3	29.8
Agree	207	62.0	70.2
Other response	39	11.7	--

29. Physical reality is an extension of mental reality.

Disagree	191	57.2	65.6
Agree	100	29.9	34.4
Other response	43	12.9	--

35. Human consciousness would not exist without the brain.

Disagree	44	13.2	14.2
Agree	266	79.6	85.8
Other response	24	7.2	--

41. There are modes of understanding latent within a person which are superior to rational thought.

Disagree	99	29.6	35.0
Agree	184	55.1	65.0
Other response	51	15.3	--

44. It is possible for there to be consciousness in which there is awareness but no object of awareness.

Disagree	111	33.2	39.8
Agree	168	50.3	60.2
Other response	55	16.5	--

(table continues)

54. The harmony of nature reflects the existence of an original creator.

Disagree	174	52.1	61.5
Agree	109	32.6	38.5
Other response	51	15.3	--

58. Personal consciousness continues after physical death.

Disagree	155	46.4	63.8
Agree	88	26.3	36.2
Other response	91	27.2	--

In general, the attitudes towards the questionnaire showed the same diversity that was found in the written notions of consciousness presented in Section 3 of the Survey Questionnaire.

5.3.1.6 Discussion of item analyses

The foregoing analyses revealed some interesting anomalies, that could be indications of the inconsistency of some respondents' beliefs. For example, 84 percent of respondents claimed that the accomplishments in their lives were determined by their own efforts (B3), yet 28 percent agreed that free will was an illusion (Q3). That means that at least 12 percent agreed with both statements. Similarly, 44 percent claimed that their consciousness was located in the center of their head (B16) while 62 percent maintained that it does not make sense to ascribe a location to consciousness (Q26). Thus, at least 6 percent showed a discrepancy between what they, personally believed to be the case, and what they were willing to state in a more philosophical manner. In a slightly different vein, 13 percent claimed that human consciousness could exist without the brain (Q35) while 26 percent believed that personal consciousness continues after physical death (Q58). Perhaps the 13 percent who agreed to life after death, but did not think that consciousness could exist without the brain, responded without having considered the implications of their contentions. Alternatively, these respondents may believe that some kind of "brain" survives physical death, as in the case of Christianity (J. Schmeiser, personal communication, 1988). Thus, not only is there a variety of notions of consciousness, but for any given individual, in some cases, their own beliefs about their experience and reality appear to be inconsistent.

5.3.5 Cluster analysis

The purpose of the empirical study was to uncover the nature of the correlations between statements about consciousness and statements about personal experiences and beliefs. A first step involved a cluster analysis in which the statements from Section 2, Personal Beliefs, and from Section 4, Consciousness and Reality, were intercorrelated. The Pearson product moment correlation coefficients calculated pairwise between the items, were then used as proximity measures for a within groups hierarchical cluster analysis. Two large clusters emerged: Items in the first cluster indexed a dimension of physicalism and conservative transcendence while the second cluster was made up of items that were concerned with an unbounded transcendence. That is to say, whereas the first cluster was made up of items that discriminated between a strongly materialist point of view and one that emphasized meaning and religious beliefs, the second cluster discriminated between the non-acceptance and acceptance of extraordinary transcendent beliefs or interpretations of personal experiences. In the case of both clusters, statements about consciousness were strongly correlated with statements about personal beliefs and experiences.

5.3.6 Factor analyses

Each of the clusters from the cluster analysis was then progressively factor analyzed as it formed. One resolution was chosen for each cluster by considering the adequacy of the factor analysis and the explanatory nature of the factors formed. Table 5.10 "Factor analysis of cluster 1: Conservative transcendence *versus* materialism", lists the four factors that were extracted for Cluster 1. The first factor, "Meaning" consists of items that discriminate between a physicalist world-view and one that emphasizes the importance of meaning. In addition, the positive pole of this factor includes the contentions that it is consciousness that endows reality with meaning, and that there is a more profound understanding of reality than that available through science. Items that refer to traditional religious beliefs loaded on the second factor which was labelled "Religiosity". Included among these are two items concerning consciousness, one of which asserts that personal consciousness continues to exist after death; the other, that consciousness is evidence of a spiritual dimension within each person. The third factor was entitled "Physicalism": the positive pole includes statements to the effect that all phenomena, including consciousness, are derived from the physical world, and can be explained in terms of the physical world. Only two items have high loadings on the fourth factor, "Determinism", both of which are statements reflecting a traditional determinist position. There are no items concerning consciousness with substantive loadings on this factor.

The factors constituting cluster 2 are listed in Table 5.11, "Factor analysis of cluster 2: Extraordinary transcendence." Factor I was entitled "Extraordinary experiences." The positive pole loads items that assert the respondent's having had transcendent, mystical or out-of-body experiences or experiences that science could not explain. A number of statements concerning consciousness are in the direction of the positive pole but these have smaller factor loadings than the experiential items and seem to emphasize the importance of the experiential aspect of consciousness. Factor II of the second cluster contains statements about consciousness

Table 5.10

Factor Analysis of Cluster 1: Conservative Transcendence vs Materialism

Factor label	Factor loading	Item
Factor I: Meaning	.704	Q31. Consciousness gives meaning to reality.
	.663	Q51. There are some truths concerning reality which, in principle, are not amenable to scientific investigation.
	.556	B11. I feel a need to find a real meaning or purpose in my life.
	−.530	Q5. There is no reality other than the physical universe.
	.519	Q57. Knowledge of people achieved through literature is more profound than any knowledge of people that can be achieved using the scientific method.
	.500	B1. I think about the ultimate meaning of life.
	.486	Q9. The existence of human consciousness is evidence of a spiritual dimension within each person.
	.446	Q54. The harmony of nature reflects the existence of an original creator.
Factor II: Religiosity	.787	Q36. There is an absolute truth which is not context-dependent.
	.634	Q54. The harmony of nature reflects the existence of an original creator.
	.588	B8. My spiritual beliefs determine my approach to life.
	.533	Q58. Personal consciousness continues after physical death.

(*table continues*)

Factor label	Factor loading	Item
	.519	Q9. The existence of human consciousness is evidence of a spiritual dimension within each person.
	.508	Q28. The reason the universe is the way it is, is to support human life.
	.462	B1. I think about the ultimate meaning of life.
Factor III: Physicalism	.740	Q46. Human consciousness is an emergent property of complex neural activity.
	.710	Q35. Human consciousness would not exist without the brain.
	.606	Q53. Even though we are not yet able to explain mental events in terms of physical processes, an explanation is, in principle, possible.
	−.531	Q56. Consciousness transcends time.
	−.477	Q58. Personal consciousness continues after physical death.
	.415	Q5. There is no reality other than the physical universe.
	−.406	Q57. Knowledge of people achieved through literature is more profound than any knowledge of people that can be achieved using the scientific method.
Factor IV: Determinism	.857	Q3. Free will is an illusion.
	.768	Q63. All thought and behavior is caused by the operation of biological and environmental events and does not occur freely.

(table continues)

Note. N=334 for 89 variables clustered using average linkage within groups hierarchical cluster analysis where median values were inserted for items where respondents failed to clearly endorse a response from "strongly disagree" to "strongly agree". The factor analysis used the principal components method of extraction with a varimax rotation. The Keyser-Meyer-Olkin Measure of Sampling Adequacy was .924; the Bartlett Test of Sphericity had a value of 2441, $p<.000005$; and the first factor extracted accounted for 38.9% of the variance, with 59.1% of the total variance being accounted for by all four factors. The first of the rotated factors accounted for 17.1% of the variance; the second rotated factor accounted for 16.4%; the third, 15.1%; and the fourth rotated factor accounted for 10.5% of the variance. Items from Section 2 of the Survey Questionnaire are numbered with numbers preceded by "B"; items from Section 4 of the Survey Questionnaire are numbered with numbers preceded by "Q".

---

and about the nature of reality and was labelled "Extraordinary beliefs". The positive pole of this factor suggests an unbounded transcendence: consciousness as part of a reality that completely transcends and conditions the physical domain and which is known through paranormal means. The third factor, "Inner growth" is concerned with the reality of subjective experience and the importance of psychological growth. Consciousness is very much a part of this factor: it is to be understood through introspection and psychological growth, although consciousness itself is the key to such growth.

Taken together, the cluster and factor analyses reveal the emergence of three major groups of beliefs, each of which determines a different view of consciousness. The materialist position holds that reality can, in principle, be explained in entirely physical terms, that knowledge is gained through science, and that consciousness, like anything else, is part of the physical world. The position of conservative transcendence holds that there is more to life than the physical aspect, knowledge can be gained through means other than the scientific method and consciousness is that which gives meaning to reality and evidence of spirituality. Extraordinary transcendence is a position in which the physical is believed to be a derivative of the mental, in which extraordinary means of obtaining knowledge are believed to be operative, and in which consciousness is viewed as a reality in its own right as well as the ingredient of a self-transformative process that includes claims of unusual experiences.[53]

---

[53]This information is also included in the summary Table 5.14.

Table 5.11

Factor Analysis of Cluster 2: Extraordinary Transcendence

Factor label	Factor loading	Item
Factor I: Extraordinary experiences	.767	B13. I have had an experience which could best be described as a transcendent or mystical experience.
	.690	B20. I have had an experience which could best be described as an out-of-body experience.
	.668	B9. I have had experiences which science would have difficulty explaining.
	.529	B5. My ideas about life have changed dramatically in the past.
	.502	B18. It is important to me to spend periods of time in contemplation or meditation.
	.502	Q7. Extrasensory perception is possible.
	.502	Q21. Reincarnation actually does occur.
	−.479	Q27. The accepted methods of science are the only proper way in which to investigate consciousness.
	.471	Q8. The inner experiential world is vaster, richer and contains more profound meanings than most people think.
	.437	Q25. In order to fully understand human consciousness, a process of psychological change is necessary which may be achieved through meditation or a spiritual way of life.
	.412	Q14. Eastern religions have much to offer our understanding of consciousness.
	.400	Q61. There is a universal consciousness of which individual consciousness is but a part.

(table continues)

Factor label	Factor loading	Item
Factor II: Extraordinary beliefs	.728	Q22. The concept of limits does not apply to consciousness.
	.714	Q29. Physical reality is an extension of mental reality.
	.588	Q61. There is a universal consciousness of which individual consciousness is but a part.
	.582	Q44. It is possible for there to be consciousness in which there is awareness but no object of awareness.
	.571	Q33. Consciousness is more real than physical reality.
	.552	Q21. Reincarnation actually does occur.
	.472	Q41. There are modes of understanding latent within a person which are superior to rational thought.
	.432	Q7. Extrasensory perception is possible.
	.399	Q14. Eastern religions have much to offer our understanding of consciousness.
	.390	Q25. In order to fully understand human consciousness, a process of psychological change is necessary which may be achieved through meditation or a spiritual way of life.
	.373	Q19. Statements about human cognition are meaningless without reference to particular states of consciousness.
	.370	Q37. Our culture can be viewed as a basic conspiracy against self-knowledge and awakening in which we collude together to reinforce one another's defenses and insanity.

(*table continues*)

Factor label	Factor loading	Item
Factor III: Inner growth	.793	Q17. Introspection is a necessary element in the investigation of consciousness.
	.597	Q25. In order to fully understand human consciousness, a process of psychological change is necessary which may be achieved through meditation or a spiritual way of life.
	.594	Q67. A process of psychological change is necessary in order to fully experience human consciousness.
	.593	Q47. Consciousness is the key to personal growth.
	.530	Q8. The inner experiential world is vaster, richer and contains more profound meanings than most people think.
	.518	Q41. There are modes of understanding latent within a person which are superior to rational thought.
	.442	B18. It is important to me to spend periods of time in contemplation or meditation.
	−.417	Q27. The accepted methods of science are the only proper way in which to investigate consciousness.
	.413	Q14. Eastern religions have much to offer our understanding of consciousness.
	.394	Q19. Statements about human cognition are meaningless without reference to particular states of consciousness.

Note. N=334 for 89 variables clustered using average linkage within groups hierarchical cluster analysis where the median values were inserted for items where respondents failed to clearly endorse a response from "strongly disagree" to "strongly agree". The factor analysis used the principal

(table continues)

components method of extraction with a varimax rotation. The Keyser-Meyer-Olkin Measure of Sampling Adequacy was .945: the Bartlett Test of Sphericity had a value of 3286, $p<.000005$; and the first factor extracted accounted for 40.6% of the variance, with 52.3% of the total variance being accounted for by all of the three factors. The first rotated factor accounted for 18.4% of the total variance; the second for 17.5%; and the third for 16.5%. Items from Section 2 of the Survey Questionnaire are numbered with numbers preceded by "B"; items from Section 4 of the Survey Questionnaire are numbered with numbers preceded by "Q".

5.3.7 Bivariate analyses: Factor scores vs Demographic Data and Notions of Consciousness

In order to find the correlations between the factors described in the last subsection and demographic data and endorsed definitions of consciousness, the following analyses were used. Factor scores were calculated for each respondent and the set of factor scores for each factor was split at the median into a low and high group. Bivariate analyses using the Chi-square distribution as a test of significance were employed to determine the relationship between all of the remaining information gathered on the questionnaire and the derived factors. This information is given in full in Table C.2, entitled, "Crosstabulation of demographic data and endorsed definitions with factor scores" in Appendix C.

5.3.7.1 Correlations between items of Section 1, Demographic Data, and factor scores

Table 5.12 summarizes the crosstabulation of demographic data with factor scores given in Table C.2 of Appendix C. Women[54] are more likely than men to emphasize the importance of meaning and to hold extraordinary beliefs or believe in inner growth, even though they are no more likely to score high on the religiosity factor or to claim to have had unusual experiences. Those who hold a doctorate or who fall within the disciplinary boundaries labelled as "hard sciences"[55] are more likely to accept materialism and reject transcendentalism. The correlations concerning religious practice clearly categorized the three belief positions. Frequency of religious practice is positively correlated with the determinism factor, indicating that those who practice their religious or spiritual activity are

---

[54]From a separate analyses, it was found that age and education were correlated as were sex and education, so that being older or male were positively correlated with holding a doctoral degree.

[55]The breakdown of the "hard sciences" by discipline is given in Table C.1.

Table 5.12

Summary of Crosstabulation of Demographic Data with Factor Scores

		Factors						
		Cluster 1				Cluster 2		
Variable (positive pole)	I	II	III	IV	I	II	III
Age					−		
Sex (female)	+					+	+
Education (doctorate)	−	−	+		−	−	−
Discipline (hard science)	−	−	+		−	−	−
Religion (none)	−	−	+		−	−	−
(traditional)	+	+	−		−		+
(own beliefs)	+	+	−		+	+	+
Religious practice (daily)	+	+	−	−	+	+	+
(occasionally)	+	+	+	+	−	+	+
(never)	−	−	+	+	−	−	−
Rigidity		+					
Written definition					+		
Written comments (positive)		+					
Request for results					+		

Note. Positive correlation statistically significant at $p<.05$ denoted by "+"; negative correlation statistically significant at $p<.05$ denoted by "−". Cluster 1, Factor I: Meaning; Cluster 1, Factor II: Religiosity; Cluster 1, Factor III: Physicalism; Cluster 1, Factor IV: Determinism; Cluster 2, Factor I: Extraordinary experiences; Cluster 2, Factor II: Extraordinary beliefs; Cluster 2, Factor III: Inner growth. This table is a summary of part of Table C.2 from Appendix C. The information concerning place of return and psychological specialty have not been included in this summary table.

---

more likely to believe in free will. Rigidity[56] and the provision of positive comments about the study[57] are both positively correlated with the Religiosity factor. Finally, providing a written definition of consciousness and requesting the results of the study are positively correlated with the claim to extraordinary experiences.

---

[56]The method for the calculation of rigidity is described in the table notes for Tables C.1 and C.2 in Appendix C.

[57]It should be kept in mind that those who may have had negative comments to make, may have been less likely to respond to the questionnaire.

5.3.7.2 Correlations between factors and Notions of Consciousness

Table 5.13 confirms and further clarifies the correlations between beliefs and notions of consciousness revealed by the factor analyses. It is evident that from the materialist point of view, consciousness is viewed as an emergent property, described in terms of information and is always of or about something. On the other hand, the materialists' characterizations of consciousness are less likely to be endorsed and subjectivist and causal notions are more likely to be adopted in the conservatively transcendent point of view. Finally, altered states, self-transformation and consciousness as a non-physical reality are more likely to be endorsed by those who subscribe to the extraordinarily transcendent position. With regard to specific notions of consciousness, it can be noted that consciousness understood as explicit knowledge or in terms of intentionality is negatively correlated with the extraordinary beliefs factor, emphasizing the

---

Table 5.13

Summary of Crosstabulation of Endorsed Definitions with Factor Scores

		Factors					
	Cluster 1				Cluster 2		
Definition	I	II	III	IV	I	II	III
1. Meaningless							
2. Emergent property	−	−	+		−	−	−
3. Information	−		+	+	−		−
4. States of consciousness	+	−			+	+	
5. End product	+						
6. Stream of consciousness	+						
7. Knowledge/awareness					−	−	+
8. Intentionality			+	−		−	+
9. Subjective component	+						
10. Subjective existence	+						
11. Transformation	+	+		−	+	+	+
12. Non-physical	+	+	−	−	+	+	+

Note. Positive correlation statistically significant at $p<.05$ denoted by "+"; negative correlation statistically significant at $p<.05$ denoted by "−". Cluster 1, Factor I: Meaning; Cluster 1, Factor II: Religiosity; Cluster 1, Factor III: Physicalism; Cluster 1, Factor IV: Determinism; Cluster 2, Factor I: Extraordinary experiences; Cluster 2, Factor II: Extraordinary beliefs; Cluster 2, Factor III: Inner growth.   This table is a summary of part of Table C.2 from Appendix C.

extraordinarily transcendent nature of the beliefs characterizing that factor. Also, the statement of intentionality appears to have overtones of efficacy, since it is negatively correlated with Determinism and positively correlated with Inner growth.

5.3.8 Summary table of results

In an effort to bring together the preceding discussions for the purpose of creating an emergent picture of the findings, Table 5.14 is presented as a summary of the key points.

Table 5.14

Summary Table of Results

	Classification of beliefs		
	Materialism	Conservative transcendence	Extraordinary transcendence
Variable			
Religious affiliation	None	Traditional	Own beliefs
Mind-body problem	Physical monism	Dualism	Berkleyan monism
Epistemology	Science	Arts[a]	Paranormal
Consciousness	Emergent property	Subjective	Importance of altered states
	Information	Gives meaning	Transcendent reality
	Of or about something	Evidence of spirit	Key to inner growth

Note. Information that did not discriminate between the three positions has not been included in this table.

[a]The epistemological beliefs associated with a conservatively transcendent position were only minimally characterized by the items in the Survey Questionnaire. The term "arts" is used here because of the high loading of Q57 on Cluster 1, Factor I.

5.4 Discussion

The results of the empirical investigation strongly support the heuristic observation that personal experiences and beliefs about reality are correlated with notions of consciousness. Before discussing the meaning and import of this finding, the data concerning the incidence of extraordinary personal beliefs and experiences is commented on. Finally, the study is situated within the context of the relevant literature.

5.4.1 Incidence and interpretation of extraordinary experiences and beliefs

Personal Beliefs, Section 2 of the Survey Questionnaire, was concerned with personally worded items that included questions about religious and extraordinary beliefs. These are mentioned in the first paragraph of this section. Impersonally worded items about extraordinary beliefs were included in Section 4, Consciousness and Reality, and are considered in the third paragraph. The remainder of the section discusses the significance of the high rates of endorsement for extraordinary experiences and beliefs.

Religious and spiritual beliefs were important for 58 percent of this sample, as shown by agreement with the statement that one's spiritual beliefs determine one's approach to life (B8).[58] A considerable number of respondents also claimed to have had extraordinary experiences: 53 percent to have had experiences that science could not explain (B9); 47 percent to have had transcendent or mystical experiences (B13); and 23 percent to have had out-of-body experiences (B20). In 1985 The Gallup Organization found that 43 percent of the general population of the United States believed that they had "had an unusual spiritual experience" (Greeley, 1987, p. 8). The higher figure obtained here is possibly due to the inclusion of priests and transpersonal psychologists in the sample, who might be more likely to report having had such experiences.

Thomas and Cooper (1980) sought to determine more precisely what it was that people have experienced when they report having had mystical experiences. They found that 34 percent of their sample reported having been "close to a powerful spiritual force" (Thomas & Cooper, 1980, p. 78), with one percent having had an experience involving overwhelming emotions and unity with God, nature or the universe; eight percent having had psychic or unusual experiences; and 16 percent having had experiences of faith or consolation which involved religious or spiritual events without paranormal elements and usually within the context of a traditional religious system.

---

[58]All of the items referred to in this paragraph are included in Table 5.7.

With regard to extraordinary beliefs, 52 percent believed that extrasensory perception is possible (Q7).[59] In 1984 Greeley found that 67 percent of the United States population claimed to have actually experienced extrasensory perception. Belief in reincarnation (Q21) was reported by 13 percent of the sample compared to the findings of the Gallup Organization in 1981 of 23 percent. Thirty-three percent of the sample indicated that the harmony of nature reflects the existence of an original creator (Q54). The Gallup Organization found that, in 1981, 95 percent of the population of the United States believed in God or a universal spirit. With regard to life after death, 26 percent of this sample agreed that personal consciousness continues after physical death (Q58), compared with Greeley's finding in 1984 and The Gallup Organization's in 1981 that 73 percent and 71 percent of the population of the United States, respectively, believed in life after death.

How is one to understand these findings? Since the incidence of extraordinary experiences is consistent with that of the general public, but that of extraordinary beliefs is much lower, one could argue that extraordinary experiences are themselves subject to interpretation. This is supported by the fact that Factors I and II of Cluster 1 and all three factors of Cluster 2 are negatively correlated with level of education, thereby suggesting that increased education leads to a less "fanciful" understanding of one's own experiences and of reality more generally. In other words, the subject population, made up of highly educated people, would be more likely to examine their ideas about reality and to discard extraordinary interpretations of their own experience that the general public would be willing to accept as a matter of superstition.

One has to be careful in making such an interpretation that one does not perceive the claim of mystical experiences as indicative of a pathological condition. Repeated efforts to find such correlations have produced negative results (Caird, 1987; Spanos & Moretti, 1988).[60] There is, in fact, some evidence to suggest that those having had extraordinary experiences are more emotionally stable (Greeley, 1987) and more open-minded (Lester, Thinschmidt & Trautman, 1987) and tolerant of ambiguity (Thomas & Cooper, 1980) than those not having had such experiences. There were no data collected in this study for the testing of the first of these contentions. The last two contentions were uncorroborated by this

---

[59]All of the items referred to in this paragraph are included in Table 5.9.

[60]The discussion here is about mystical experiences in general. Reports of diabolical experiences are correlated with psychopathology (Spanos & Moretti, 1988).

research.[61]

While extraordinary experiences are understood to be such only under certain interpretations, such experiences, for those who have them, can be so compelling that they can lead one to re-examine one's understanding of reality. In the particular case of those who claim to have had near-death experiences, Ring (1987) has stated:

> NDErs almost universally allege to have lost all fear of death *and* to be convinced that the end of life is anything but. Death, they say, as in a single voice, is but a transition into a higher, transcendental realm of being. There is no death. (p. 172; emphasis in original)[62]

The results of the present investigation are compatible with such an interpretation because of the prominent inclusion of Item B5 in Cluster 2, Factor I. Those who endorsed this item, stating that their ideas about life had changed dramatically in the past, were also those who claimed to have had extraordinary experiences.

These interpretations of the incidence of claims of extraordinary experiences and extraordinary beliefs are consistent with the results of a study investigating a person's conceptions of the afterlife carried out by Gardner and Baruss (1988). Content analyses of structured interviews with 28 people, from a broad spectrum of educational backgrounds and social and economic status, indicated that those who believed in an afterlife claimed to believe in it for a number of reasons. Some participants had been brought up in a religious system which they had never questioned. Others appeared to have a need to believe in an afterlife, wishing or hoping that there was one. A third group of respondents reported that they had had experiences which had convinced them of the possibility of an afterlife. These experiences were sometimes claims to mystical experiences generally rather than to near-death or other experiences specific to the issue of afterlife. Thus, both the present survey concerning consciousness and the Gardner and Baruss study concerning conceptions of the afterlife, suggest that transcendent interpretations of reality may be determined in part by the nature of one's own experiences, and that claims of transcendentalism may result from a number of widely different situations.

---

[61]This observation is based on the lack of correlation between claims to unusual experiences and scores on the short form of Kirton's revision of the Budner Intolerance of Ambiguity Scale. It is possible, of course, that had a different instrument been available, such a correlation may have been found.

[62]An NDEr is a person who claims to have had a near-death experience.

It is important to note, at this point, that there is no effort made here to legislate on the authority or validity of claims of extraordinary experiences. How one does that already depends upon one's understanding of reality. The purpose in this book is simply to discuss the claims to such experiences, and some of the correlations and implications of such claims. This issue is brought up again in the next subsection as well as in the concluding chapter of this book.

5.4.2 The significance of the finding of the relationships between notions of consciousness and personal beliefs and experiences

The purpose of the empirical investigation was to examine, using a survey questionnaire, the variety of notions of consciousness and their relationship to personal experiences and beliefs about reality. Cluster and factor analyses of the data revealed that the statements that people make about consciousness can be largely understood in terms of a few constructs. These constructs, in general, fall along a physical-transcendent dimension as hypothesized. Also as hypothesized, a scientific/objective/material position is correlated with consciousness understood as an emergent property or in terms of information-processing, and negatively correlated with notions of consciousness given in terms of altered states of consciousness. What is surprising, is that the transcendental pole of the physical-transcendental dimension was so clearly defined. In particular, it was not expected that two distinct transcendent positions would emerge[63] or that they would be so well articulated (Tables 5.10 to 5.14).

The use of the notion of transcendence should be clarified here. As with the problem of the validity of extraordinary experiences mentioned previously, the effort here is not to decide the issue of whether or not transcendent experiences are possible. That is not the point. The point is that some people claim that they are possible, and discuss issues regarding consciousness from that perspective, and that that is something that has to be considered when dealing with the literature concerning consciousness.

More generally, there is an ongoing debate in religious studies between humanist and social science factions as to whether or not reference should be made, implicitly or explicitly, to a purported dimension of reality different from that of ordinary everyday experiences. Dawson (1987) has suggested that one can formally employ the category of the transcendent without thereby asserting its existence. The situation

---

[63]It is correct to say that these two positions emerge, but they are not isolated from one another in the same way that they are both isolated from the materialist position. While the factors within each cluster are orthogonal, they are correlated across clusters. In particular, both are inherently concerned with transcendence.

similar to that of the experience of a subjective self, which is seen as a vacuous experience – essentially as a problem of failed reference in the use of language – within contemporary philosophy of mind (Lycan, 1987; Natsoulas, 1983b). This does not, however, prohibit the examination of the use of such a category by those who investigate the nature of consciousness.

In fact, it has been shown by this research that the status that one gives to the category of the transcendent varies from person to person. This characterizes a fundamental schism within the ranks of the highly educated who are in a position to discuss consciousness in the academic literature, and leads to essentially different and irreconcilable explanations concerning the nature of consciousness. This is a situation that is unlikely to change.[64]

What are the implications of this situation for the study of consciousness? The prediction is that the study of consciousness will remain splintered. Some people will continue to investigate their version of consciousness from a traditionally scientific point of view and discredit any other efforts to understand consciousness. Others will continue to address the subject from a more philosophical stance. Others again, will remain relegated to the counterculture, where they will continue to introspect their own inner experience, occasionally finding expression for their ideas within the academic arena.

The significance of this research is to have empirically demonstrated that (the definition, study and explanation of consciousness is grounded in personal convictions that may themselves be rooted in a person's particular beliefs and experiences of reality.) Thus, the understanding of consciousness will continue to be ultimately, generally a personal matter with different and conflicting notions of consciousness entertained by different people. Those differences and contradictions will continue to be reflected in the academic literature.

5.4.3 The relevance of the findings to the psychological literature

In concluding the discussion of the findings, it is appropriate to locate the results of this study within the literature outlined in the introduction to the chapter, as well as to one additional relevant source.

Insofar as the present study demonstrates empirically a variety of beliefs and notions concerning consciousness, it is consistent with the contentions of Heidegger (1926/1962), Harvey, Hunt and Schroeder (1961),

---

[64]It is also important to note here that it is not a matter of legislating what the situation should be, but rather, of describing what the situation, in fact, is.

Rokeach (1960, 1976) and Straker (1985) that one's understanding of reality is largely mediated by one's interpretive schemata. In particular, consistent with the ideas of Osborne (1981) and Frank (1977), the physical-transcendental dimension turns out to be pivotal to understanding the range of positions with regard to consciousness in the Western intellectual tradition. However, further to Osborne, the transcendental pole is characterized in detail in this study, revealing some of the diverse elements of a transcendent position. Consistent with Frank, there are no major differences in the altruistic ethic between the material and transcendental positions as shown by the absence of items Q10, "Our objective as human beings is to maximize the material and psychological benefits of each individual person," and Q42, "We are morally obligated to reduce pain and suffering in the world," from the factors defining the belief positions. The observations of Frank with regard to the open-mindedness of the scientific-humanist position also appear to be supported by this research, in that the only correlation with rigidity scores is a positive correlation with the Religiosity Factor, which is one aspect of a transcendental position.

The work of Coan (1968), Krasner and Houts (1984), and Kimble (1984), who found similar physical-transcendent dimensions within the psychological community, is supported by this research in that such a dimension is revealed here to be operative for a more general academic and professional population.

The present research also extends aspects of Unger, Draper and Pendergrass' (1986) work in two ways: (a) the Survey Questionnaire has a more thorough set of items concerning philosophical issues than the Attitudes About Reality Scale; and, (b) the subject population for this study consisted of highly educated academics and professionals rather than college students. As in the case of Unger, Draper and Pendergrass' work, the results of this study demonstrate that factors involving the personal are correlated with ideological positions.

Harman (1987a) has maintained that an interpretation of reality depends upon the metaphysical stance that one adopts. He has outlined three such positions. The first of these he has called "Materialistic monism," a position in which matter gives rise to mind. The second is a dualist position in which it is maintained that both material and mental realities exist and must be explored by means that are appropriate to each. Finally, he has discussed a third metaphysic, which he has called "Transcendental monism," whereby the "ultimate stuff of the universe" (p. 8) is consciousness, and the physical world is like a dream image. While these three positions are essentially just a restatement of the three positions with regard to the mind-body problem, it is significant that Harman discusses them as substantive determinants of the way in which issues in consciousness are treated today. The present study supports Harman's surmise concerning the presence and significance of those three implicit metaphysical positions and further elaborates them.

In conclusion, the results of this study support, further clarify and extend work that has been done with regard to the role of personal beliefs in the academic understanding of reality. In addition, this present work stands alone in demonstrating empirically how unusual personal experiences as well as such implicit beliefs are correlated with notions of consciousness.

CHAPTER 6

CONCLUSIONS

Once we admit that the ways of reasoning vary with the ways of the reasoners, the scope for common ground seems too narrow to escape relativism, and the admission marks the fact that there are different institutions, different practices and different styles in approaching the world. Tolerance we may have, but no claim to universality for our own ways. (Newell, 1986, p. 101)

This final chapter consolidates the material in this book by presenting an overview of the preceding chapters, discusses the thesis and concludes with a number of suggestions for further research.

6.1 Overview

This project arose out of a recognition of the disparity of views concerning consciousness present in the academic literature and the need to clarify such diversity. Without claiming the correctness of any one version of consciousness, the undertaking was carried out to investigate the role of the personal in the understanding of consciousness using the standard theoretical and empirical methods of the behavioral sciences.

Chapter 1 provided an introduction to the book by giving the motivation for it, by stating its thesis and by indicating the scope of the project. Chapters 2, 3 and 4 were theoretical in nature. They further elaborated the issues raised in the thesis and provided material for the empirical study as well as an interpretive framework for understanding the findings from such a study. Chapter 5 consisted of the empirical work. Conclusions from the theoretical and empirical work are then drawn in Chapter 6.

In Chapter 1, Section 1, some examples were given of statements about consciousness that have appeared in the literature. In addition, examples were included that indicated that particular versions of consciousness were allied more generally to beliefs about the nature of reality and beliefs about how that reality was to be known. In Section 3, the suggestion was made that notions of consciousness are correlated with parameters usually considered part of one's personal nature, such as one's beliefs about reality, religious beliefs and interpretations of personal

137

experiences. It was stated that the purpose of the project was, first, to discuss this contention theoretically and, second, to seek empirical support for it. Section 3 gave an outline of the progression that was to be followed in the book.

In Chapter 2 the problem of consciousness was identified as the apparent disparity between the purportedly subjective nature of consciousness and the objective nature of reality as it comes to be known by science. The first section explicitly discussed this apparent gap and the problems caused by subjectivity. Science as a methodology for studying consciousness was discussed in the first part of the second section, and suggestions that have appeared in the literature concerning alternative means of studying consciousness were mentioned in the second half. The third section reviewed the arguments and empirical work that have lent credence to the contention that one's approach to the study of consciousness and its understanding are significantly dependent upon the context within which one functions, including the context of one's personal beliefs and experiences. While the first two sections of the chapter were concerned with the apparent problem of consciousness, the third section gave a perspective from which to organize the problem. As such it served as an introduction to the empirical study of Chapter 5.

Before proceeding with the empirical study it was necessary to accomplish two things: to clarify the definition of the term consciousness and to detail some of the notions of consciousness. A metanalysis of notions of consciousness was carried out in Chapter 3. It was found that the term consciousness has three main referents. *Consciousness$_1$* refers to an organism's basic ability to process information. Subjective awareness of anything or its demonstration behaviorally constitutes the referent of *consciousness$_2$*. The designation *consciousness$_3$* is to be used for the sense of existence that is a concomitant of subjective experience.

Chapter 4 was an attempt to circumscribe some of the notions of consciousness. It started in Section 1 by considering the evolution of James's ideas about consciousness, from his belief in the causal capacity of consciousness, through his interest in its mundane manifestations to a consideration of its alterations. In Section 2, the role of matter in the understanding of consciousness was introduced in two ways. The first of these was through the examination of the eliminative materialist position which maintains that the concept of consciousness has no referent and that discussions about mental events should be given in neurophysiological terms. The second was a review of some of the physiological phenomena that have appeared to have a bearing on conscious functioning. The third section introduced the Turing test as a criterion for the presence of consciousness, as well as Dennett's version of consciousness in terms of a computer program's printout faculty. The Turing test and computationalism are the key ingredients of the understanding of consciousness in cognitive science. Subjectivist notions of consciousness were considered in Section

4, by discussing Husserl's conscious mental acts and tra versions of consciousness. The chapter ended by mentior _ .y s contention that a consciousness revolution has taken place due to a new understanding of causality, and by cataloguing some of the contexts, issues and perspectives concerning consciousness.

Chapter 5 was a presentation of the empirical work that formed the focus of this project. A survey instrument was developed that could be used for determining any relationships between a person's ideas about consciousness and their beliefs about reality and purported paranormal experiences. The development of the questionnaire proceeded in three stages. Initially a Preliminary Questionnaire was designed by selecting statements about consciousness from the literature and determining which of them made sense to a well-educated population. Some of the items from the Preliminary Questionnaire along with items concerning personal beliefs and purported paranormal experiences were included in a Pilot Questionnaire. The Pilot Questionnaire was revised and the Survey Questionnaire was circulated to a sample of people who could potentially write about consciousness in the academic literature. The responses to the Survey Questionnaire were then cluster and factor analyzed. Three main positions emerged: a materialist position, a position of conservative transcendence and a position of extreme transcendence. Factor scores were calculated, split at the median and compared with demographic data and endorsed definitions of consciousness. Bivariate analyses confirmed and further defined each of the three positions which are strongly correlated with specific statements about consciousness. The materialist position, characterized by belief in physical reality as the only reality, is correlated with explanations of consciousness in terms of emergent properties, information and intentionality. Conservative transcendence, a position in which it is believed that there is more to life than the physical world, entails the importance of subjectivity and consciousness as providing meaning and evidence for spirituality. From an extremely transcendent position, consciousness is considered to be the primary reality to be understood through alterations of consciousness and self-transformation for which consciousness itself is the key. The implications of the importance of purported paranormal experiences for the extreme transcendentalist view and the significance and relevance of the study to the psychological literature were discussed.

Thus the book has a natural progression, from the identification of a problem with the study of consciousness in Chapters 1 and 2, through an analysis of the definitions and notions of consciousness in Chapters 3 and 4, to the development and implementation of a survey instrument in Chapter 5.

6.2 The personal nature of notions of consciousness

There is no consensus in the academic literature concerning the notion of consciousness. In particular, there is no agreement as to how to understand the subjective aspect of consciousness. In many cases it is argued that subjectivity does not cause a problem. In practice, however, it clearly does present a problem. It has been shown in this book that explanations of consciousness vary with the personal beliefs and experiences of those who give them.

The situation is analogous to that in physics and mathematics. Heisenberg's Uncertainty Principle in physics and Godel's Incompleteness Theorem in mathematics have demonstrated that there are limits to what can be determined within a given system. The joke in mathematics, for example, is that one no longer gives a proof or finds a counter-example for a proposition in mathematics, but proves undecidability. In other words, rather than seeking to prove a statement in mathematics, it is said that one shows that it is neither provable nor disprovable in a given elementary theory of mathematics. In neither physics nor mathematics does the situation affect the everyday functioning of most physicists and mathematicians. Similarly in psychology, very few psychologists are concerned with understanding the nature of consciousness; but those who are, encounter this problem of indeterminism.[65] The nature of consciousness cannot be completely determined in a consensual manner, but its understanding must, in part, be deferred to one's own personal beliefs and experience.

This is an unnerving situation. Could one not avoid this problem by restricting oneself to a sufficiently circumscribed position with regard to consciousness, say cognitive science, the currently respected consensus position with regard to the study of human cognition? It is interesting to note, however, that a position which is manifestly objectively scientific in perspective has, seemingly reluctantly, had to admit events from personal experience as evidence of the nature of cognitive processes. Dennett, for example, in order to validate the model of consciousness given in Chapter 4, has called on his own experience:

> How on earth should one . . . address [the question of whether an apparent zombie has an inner conscious life]? Is there a better course than mere doctrinaire verificationism on the one hand, or shoulder-shrugging agnosticism on the other? This is of course just 'the problem of other minds', and I propose that progress can be made on it by reexamining *what one knows about one's own case* in the light of the most promising theories of psychology. What convin-

---

[65]It is interesting to note that in all three cases, the systems break down at the "edges" when self-reference is introduced. In physics, the device with which one measures is a physical device, in Godel's Incompleteness Theorem, the Godel sentence refers to itself and in psychology, "consciousness" is used for understanding itself.

ces *me* that a cognitivistic theory could capture all the dear features I discover in my inner life is not any 'argument', and not just the programmatic appeal of thereby preserving something like 'the unity of science', but rather a detailed attempt to describe to myself exactly those features of my life *and the nature of my acquaintance with them* that I would cite as my 'grounds' for claiming that I *am* – and do not merely *seem to be* – conscious. What *I* discover are facts quite congenial to cognitivistic theorizing, and my tactic here has been to try, by persuasive redescription, to elicit the same discoveries in others. (Dennett, 1978, p. 173; emphases in original)

Having prescribed the test, Dennett should not be surprised, given the history of the problem of introspection, if others, after examining their own experience, come to conclusions quite different from his.[66] Perhaps after a near-death experience, Dennett may change his mind about his model's ability to explain consciousness.

Mandler, in his review of research concerning consciousness in cognitive psychology, as mentioned in Chapter 4, has made the same point that is being made here:

Private experiences are important aspects of the fully functioning mental system. It is possible to get transformed reports about those events, and it should be possible to develop appropriate theories that relate the contents of consciousness, their transformations, and their report. However, it is not possible to build a *viable* theory that makes precise predictions about private experience, since the outcome of those predictions cannot be properly evaluated by the psychologist-observer.

This position does admit the development of private theories, by individuals, about themselves. To the individual, one's experience *is* a datum, and consequently personal theories about one's own structures are, within limits, testable by direct experience. These individual, personal theories of the self are both pervasive and significant in explaining human action, but they cannot, without peril, be generalized to others or to the species as a whole. (Mandler, 1985, p. 56; emphases in original)

As Mandler has expressed it, the deference to introspective observations is continuous with observations of external events. Just as one can learn to hypothesize, observe external events, and theorize as part of a scientific endeavor, one could hypothesize, "observe internal events" and theorize as part of a modified science endeavor. In this manner, obser-

---

[66]One is immediately reminded of James's contention, that upon examination of his experience, he found that thinking, which is what consciousness was, was just the breath.

vations for oneself are an extension of the method of participant obser-vation in the behavioral sciences.[67] Rather than becoming an active member of a cult, for example, in order to understand its dynamics, one could become an active thinker trying to understand one's own conscious-ness. Thus, even within the restricted domain of cognitive science, unintentionally and intentionally, there has been latitude given for differences in understanding consciousness that would reflect real dif-ferences in personal experience. Furthermore, this latitude is not an aberration but a development of the spirit and endeavor of science.

But none of this is a surprise to many psychiatrists and counselling and clinical psychologists. Both Kelly (1955) and Beck (1976) have pointed out that each person is an amateur scientist solving the problems of her life, and that psychopathology results from incorrect strategies of reason-ing. In addition, one's client in psychotherapy is often required to examine their experience to determine its meaningfulness for them and to develop an understanding of reality that is compatible with that (Assagioli, 1965; Maslow, 1968; Rogers and Stevens, 1967). It is a heuristic observation that this aspect of psychotherapy, which properly belongs to the humanistic tradition, appears to have come to form the backbone of a generic form of psychotherapy practiced by many counsellors and psycho-therapists in North America. It is not surprising then, that affiliation with clinical or transpersonal psychology is significantly correlated with high scores on Factor III of Cluster 2. Having been empowered, or having empowered oneself, to personally come to grips with reality, how is one to understand oneself, including one's consciousness, except through self-exploration and in terms that are meaningful to oneself?

At this point, the discussion comes back to the issue of introspec-tion and the problem of conviction which were discussed in Chapter 2. Pursuing that issue leads one outside the scope of this book and into the next subsection.

6.3 Suggestions for further research

Upon consideration of the issues raised in the course of this project, a number of directions for further research suggest themselves at its close. These fall into three major categories: those concerned with the role of beliefs in human understanding; those concerned with personal experien-ces, in particular, purported transcendental experiences; and those that directly concern the study of the understanding of consciousness. After briefly discussing the limitations of this book, each of these categories is discussed in turn.

---

[67]Participant observation is discussed, for example, by Rosenthal and Rosnow (1984).

Each of the chapters two through five in this book is only a beginning for dealing with the issues raised in that chapter. This is necessarily the case since the effort of this project has been to bring together, in a multidisciplinary manner, the academic literature concerning consciousness. In particular, a more comprehensive cataloguing and exposition of the notions of consciousness would be useful to those who are conducting research in the area of consciousness. An additional limitation results from the use of nomothetic methods for the empirical investigation of Chapter 5 which necessarily restrict the kinds of deeper questions that one would like to ask concerning a person's beliefs about reality. For example, how are incompatible beliefs structured for any given individual? What are the factors that are involved in a change of world-view? The idiographic methods mentioned in Chapter 2 could be utilized to address such questions. Other, more specific suggestions for future research are given below.

In Chapter 2 some of the empirical work concerning the role of beliefs in academic research was reviewed. More work along these lines is required, so that the formation and maintenance of beliefs and their impact on science and academic activity can be properly assessed. More generally, a psychology of science is necessary, so that the variables influencing the hypothesizing, observing and theorizing of scientists can be better understood. Similarly, there is need for a psychology of philosophy which could catalogue the forms and kinds of contentions and arguments that philosophers make and which could find the parameters that lead to specific schools of thought.

One class of beliefs that turns out to be important in this study is that of religious beliefs. In particular, it may be necessary to distinguish between religious beliefs that are held because one has grown up with them, religious beliefs that are held out of wishfulness for a better life and religious beliefs that have apparently resulted from a reconsideration of reality. Such categories have emerged from a study by Gardner and Baruss (1988) in which 28 people were interviewed concerning their beliefs about the afterlife. The dynamics of religious beliefs need to be better understood, especially where they are held with great conviction.

Related to the issue of beliefs is the area of research which concerns the range of possible personal experiences. In particular, experiences in altered states of consciousness and exceptional states of being need to be carefully examined. This point has been made repeatedly (e.g., Dane & DeGood, 1987; Hurley, 1988; Mavromatis, 1987; Tart, 1980; Walsh, 1984a). As discussed in Chapter 5, such states are being reported more frequently and appear to strongly influence the personal beliefs and convictions about reality held by those who claim to have experienced them. As discussed in Chapter 4, the suggestion has sometimes been made that altered states of consciousness are developmentally more mature than ordinary states of consciousness. The conviction that such states are in some sense synthetic rather than regressive needs to be examined. In particular, in this study, it was found that those who reported having had paranormal experiences were also more likely to have reported having had a dramatic change of ideas about life in the past. What are the dynamics and parameters of such conversion experiences?

Finally, the understanding of consciousness itself needs to be further clarified. A great deal of theoretical work is necessary to find and explicate the relationships among the variety of notions of consciousness that have been mentioned in this book. The empirical study itself should be replicated. The factors that were obtained could be item analyzed and developed as scales that could be used in further research. In depth examinations of versions of consciousness could be obtained through interviews and through the use of the Preliminary Questionnaire, with those who have sufficiently developed views of consciousness.

Finally, one has to consider the problem of the nature of consciousness. That, however, will be pursued by individuals in whatever way they deem to be appropriate and will continue to result in a variety of explanations of consciousness.

APPENDIX A

CONSCIOUSNESS QUESTIONNAIRES

Preliminary Questionnaire

For each of the following items, write the number of the response that best reflects your understanding of that item, using the following scale:

1. This statement does not make sense to me;
2. This statement is not relevant to my understanding of consciousness;
3. This statement is relevant to my understanding of consciousness, but I don't know whether or not I agree with it;
4. I agree with the statement;
5. I disagree with the statement.

Include any comments about the items.

1. More research is needed in the area of human consciousness.
2. It is not possible, at present, to evaluate the importance of consciousness in a scientific description of the world.
3. The notion of consciousness is useful in military settings.
4. Alternative approaches and innovative theories are needed for the study of consciousness.
5. The subject of consciousness is a nebulous one.
6. Western conceptions of consciousness are limiting.
7. The problem of consciousness is a central problem in psychology.
8. Consciousness is a fundamental aspect of human functioning.
9. Consciousness can best be regarded as an epiphenomenon of a behaving organism.
10. Scientists can gain many valuable insights into consciousness through meditation or other procedures designed to expand or illuminate private experience.
11. A view of consciousness that does justice to the variety of complications surrounding it will almost certainly demand a revolution in our habits of thought.
12. It does not make sense to talk about consciousness in quantitative terms.
13. Consciousness is not a function of psychic existence but its very structure.

14. Consciousness is without form, structure, or content.
15. Consciousness is a concomitant of all thought, feeling and volition.
16. The inner experiential world is more vast, richer and contains more profound meanings than most people think.
17. Consciousness is a natural phenomenon, neither synthetic nor artificial.
18. The existence of human consciousness is evidence of a spiritual dimension within each person.
19. Consciousness is an awareness, beyond words and concepts, within the immediate, direct and present moment of experience.
20. One aspect of consciousness is the awareness of external events.
21. Awareness is a term equivalent to consciousness.
22. One's own consciousness can be understood through a process of introspection.
23. A stream of consciousness is accessible through meditation.
24. Ultimately, the only way to understand human consciousness is through meditation or a religious way of life.
25. Mind can only be experienced as an ongoing process.
26. It is possible to talk about dimensions of consciousness.
27. It makes sense to talk about passive and active modes of consciousness.
28. There is a continuum of consciousness between events that are conscious and those that are not.
29. Ordinary consciousness comprises only a minute fraction of the total activity of the mind.
30. Consciousness can occur only in a relatively intact human organism.
31. Consciousness is not unique to each human being but is universal in nature.
32. The concept of limits does not apply to consciousness.
33. It doesn't make sense to ascribe consciousness to animals.
34. A person's consciousness can be said to be located inside their skull.
35. Consciousness refers to knowing within oneself, alone.
36. Consciousness is distributed diffusely throughout the brain in a statistical fashion.
37. It does not make sense to ascribe a location to consciousness.
38. Consciousness can best be thought of as a field which permeates all space.
39. We can understand consciousness in the same way that we can understand the contents of consciousness.
40. The accepted methods of science are the only proper way in which to investigate consciousness.
41. It will never be fully possible to understand human consciousness.
42. The whole issue of human consciousness is rather puzzling.
43. Consciousness provides meaning.
44. Consciousness is more real than physical reality.
45. Consciousness is not an unvarying, independent entity.
46. Consciousness is a varying quantity.
47. Within each person, consciousness varies from moment to moment.

48. The terms consciousness and mind refer to the same reality.
49. The quality of a person's thinking is a function of the scope of their consciousness.
50. Consciousness is proof of the reality of mental existence.
51. Human consciousness expresses itself through the physical medium of the brain, but is not dependent on it.
52. Human consciousness would not exist without the brain.
53. Consciousness involves knowing what we are doing.
54. Consciousness is much more than just self-awareness.
55. It makes sense to talk about the intensity of consciousness.
56. Consciousness can understand the external world, but not itself.
57. Consciousness is a basic sensory responsiveness to and awareness of our situation.
58. In terms of their inner nature, conscious entities are not only passively related to their external environment, but actively related to it.
59. One aspect of consciousness is a physiological reaction to stimuli interacting with the nervous system.
60. Consciousness generates programs of behavior to adjust the organism to its environment.
61. An organism is conscious of an aspect of its environment if it reacts differentially with respect to variations within that aspect.
62. Conscious events become memories.
63. Human consciousness depends upon language.
64. Consciousness always entails consciousness of something.
65. There is a distinction between consciousness as a phenomenon and the contents of consciousness.
66. Consciousness entails the faculty of being mentally aware of anything.
67. It is possible for there to be consciousness in which there is awareness but no contents of awareness.
68. Conscious beings have free will.
69. Consciousness plays a causal role in determining neural activity and behavior.
70. Across the course of history, consciousness itself has changed.
71. It is possible to experience a state of superconsciousness which has qualities different from personal consciousness.
72. It is possible to be in a state of consciousness in which a whole and boundless relationship with everything is experienced.
73. Strong emotions should be regarded as an altered state of consciousness.
74. Much of what is unconscious can be brought into consciousness.
75. A transcendent state of consciousness is possible but can be explained simply in terms of physiological mechanisms.
76. Different planes of consciousness are each valid in their own right.
77. Consciousness is an accidental property of complex neural tissue.
78. Consciousness is an emergent property of information-processing systems.
79. Consciousness entails an interaction between levels of an information-

processing system in which higher levels reach back down towards lower levels, influencing them, while at the same time being themselves determined by the lower levels.

80. Human consciousness is an emergent property of cellular interaction.

81. Conscious experience is associated with control processes of the brain.

82. The evolution of consciousness can be attributed solely to the gradual accumulation of knowledge.

83. A reductionistic explanation of consciousness, in order to be comprehensible, must bring in soft concepts such as levels, mappings and meanings.

84. Consciousness represents a principle of economy that makes information-processing more efficient and reduces the number of elements necessary to perform a task.

85. Consciousness sets goals and activates behavioral action systems appropriate to accomplishing these goals.

86. Consciousness is the cathexis or attention-dispensing function of the ego system in a person.

87. Consciousness is a limited capacity mechanism of attention.

88. Attention refers to processes that organize the contents of consciousness into one or another conscious state.

89. Someday we will be able to say that computers are conscious.

90. There is no a priori reason why certain classes of machines would not be conscious, without thereby losing their status as machines.

91. The understanding we have of our own conscious experience is self-evident.

92. Conscious experience is experience that is, at least in principle, reportable.

93. Consciousness allows for immediacy of knowledge about oneself.

94. It is possible to study consciousness empirically by analyzing verbal reports of subjective experiences.

95. Consciousness is subjective knowledge, by and for oneself.

96. Consciousness entails the subject's awareness of themselves as subject.

97. Subjective experience is the product of the contents of consciousness.

98. Consciousness is identical with the report of consciousness.

99. The internal world of purely private data constitutes a stream of consciousness by appeal to which we can alone justify claims to knowledge of the external world in which we live and move and have our being.

100. The term consciousness should be reserved for those aspects of the environment or of the subject's own experience upon which they are in a position to make a verbal report.

101. If an organism is capable of responding to the same elements in different contexts and hence with different behaviors, that organism is conscious of something.

102. If different complexes of cues, often corresponding to the same definable object, elicit similar differential behavior, then that organism can be said to be conscious of the relevant object.

103. If a subject, normally capable of demonstrating consciousness by

producing a verbal report of awareness is unable to do so, then intelligent, adaptive, responsive and rational behavior may be cautiously accepted as providing such a demonstration.

104. The unity of consciousness is an illusion.
105. The unity of self arises from the irreducible awareness of being.
106. All sufficiently healthy human beings experience consciousness.
107. The experience of consciousness is the same for all human beings who experience it.
108. The question of whether others are conscious as oneself, can never be conclusively answered.
109. Consciousness does not change with time.
110. Consciousness transcends time.
111. Consciousness changes with the maturational process.
112. Consciousness ends with biological death.
113. Time is always a continuous element for consciousness.
114. It is possible to consciously experience a sense of timelessness.
115. Personal consciousness continues after physical death.
116. Eastern religions have much to offer our understanding of consciousness.
117. The great religions are state-specific technologies and roadways to higher states of consciousness.
118. Consciousness is contingent upon another's awareness of one's perceptions of them and one's perception of this awareness.
119. Consciousness is essentially the result of social processes.
120. Consciousness is joint or mutual knowledge.
121. Each person needs to be initiated into consciousness as part of a social process.
122. Consciousness is mutual knowledge possessed by joint agents in a shared plan.
123. Human consciousness can best be understood in terms of human interaction.
124. Our culture can be viewed as a vast conspiracy against self-knowledge and awakening in which we collude together to reinforce one another's defenses and insanity.
125. The evolution of consciousness can be facilitated by psychotherapy.
126. A greater understanding of consciousness can lead to military applications.
127. The subject of consciousness is a legitimate subject of study.
128. The concept of consciousness is respectable, useful and probably necessary.
129. Human consciousness is intimately linked to the development of values.
130. Consciousness is an entity deducible from more primitive terms and propositions.
131. Mathematics is a language that may eventually be used for talking about consciousness.
132. Consciousness combines, but does not synthesize sense modalities.
133. Consciousness is never complete, but always partial and subject to

error.

134. Consciousness within a person is characterized by an ability to make distinctions.

135. Consciousness is related to the ability to symbolize.

136. The highest and most complex form of relationship is expressed in consciousness.

137. We can assign consciousness the attribute of creativity, in that it leads to the adoption of new procedures.

138. Experiences that are not consciously processed may show up in dreams.

139. It is possible for there to be more than one subject of consciousness in a person.

140. Quantum mechanics will eventually be able to explain consciousness.

141. There is a universal consciousness of which individual consciousness is but a part.

142. Consciousness consists of real conversations with other individuals or imaginary conversations with archetypes of other people.

143. Consciousness can be used to speed the process of healing and in some cases to precipitate it.

144. It makes sense to talk about the differences between masculine and feminine consciousness.

145. Consciousness is indefinable.

146. Consciousness can be known only within oneself.

147. Consciousness of one's own being is not something that one possesses or something that one can create within oneself by desire or decision alone.

148. Ordinary consciousness can be likened to being asleep.

149. Consciousness permeates all of nature.

150. The totality of human consciousness has grown from the impulse of a love of knowledge.

151. Consciousness is located first in the senses.

152. Consciousness is cyclic in nature.

153. Psychological activity must always be understood as occurring within a specific state of consciousness.

154. The experience of self can vary from one state of consciousness to another.

155. The nature of truth can vary from one state of consciousness to another.

156. Everything is at some point changing into its opposite.

157. The subject of consciousness is a confusing one.

158. Consciousness is mysterious.

159. Indicate here, in descending order of importance, the 10 questionnaire items which you feel best characterize your understanding of consciousness:

160. Discipline:

Sources for items of Preliminary Questionnaire

1. Derived from Pekala and Levine (1981-82), p. 32.
2. Reworded from Josephson (1980), p. 115.
3. Derived from Alexander (1980).
4. Derived from Osborne (1981), p. 289, and Pelletier (1978), p. 250.
5. Derived from Ramachandran (1980), p. 1.
6. Derived from Ring (1974), p. 125.
7. Derived from Hilgard (1980), p. 2.
8. Quotation from Osborne (1981), p. 289.
9. Statement of the epiphenomenalist position given, for example, in Flanagan (1984), p. 38.
10. Derived from Walsh (1984a).
11. Derived from Dennett (1978), p. 178.
12. Derived from Miller and Buckhout (1973), pp. 93 – 95 and Fischer (1978-79), p. 162.
13. Quotation (essentially) from Fischer (1978-79), p. 162.
14. Reworded from Fischer (1978-79), p. 162.
15. Derived from Natsoulas (1978a).
16. Reworded from Walsh (1984a), pp. 54 – 55.
17. Quotation (essentially) from Weinland (1974), p. 77.
18. Derived from Weinland (1974), p. 34.
19. Quotation (essentially) from Tulku cited by Helminiak (1984), p. 221.
20. Derived from Klein (1959), p. 15.
21. Reworded from Lowenhard (1981), p. 22.
22. Derived from James (1890/1983).
23. Derived from Walsh (1976, 1984a).
24. Derived from Chang (1978), Merrell-Wolff (1973a, 1973b) and Walsh (1984a).
25. Derived from Denzin (1982), p. 41, Muses (1968a), p. 30 and Walsh (1976), pp. 100 – 101.
26. Derived from Pekala and Levine (1981-82), p. 33.
27. Derived from Hilgard (1980), p. 18.
28. Derived from Pelletier (1978), p. 243 and White (1982), p. 14.
29. Reworded from Harman (1981a), p. 114.
30. Restatement and restriction of Postulate 9 by Lowenhard (1981), p. 25.
31. Derived from Rama (1981), p. 320.
32. Derived from Walsh (1984a), p. 31.
33. Pervasive problem, discussed, for example, by Appleton (1976) and Thomas (1983), p. 7.
34. Antithesis of statement by Holt (1914), p. 181.
35. Seventeenth century usage of the term "conscious" according to Fischer (1978-79), p. 161.
36. Reworded from John (1980), p. 132.
37. Derived from Beaumont (1981), p. 194.
38. Derived from Battista (1978), p. 59, Beaumont (1981), p. 194 and Gurwitsch (1964).
39. Paraphrase of quotation from Jaynes cited in Osborne (1981), p. 279.

40. Pervasive problem, discussed, for example, by Walsh (1980).
41. Pervasive problem, discussed, for example, by Walsh (1980).
42. Observation made after substantial reading about consciousness.
43. Generalization of Muses (1970), p. 43.
44. Derived from Briggs and Peat (1984), Harman (1981a) and Merrell-Wolff (1973a).
45. Quotation from Jackson cited by Penfield (1975), p. 92.
46. Quotation from Jackson cited by Penfield (1975), p. 92.
47. Derived from James (1890/1983) and Items 45 and 46.
48. Derived from Holt (1914), p. 183.
49. Reworded from Lunzer (1979), p. 3.
50. Derived from C. Taylor (1982), p. 38.
51. Statement compatible with Berkleyan monism, discussed, for example, by Flanagan (1984), p. 20.
52. Permutation of Item 51.
53. Restriction of statement by Sloan (1980), p. 4.
54. Paraphrase of Walker (1970), p. 139.
55. Derived from Natsoulas (1981), pp. 159 – 161.
56. Derived from statement made by Wheeler cited by Jahn (1981), p. 2.
57. Reworded from Toulmin (1982), p. 57.
58. Reworded from Shotter (1982), p. 32.
59. Derived from Holt (1914), p. 182.
60. Paraphrased from John (1976), p. 4.
61. Reworded from Lunzer (1979), p. 1.
62. Quotation from White (1982), p. 24.
63. Generalization of statement by Eccles and Robinson (1984), p. 47.
64. Intentionality hypothesis as stated by Natsoulas (1978a), p. 910.
65. Derived from Merrell-Wolff (1973b), p. 174 and Osborne (1981), p. 285.
66. Reworded from *Oxford English Dictionary* as cited in Natsoulas (1978a), p. 910.
67. Permutation of Item 65.
68. Pervasive problem, discussed, for example, by Weinland (1974), p. 51.
69. Antithesis of position held by Bindra (1970).
70. Quotation from Martindale (1977 – 78), p. 265.
71. Derived from Assagioli (1965) and Merrell-Wolff (1973a, 1973b).
72. Reworded from Battista (1978), p. 61.
73. Derived from Hilgard (1980), p. 27, Muses (1968b), p. 151 and Tart (1985), p. 3.
74. Derived from Berger (1977), pp. 131 – 133 and Pelletier (1978), pp. 86 – 88.
75. Derived from Mandell (1980).
76. Derived from Roberts (1984, 1985) and Tart (1985).
77. Statement mentioned but not endorsed by Gregory (1980), pp. 33 – 34.
78. Paraphrase of Hofstadter (1979), p. 709.
79. Paraphrase of Hofstadter (1979), p. 709.
80. Restatement of Item 78 modified by arguments by Searle (1981) and Lowenhard (1981) that consciousness may be specific to biological organisms.

81. Reworded from White (1982), p. 24.
82. Reworded from Martindale (1977-78), p. 263.
83. Reworded from Hofstadter (1979), p. 709.
84. Reworded from Lowenhard (1981), p. 25.
85. Reworded from Shallice's statement cited in Carr (1979), p. 124.
86. Quotation with additional wording from Klein (1959), p. 15.
87. Paraphrase of Posner and Snyder quoted in Mandler (1985), p. 49.
88. Paraphrase of Pribram (1980), p. 49.
89. Pervasive belief, discussed, for example, by Kelly (1979), p. 19 and Brams (1983), p. 3.
90. Reworded from Wasserman (1983), p. 3.
91. Quotation from White (1982), p. 1.
92. Derived from White (1982), pp. 13, 14.
93. Derived from White (1982).
94. Derived from Dennett (1982).
95. Reworded from Fischer (1978-79), p. 168.
96. Paraphrase of Helminiak (1984), p. 214.
97. Paraphrase of John (1976), p. 4.
98. Derived from Eccles and Robinson (1984), p. 47.
99. Reworded statement challenged by Toulmin (1982), p. 70.
100. Reworded from Lunzer (1979), pp. 1, 2.
101. Quotation from Lunzer (1979), p. 2.
102. Reworded from Lunzer (1979), p. 2.
103. Reworded from Beaumont (1981), p. 194.
104. Derived from Natsoulas (1981), pp. 152 – 155.
105. Derived from Eccles and Robinson (1984), p. 41.
106. Pervasive belief, discussed, for example, by Muses (1968b), pp. 150 – 151.
107. Derived from Martindale (1977-78), p. 265.
108. Pervasive problem, discussed, for example, by Flanagan (1984), p. 71.
109. Antithesis of developmental (Hall, 1976, p. 50) and evolutionary (Martindale,1977-78, p. 265) views.
110. Quotation (essentially) from Globus and Franklin (1980), p. 470.
111. Derived from Hall (1976), p. 50.
112. Derived from Sperry (1983), p. 30.
113. Derived from Block (1979), p. 179.
114. Reworded from Block (1979), p. 209.
115. Antithesis of Item 112.
116. Implied by Osborne (1981), pp. 278 – 279.
117. Reworded from Walsh (1984a), p. 55.
118. Reworded from Denzin (1982), p. 42.
119. Derived from Harre (1984).
120. *Oxford English Dictionary*'s first entry for definitions of consciousness cited by Natsoulas (1978a), p. 909.
121. Derived from Natsoulas (1978a), pp. 909 – 910.
122. Derived from Natsoulas (1978a), p. 909.
123. Implication of Items 118 – 122.
124. Quotation (essentially) from Walsh (1984a), p. 58.

125. Derived from Ujhely (1982).
126. Derived from Alexander (1980).
127. Reworded from Natsoulas (1978a), p. 907.
128. Derived from Mandler (1975), p. 229.
129. Derived from Hall (1976), pp. 2, 7.
130. Reworded from Holt (1914), p. 166.
131. Derived from Muses (1968b), pp. 149, 150.
132. Reworded from Denzin (1982), p. 41.
133. Reworded from Denzin (1982), p. 41.
134. Derived from Globus and Franklin (1980), p. 469.
135. Derived from Gregory (1980), pp. 46 – 47.
136. Quotation from Salk (1984), p. 8.
137. Reworded from Josephson (1980), p. 117.
138. Derived from Klein (1959), p. 10.
139. Derived from Natsoulas (1978a), p. 913.
140. Derived from Pelletier (1978), p. 132.
141. Paraphrase of Rama (1981), p. 320.
142. Reworded from Ramachandran (1980), p. 4.
143. Derived from Ujhely (1982), p. 3.
144. Derived from Ujhely (1982), p. 4.
145. Observation made after considering Items 1 – 144.
146. Permutation of Item 35.
147. The problem of the introspected subject, e.g., Natsoulas (1978b).
148. Derived from Ouspensky (1972).
149. Derived from Pelletier (1978), p. 243.
150. Reworded from Oxley (1982), p. 92.
151. Locke's dictum cited by Strange (1978), p. 11.
152. Taoist belief as given by Taylor (1978), p. 35.
153. Derived from Roberts (1984).
154. Derived from Roberts (1984), p. 8.
155. Derived from Roberts (1984), p. 8.
156. Taoist belief reworded from Taylor (1978), p. 35.
157. Observation made after considering Items 1 – 156.
158. Derived from Pope and Singer (1978), p. 3.

Survey Questionnaire

Section 1: Demographic Data

Age:
Sex:
Highest level of education:
    Subject area:
Profession:
    Discipline, if applicable:
Current professional or research interests:
Religious or spiritual orientation (none/Jewish/Christian/own beliefs):
    Specify if other:

Religious or spiritual practice carried out at least (daily/weekly/monthly/annually/hardly ever):

Section 2: Personal Beliefs

The following statements refer to your personal experiences. Though some of the items may seem unusual, we ask that you write the number of the response for each item that best reflects your experience using the following scale:

1. If a statement does not at all correspond to your experience;
2. If you are not sure whether or not a statement applies to you, but don't think that it does;
3. If you think that a statement does apply to you but you are not certain of that;
4. If a statement clearly does apply.

1. I think about the ultimate meaning of life.
2. I feel that some element which I can't quite define is missing from my life.
3. My accomplishments in life are largely determined by my own efforts.
4. I believe that there is no such thing as a problem that can't be solved.
5. My ideas about life have changed dramatically in the past.
6. No one else can have access to my experience in the way that I have access to it.
7. I find that my consciousness changes from moment to moment.
8. My spiritual beliefs determine my approach to life.
9. I have had experiences which science would have difficulty explaining.
10. I believe that a good job is one for which what is to be done and how it is to be done are always clear.
11. I feel a need to find a real meaning or purpose in my life.
12. There is a difference between my being conscious and that which I am conscious of.
13. I have had an experience which could best be described as a transcendent or mystical experience.
14. I think that others are conscious in the same way that I am conscious.
15. I believe that I am absolutely free to make all choices in my life.
16. It seems to me that my consciousness is located in the center of my head.
17. I find that in the long run I get more done by tackling small, simple problems rather than large and complicated ones.
18. It is important to me to spend periods of time in contemplation or meditation.
19. My experience of myself varies in accordance with my state of consciousness.
20. I have had an experience which could best be described as an out-of-body experience.

21. I prefer the familiar to the unfamiliar.

Section 3: Notions of Consciousness

After reading the following twelve statements about consciousness, place an "x" beside those that most accurately reflect your understanding. If you are not satisfied with any of these statements, or would like to elaborate on one of them, please provide us with your notion of consciousness by writing it in the space below.

1. The concept of consciousness is neither desirable nor useful.
2. Consciousness is an emergent property of sufficiently complex neural systems.
3. Consciousness is further information in certain information-processing systems.
4. What is meant by consciousness changes with changes in the state of consciousness. Thus, the term consciousness only has meaning with reference to a particular state of consciousness.
5. Consciousness is the end product of unconscious and preconscious mental events.
6. Consciousness is a stream of thoughts, feelings and sensations, some of which are more directly the focus of attention than others.
7. Consciousness is the explicit knowledge of one's situation, mental states or actions as opposed to lack of such awareness. It is the opposite of automatic functioning.
8. Consciousness is characterized by reference to an object of thought, inherent in every conscious act. That is to say, consciousness is always consciousness of something.
9. Consciousness is the subjective component of a mental act which allows one to be subject to an object of thought.
10. Consciousness is a subjective experience, not accessible to outside observers, that attests to our existence.
11. Consciousness is a personal experience that requires a process of self-transformation to be adequately understood.
12. Consciousness is a non-physical reality that can have causal effects on physical systems.

Section 4: Consciousness and Reality

The following statements about consciousness, human knowledge and reality have been extracted from a number of sources. Although you may find some of them ill-conceived or improperly stated, we ask that you answer them as best you can using the following response categories:

1. Strongly disagree;
2. Disagree;
3. Moderately disagree;
4. Moderately agree;

5. Agree;
6. Strongly agree;
7. Don't know.

For each statement write the number of the one response that best reflects your own ideas. The category "don't know" is meant to be used in cases of indecision when you cannot choose between disagreement and agreement, or when you have no opinion about an item. Feel free to include comments about specific items.

1. Consciousness is mysterious.
2. Science can legitimately concern itself with subjective events only to the extent that these events have objectively observable correlates.
3. Free will is an illusion.
4. Consciousness is a fundamental aspect of human functioning.
5. There is no reality other than the physical universe.
6. Consciousness entails one's awareness of oneself as subject.
7. Extrasensory perception is possible.
8. The inner experiential world is vaster, richer and contains more profound meanings than most people think.
9. The existence of human consciousness is evidence of a spiritual dimension within each person.
10. Our objective as human beings is to maximize the material and psychological benefits of each individual person.
11. Life does not exist on other planets.
12. One's personal experience is ultimately the test of any contention about reality.
13. Awareness is a term equivalent to consciousness.
14. Eastern religions have much to offer our understanding of consciousness.
15. Scientific theories necessarily make metaphysical assumptions.
16. Mind and body are separate, and both are real.
17. Introspection is a necessary element in the investigation of consciousness.
18. The problem of the relationship between the body and the mind is a metaphysical problem which cannot be solved empirically.
19. Statements about human cognition are meaningless without reference to particular states of consciousness.
20. We invent reality just as much as we discover it.
21. Reincarnation actually does occur.
22. The concept of limits does not apply to consciousness.
23. Mind and body are separate, but work in parallel.
24. In trying to understand consciousness one must take into account evidence from subjective experience as well as objective observation.
25. In order to fully understand human consciousness, a process of psychological change is necessary which may be achieved through meditation or a spiritual way of life.
26. It does not make sense to ascribe a location to consciousness.

27. The accepted methods of science are the only proper way in which to investigate consciousness.
28. The reason the universe is the way it is, is to support human life.
29. Physical reality is an extension of mental reality.
30. It will never be possible to fully understand human consciousness.
31. Consciousness gives meaning to reality.
32. Human values are the most powerful force now shaping world events.
33. Consciousness is more real than physical reality.
34. It is possible in principle to discover exact laws which govern human behavior.
35. Human consciousness would not exist without the brain.
36. There is an absolute truth which is not context-dependent.
37. Our culture can be viewed as a basic conspiracy against self-knowledge and awakening in which we collude together to reinforce one another's defenses and insanity.
38. Consciousness is proof of the reality of mental existence.
39. Science necessarily involves personal beliefs.
40. Human consciousness is derived from language.
41. There are modes of understanding latent within a person which are superior to rational thought.
42. We are morally obligated to reduce pain and suffering in the world.
43. Mind and body, though separate, act causally on each other.
44. It is possible for there to be consciousness in which there is awareness but no object of awareness.
45. Science will never be fully able to explain human nature.
46. Human consciousness is an emergent property of complex neural activity.
47. Consciousness is the key to personal growth.
48. Consciousness plays a causal role in determining neural activity and behavior.
49. Death is simply part of the process of life.
50. Someday we will be able to say that computers are conscious.
51. There are some truths concerning reality which, in principle, are not amenable to scientific investigation.
52. Consciousness is self-evident; it does not require further proof for its existence.
53. Even though we are not yet able to explain mental events in terms of physical processes, an explanation is, in principle, possible.
54. The harmony of nature reflects the existence of an original creator.
55. Conscious experience is experience that is, at least in principle, reportable.
56. Consciousness transcends time.
57. Knowledge of people achieved through literature is more profound than any knowledge of people that can be achieved using the scientific method.
58. Personal consciousness continues after physical death.
59. The subject of consciousness is a legitimate subject of study.
60. Science is not value free.

61. There is a universal consciousness of which individual consciousness is but a part.
62. The question of the real physical existence or non-existence of objects of experience cannot be answered.
63. All thought and behavior is caused by the operation of biological and environmental events and does not occur freely.
64. The meaning of life is inherent in the world around us.
65. Consciousness cannot be defined or explained.
66. Reality is the result of an interaction between consciousness and the physical domain.
67. A process of psychological change is necessary in order to fully experience human consciousness.

Section 5: Written Comments

Comments:

If you wish to receive a copy of this questionnaire, fill in your name and address below:

Sources for items of Survey Questionnaire

Items from Section 2, Personal Beliefs

B1. Item 4 from Life Attitude Profile (LAP) – Form 5 by Reker and Peacock (G. Reker, personal communications, 1985, 1986).
B2. Item 6 from Life Attitude Profile (LAP) – Form 5 by Reker and Peacock (G. Reker, personal communications, 1985, 1986).
B3. Item 11 from Life Attitude Profile (LAP) – Form 5 by Reker and Peacock (G. Reker, personal communications, 1985, 1986).
B4. Reworded item from Budner's Intolerance of Ambiguity Scale as given by Kirton (1981), p. 411.
B5. Statement concerning personal nature of understanding.
B6. Statement of the problem of privileged access.
B7. Reworded Item 47 from Preliminary Questionnaire.
B8. Reworded Item 8 from Intrinsic/Extrinsic Scale of religious orientation (Feagin, 1964, p. 5).
B9. Statement of occurrence of unusual experiences.
B10. Reworded item from Budner's Intolerance of Ambiguity Scale (Kirton, 1981, p. 411).
B11. Reworded Item 7 from Life Attitude Profile (LAP) – Form 5 by Reker and Peacock (G. Reker, personal communications, 1985, 1986).
B12. Reworded Item 65 from Preliminary Questionnaire.
B13. Statement of occurrence of unusual experiences.
B14. Reworded Item 107 from Preliminary Questionnaire.
B15. Reworded Item 17 from Life Attitude Profile (LAP) – Form 5 by Reker and Peacock (G. Reker, personal communications, 1985, 1986).

B16. Reworded Item 34 from Preliminary Questionnaire.
B17. Reworded item from Budner's Intolerance of Ambiguity Scale (Kirton, 1981, p. 411).
B18. Reworded Item 20 of Intrinsic/Extrinsic Scale of religious orientation (Feagin, 1964, p. 6).
B19. Reworded Item 154 from Preliminary Questionnaire.
B20. Statement of occurrence of unusual experiences.
B21. Reworded Item 43 from Preliminary Questionnaire.
B22. Reworded item from Budner's Intolerance of Ambiguity Scale (Kirton, 1981, p. 411).

Items from Section 3, Notions of Consciousness

C1. Churchland (1983) and antithesis of Item 128 of Preliminary Questionnaire.
C2. Reworded Item 80 of Preliminary Questionnaire (*consciousness$_1$*).
C3. Klein (1984) and reworded Item 78 of Preliminary Questionnaire (*consciousness$_1$/consciousness$_2$*).
C4. Variation of Items 76 and 153 of Preliminary Questionnaire.
C5. Mandler (1985) (*consciousness$_2$*).
C6. James (1890/1983) Chapter IX (*consciousness$_2$*).
C7. Reworded Items 19 to 21 of Preliminary Questionnaire and Pribram (1976), p. 306 (*consciousness$_2$*).
C8. Reworded Item 64 of Preliminary Questionnaire (*consciousness$_2$*).
C9. One antithesis of Item 97 of Preliminary Questionnaire (*consciousness$_3$*).
C10. Variation of Items 19, 95 and 96 of Preliminary Questionnaire (*consciousness$_3$*).
C11. Variation of Items 22, 24, 99, 117, 124 and 146 of Preliminary Questionnaire (*consciousness$_3$*).
C12. Variation of Items 18, 44, 51, 71 and 72 of Preliminary Questionnaire (*consciousness$_3$*).

Items from Section 4, Consciousness and Reality

Q1. Item 158 of Preliminary Questionnaire.
Q2. Statement of methodological behaviorism similar to Item 23 of Krasner and Houts's version of Coan's Theoretical Orientation Survey (Krasner, personal communication, 1986).
Q3. Antithesis of Item 68 of Preliminary Questionnaire.
Q4. Item 8 of Preliminary Questionnaire.
Q5. Statement of physical monism (discussed, for example, by Flanagan, 1984).
Q6. Reworded Item 96 of Preliminary Questionnaire.
Q7. Reworded item from Extraordinary Belief Inventory (L. Otis, personal communication, 1986).
Q8. Reworded Item 16 from Preliminary Questionnaire.
Q9. Item 18 from Preliminary Questionnaire.

Q10. Derived from C. Jillings (personal communication, 1985).
Q11. Adapted from Extraordinary Belief Inventory (Otis, personal communication, 1986).
Q12. Thesis of this book.
Q13. Item 2 from Preliminary Questionnaire.
Q14. Item 16 from Preliminary Questionnaire.
Q15. Item 41 from Epistemological Style Questionnaire by Krasner and Houts (L. Krasner, personal communication, 1986).
Q16. Mind-body dualism (discussed, for example, by Flanagan, 1984).
Q17. Permutation of Items 22 and 24 of Preliminary Questionnaire.
Q18. Relationship of mind-body problem to science (discussed, for example, by Flanagan, 1984).
Q19. Variation of Item 153 of Preliminary Questionnaire.
Q20. Reworded from LeShan and Margenau (1982), p. 236.
Q21. Reworded item from Extraordinary Belief Inventory (L. Otis, personal communication, 1986).
Q22. Item 32 from Preliminary Questionnaire.
Q23. Parallelist version of mind-body problem (discussed, for example, by Flanagan, 1984).
Q24. One antithesis of Q2.
Q25. Variation of Item 22 from Preliminary Questionnaire.
Q26. Item 37 from Preliminary Questionnaire.
Q27. Item 40 from Preliminary Questionnaire.
Q28. Statement of Anthropic Principle (Guillen, 1984).
Q29. Berkleyan monism (or "mental monism," discussed, for example, by Flanagan, 1984).
Q30. Item 41 from Preliminary Questionnaire.
Q31. Reworded Item 43 from Preliminary Questionnaire.
Q32. Reworded from Sperry (1982), p. 8.
Q33. Item 44 from Preliminary Questionnaire.
Q34. Extracted from Item 2 of Kimble's Epistemic Differential (G. Kimble, personal communication, 1985).
Q35. Item 52 from Preliminary Questionnaire.
Q36. Derived from Oxley (1982), p. 20.
Q37. Reworded Item 124 from Preliminary Questionnaire.
Q38. Item 50 from Preliminary Questionnaire.
Q39. Variation of Q15.
Q40. Reworded Item 63 from Preliminary Questionnaire.
Q41. Contention made by Assagioli (1965) and Merrell-Wolff (1973a, 1973b).
Q42. Reworded Item 16 from Values Survey by Krasner and Houts (L. Krasner, personal communication, 1986).
Q43. Interactionist position with regard to mind-body problem (discussed, for example, by Flanagan, 1984).
Q44. Item 67 from Preliminary Questionnaire.
Q45. Variation of Q30.
Q46. Derived from Item 80 of Preliminary Questionnaire.
Q47. Derived from Merrell-Wolff (1973a, 1973b) and Walsh (1984a).

Q48. Item 69 from Preliminary Questionnaire.
Q49. Item 33 from Life Attitude Profile (LAP) – Form 5 by Reker and Peacock (G. Reker, personal communications, 1985, 1986).
Q50. Item 89 from Preliminary Questionnaire.
Q51. Variation of Q45.
Q52. Combination of Q6 and Q12.
Q53. Promissory materialism (discussed, for example, by Flanagan, 1984).
Q54. Reworded Item 43 from Values Survey by Krasner and Houts (L. Krasner, personal communication, 1986).
Q55. Item 92 from Preliminary Questionnaire.
Q56. Item 110 from Preliminary Questionnaire.
Q57. Reworded Item 49 of Epistemological Style Questionnaire by Krasner and Houts (L. Krasner, personal communication, 1986).
Q58. Item 115 from Preliminary Questionnaire.
Q59. Item 127 from Preliminary Questionnaire.
Q60. Variation of Q15 and Q39.
Q61. Item 141 from Preliminary Questionnaire.
Q62. Reworded from Wetherick (1979), p. 100.
Q63. Derived from R. J. Moore (personal communication, 1986).
Q64. Reworded Item 18 from Life Attitude Profile (LAP) – Form 5 by Reker and Peacock (G. Reker, personal communications, 1985, 1986).
Q65. Variation of Item 158 from Preliminary Questionnaire.
Q66. Derived form Ziemelis (1986), p. 68.
Q67. Derived from Merrell-Wolff (1973a, 1973b) and Walsh (1984a).

APPENDIX B

RESPONDENTS' WRITTEN RESPONSES

Respondents' written definitions of consciousness

"Consciousness is indubitable reality. To deny it is to affirm it, because denial is itself an act or a state of consciousness."

"In general, I am a materialist of an eliminativist variety. While I think that mental events reduce to brain (or central nervous system) events, I *don't* think that the terms of folk psychology embedded in our common usage are always terms which *refer* to significant neurological entities."

"To me, the notion of consciousness is like a room in a house containing a light and a switch. When the switch is 'on' ([therefore] the light), I am conscious. When it is 'off', I am not."

"The above statements leave no room for the Marxist view of consciousness as a socio-historical 'production'. This would be closest to my own view."

"THE CATEGORIES OF THIS QUESTIONNAIRE (LIKE ALL OTHERS) ARE INADEQUATE FOR THE TASK OF *DISCOVERING THE NEW*; FOR THEY REFER TO *MATCHING THE OLD* (I. E. THE BIAS OF SCIENCE) RATHER THAN *MAKING THE NEW* (I. E. THE ROLE OF ART)"

C4: "nonsense!"; C5: "nonsense!"; C9: "empty verbiage"; C11: "nonsense!"; C12: "bullshit"

"Consciousness is explicit awareness of one's own [?], presence, experience and of more or less 'real' or 'ideal' objects, and 'levels' of that subjective experience from the grossest material to the highest spiritual realms."

"Consult my book . . ."

"Consciousness represents the interface between 'divine programming' and 'human implementation'."

163

"This is too complicated"

Respondents' written comments

"I don't wish to answer these questions. I think they're silly!"

"I am encouraged that science is taking consciousness seriously as something to be studied. On the other hand I am not that hopeful that this type of questionnaire will shed much light on the reality of consciousness."

"I spent 7 – 10 years studying + researching issues related to self-actualization, ESP, consciousness (e.g. humanistic + transpersonal) and it was a waste of time. These areas have made no progression, they lack rules of testability, theories are flimsy + undeveloped. We have more ESP ability in language than in any findings from the mystics."

"Very complicated and not very interesting . . . why bother"

"Nobody seems to be funding consciousness research. This is absurd."

"It is easy to contradict oneself answering to this questionnaire for some statements can be considered partly true but not completely."

"An excellent instrument. Very difficult to word. Will require precision in such instruments again & again. Go for it!"

"The main difficulty I had was words changing in meaning. For example, science as scientism (the materialistic ideology) has no place for consciousness or its study, but I do not think science must be mechanistic, not that it is uniformly so at present."

"It's interesting to see how confused one can be about these matters."

"It will be interesting to see what people think about these things. But their opinions often differ from the presuppositions of their thinking. Few admit to being materialists, but many reason as if they were."

STATISTICAL ANALYSES

Table C.1

Frequencies of Responses for Survey Questionnaire

Item	Frequency	%	Valid %
Demographic Items			
Place of return			
University of Saskatchewan	40	12.0	12.0
Reply mail, Canada	185	55.4	55.4
United States	54	16.2	16.2
Electronic mail	55	16.5	16.5
Age			
Up to 29 years	38	11.4	11.4
30 to 44 years	149	44.6	44.7
45 to 59 years	115	34.4	34.5
60 to 99 years	31	9.3	9.3
Missing	1	0.3	--
Sex			
Female	89	26.6	26.7
Male	244	73.1	73.3
Missing	1	.3	--
Education			
High school	2	0.6	0.6
Postsecondary	10	3.0	3.0
Bachelor's degree	25	7.5	7.5
Master's degree	73	21.9	21.9
MD or equivalent	22	6.6	6.6
PhD or equivalent	201	60.2	60.4
Missing	1	0.3	--

(*table continues*)

Item	Frequency	%	Valid %
Doctorate			
No doctorate	110	32.9	32.9
Doctorate	223	66.8	67.0
Missing	1	0.3	--
General area of discipline			
Hard sciences	109	32.6	32.7
Human sciences	149	44.6	44.7
Humanities	75	22.5	22.5
Missing	1	0.3	--
Discipline			
Hard sciences			
Animal sc/vet med	2	0.6	0.6
Biochemistry	3	0.9	0.9
Biology	7	2.1	2.1
Chemistry	3	0.9	0.9
Comp science	17	5.1	5.1
Crop science	1	0.3	0.3
Engineering	6	1.8	1.8
Geology	1	0.3	0.3
Math/Statistics	2	0.6	0.6
Meteorology	1	0.3	0.3
Physics	40	12.0	12.0
Psychology:exp/animal	10	3.0	3.0
Psychology:physiological	12	3.6	3.6
Psychology:statistics	4	1.2	1.2
Human sciences			
Anthropology/archaeology	1	0.3	0.3
Dentistry	2	0.6	0.6
Economics	2	0.6	0.6
Education	5	1.5	1.5
Geography	1	0.3	0.3
Law	3	0.9	0.9
Management/business	2	0.6	0.6
Medicine	4	1.2	1.2
Neurology	1	0.3	0.3
Nursing	7	2.1	2.1
Pharmacy	2	0.6	0.6
Physical education	2	0.6	0.6
Psychiatry	16	4.8	4.8
Psychology (not further specified)	6	1.8	1.8
Psychology:clinical	47	14.1	14.1
Psychology:cognitive	19	5.7	5.7

(*table continues*)

Item	Frequency	%	Valid %
Psychology:developmental	12	3.6	3.6
Psychology:history	1	0.3	0.3
Psychology:ind/commer/org	4	1.2	1.2
Psychology:psychometrics	2	0.6	0.6
Psychology:soc/pers/commun	7	2.1	2.1
Sociology	3	0.9	0.9
Humanities			
English/languages	5	1.5	1.5
History	9	2.7	2.7
History of science	5	1.5	1.5
Music/theatre	2	0.6	0.6
Philosophy	21	6.3	6.3
Philosophy of science	7	2.1	2.1
Psychology:transpersonal	16	4.8	4.8
Religion/spirituality	10	3.0	3.0
Missing	1	0.3	--
Psychologists[a]			
Experimental/physiological	26	18.6	19.5
Clinical/applied	53	37.9	39.8
Soc/pers/commun/dev	19	13.6	14.3
Cognitive	19	13.6	14.3
Transpersonal	16	11.4	12.0
Missing	7	5.0	--
Religious affiliation			
None	82	24.6	26.3
Traditional	141	42.2	45.2
Own beliefs	89	26.6	28.5
Other or missing	22	6.6	--
Frequency of religious practice			
Daily	84	25.1	27.8
Occasionally	82	24.6	27.2
Never	136	40.7	45.0
Missing	32	9.6	--

Personal Beliefs

Item	Frequency	%	Valid %
1. I think about the ultimate meaning of life.			
No	56	16.8	16.8
Yes	278	83.2	83.2

(table continues)

Item	Frequency	%	Valid %

2. I feel that some element which I can't quite define is missing from my life.

No	229	68.6	68.8
Yes	104	31.1	31.2
Missing	1	0.3	--

3. My accomplishments in life are largely determined by my own efforts.

No	52	15.6	15.7
Yes	280	83.8	84.3
Missing	2	0.6	--

4. I believe that there is no such thing as a problem that can't be solved.

No	210	62.9	62.9
Yes	124	37.1	37.1

5. My ideas about life have changed dramatically in the past.

No	144	43.1	43.2
Yes	189	56.6	56.8
Missing	1	0.3	--

6. No one else can have access to my experience in the way that I have access to it.

No	50	15.0	15.1
Yes	281	84.1	84.9
Missing	3	0.9	--

7. I find that my consciousness changes from moment to moment.

No	163	48.8	50.5
Yes	160	47.9	49.5
Missing	11	3.3	--

8. My spiritual beliefs determine my approach to life.

No	136	40.7	41.3
Yes	193	57.8	58.7
Missing	5	1.5	--

9. I have had experiences which science would have difficulty explaining.

No	153	45.8	46.4
Yes	177	53.0	53.6
Missing	4	1.2	--

10. I believe that a good job is one for which what is to be done and how it is to be done are always clear.

No	243	72.8	73.9
Yes	86	25.7	26.1
Missing	5	1.5	--

11. I feel a need to find a real meaning or purpose in my life.

No	162	48.5	48.9
Yes	169	50.6	51.1
Missing	3	0.9	--

(*table continues*)

Item	Frequency	%	Valid %

12. There is a difference between my being conscious and that which I am conscious of.

No	60	18.0	18.2
Yes	269	80.5	81.8
Missing	5	1.5	--

13. I have had an experience which could best be described as a transcendent or mystical experience.

No	174	52.1	52.6
Yes	157	47.0	47.4
Missing	3	0.9	--

14. I think that others are conscious in the same way that I am conscious.

No	66	19.8	20.2
Yes	261	78.1	79.8
Missing	7	2.1	--

15. I believe that I am absolutely free to make all choices in my life.

No	201	60.2	61.5
Yes	126	37.7	38.5
Missing	7	2.1	--

16. It seems to me that my consciousness is located in the center of my head.

No	175	52.4	54.5
Yes	146	43.7	45.5
Missing	13	3.9	--

17. I find that in the long run I get more done by tackling small, simple problems rather than large and complicated ones.

No	182	54.5	55.3
Yes	147	44.0	44.7
Missing	5	1.5	--

18. It is important for me to spend periods of time in contemplation or meditation.

No	89	26.6	26.7
Yes	244	73.1	73.3
Missing	1	0.3	--

19. My experience of myself varies in accordance with my state of consciousness.

No	83	24.9	26.0
Yes	236	70.7	74.0
Missing	15	4.5	--

20. I have had an experience which could best be described as an out-of-body experience.

No	254	76.0	76.7
Yes	77	23.1	23.3
Missing	3	0.9	--

(*table continues*)

Item	Frequency	%	Valid %

21. If I weren't conscious, my life would have no meaning for me.

No	42	12.6	12.9
Yes	283	84.7	87.1
Missing	9	2.7	--

22. I prefer the familiar to the unfamiliar.

No	158	47.3	48.9
Yes	165	49.4	51.1
Missing	11	3.3	--

Rigidity[b]

Level of rigidity

0	64	19.2	19.2
1	77	23.1	23.1
2	79	23.7	23.7
3	63	18.9	18.9
4	32	9.6	9.6
5	9	2.7	2.7
6	6	1.8	1.8
7	1	0.3	0.3
8	3	0.9	0.9

Notions of Consciousness

1. The concept of consciousness is neither desirable nor useful.

Not endorsed	326	97.6	97.6
Endorsed	8	2.4	2.4

2. Consciousness is an emergent property of sufficiently complex neural systems.

Not endorsed	171	51.2	51.2
Endorsed	163	48.8	48.8

3. Consciousness is further information in certain information-processing systems.

Not endorsed	270	80.8	80.8
Endorsed	64	19.2	19.2

4. What is meant by consciousness changes with changes in the state of consciousness. Thus, the term consciousness only has meaning with reference to a particular state of consciousness.

Not endorsed	245	73.4	73.4
Endorsed	89	26.6	26.6

5. Consciousness is the end product of unconscious and preconscious mental events.

Not endorsed	267	79.9	79.9
Endorsed	67	20.1	20.1

(table continues)

Item	Frequency	%	Valid %

6. Consciousness is a stream of thoughts, feelings and sensations, some of which are more directly the focus of attention than others.

Not endorsed	124	37.1	37.1
Endorsed	210	62.9	62.9

7. Consciousness is the explicit knowledge of one's situation, mental states or actions as opposed to lack of such awareness. It is the opposite of automatic functioning.

Not endorsed	132	39.5	39.5
Endorsed	202	60.5	60.5

8. Consciousness is characterized by reference to an object of thought, inherent in every conscious act. That is to say, consciousness is always consciousness of something.

Not endorsed	210	62.9	62.9
Endorsed	124	37.1	37.1

9. Consciousness is the subjective component of a mental act which allows one to be subject to an object of thought.

Not endorsed	249	74.6	74.6
Endorsed	85	25.4	25.4

10. Consciousness is a subjective experience, not accessible to outside observers, that attests to our existence.

Not endorsed	208	62.3	62.3
Endorsed	126	37.7	37.7

11. Consciousness is a personal experience that requires a process of self-transformation to be adequately understood.

Not endorsed	266	79.6	79.6
Endorsed	68	20.4	20.4

12. Consciousness is a non-physical reality that can have causal effects on physical systems.

Not endorsed	225	67.4	67.4
Endorsed	109	32.6	32.6

Comments concerning definitions of consciousness

Comments not provided	263	78.7	78.7
Comments provided	71	21.3	21.3

Consciousness and Reality

1. Consciousness is mysterious.

Disagree	110	32.9	34.0
Agree	214	64.1	66.0
Other response	10	3.0	--

(*table continues*)

Item	Frequency	%	Valid %

2. Science can legitimately concern itself with subjective events only to the extent that these events have objectively observable correlates.

Disagree	127	38.0	39.8
Agree	192	57.5	60.2
Other response	15	4.5	--

3. Free will is an illusion.

Disagree	212	63.5	69.5
Agree	93	27.8	30.5
Other response	29	8.7	--

4. Consciousness is a fundamental aspect of human functioning.

Disagree	14	4.2	4.2
Agree	316	94.6	95.8
Other response	4	1.2	--

5. There is no reality other than the physical universe.

Disagree	211	63.2	71.8
Agree	83	24.9	28.2
Other response	40	12.0	--

6. Consciousness entails one's awareness of oneself as subject.

Disagree	48	14.4	14.8
Agree	277	82.9	85.2
Other response	9	2.7	--

7. Extrasensory perception is possible.

Disagree	99	29.6	36.5
Agree	172	51.5	63.5
Other response	63	18.9	--

8. The inner experiential world is vaster, richer and contains more profound meanings than most people think.

Disagree	49	14.7	16.9
Agree	241	72.2	83.1
Other response	44	13.2	--

9. The existence of human consciousness is evidence of a spiritual dimension within each person.

Disagree	137	41.0	46.8
Agree	156	46.7	53.2
Other response	41	12.3	--

10. Our objective as human beings is to maximize the material and psychological benefits of each individual person.

Disagree	99	29.6	35.5
Agree	180	53.9	64.5
Other response	55	16.5	--

11. Life does not exist on other planets.

Disagree	143	42.8	88.3
Agree	19	5.7	11.7
Other response	172	51.5	--

(*table continues*)

Item	Frequency	%	Valid %
12. One's personal experience is ultimately the test of any contention about reality.			
Disagree	168	50.3	55.6
Agree	134	40.1	44.4
Other response	32	9.6	--
13. Awareness is a term equivalent to consciousness.			
Disagree	107	32.0	34.1
Agree	207	62.0	65.9
Other response	20	6.0	--
14. Eastern religions have much to offer our understanding of consciousness.			
Disagree	70	21.0	24.7
Agree	213	63.8	75.3
Other response	51	15.3	--
15. Scientific theories necessarily make metaphysical assumptions.			
Disagree	79	23.7	26.2
Agree	222	66.5	73.8
Other response	33	9.9	--
16. Mind and body are separate, and both are real.			
Disagree	223	66.8	73.6
Agree	80	24.0	26.4
Other response	31	9.3	--
17. Introspection is a necessary element in the investigation of consciousness.			
Disagree	36	10.8	11.4
Agree	281	84.1	88.6
Other response	17	5.1	--
18. The problem of the relationship between the body and mind is a metaphysical problem which cannot be solved empirically.			
Disagree	157	47.0	54.9
Agree	129	38.6	45.1
Other response	48	14.4	--
19. Statements about human cognition are meaningless without reference to particular states of consciousness.			
Disagree	126	37.7	45.2
Agree	153	45.8	54.8
Other response	55	16.5	--
20. We invent reality just as much as we discover it.			
Disagree	82	24.6	25.8
Agree	236	70.7	74.2
Other	16	4.8	--

(*table continues*)

Item	Frequency	%	Valid %
21. Reincarnation actually does occur.			
Disagree	192	57.5	82.1
Agree	42	12.6	17.9
Other	100	29.9	--
22. The concept of limits does not apply to consciousness.			
Disagree	154	46.1	62.3
Agree	93	27.8	37.7
Other response	87	26.0	--
23. Mind and body are separate, but work in parallel.			
Disagree	232	69.5	77.9
Agree	66	19.8	22.1
Other response	36	10.8	--
24. In trying to understand consciousness one must take into account evidence from subjective experience as well as objective observation.			
Disagree	15	4.5	4.7
Agree	304	91.0	95.3
Other response	15	4.5	--
25. In order to fully understand human consciousness, a process of psychological change is necessary which may be achieved through meditation or a spiritual way of life.			
Disagree	157	47.0	54.7
Agree	130	38.9	45.3
Other response	47	14.1	--
26. It does not make sense to ascribe a location to consciousness.			
Disagree	88	26.3	29.8
Agree	207	62.0	70.2
Other response	39	11.7	--
27. The accepted methods of science are the only proper way in which to investigate consciousness.			
Disagree	212	63.5	69.3
Agree	94	28.1	30.7
Other response	28	8.4	--
28. The reason the universe is the way it is, is to support human life.			
Disagree	236	70.7	84.9
Agree	42	12.6	15.1
Other response	56	16.8	--
29. Physical reality is an extension of mental reality.			
Disagree	191	57.2	65.6
Agree	100	29.9	34.4
Other response	43	12.9	--
30. It will never be possible to fully understand human consciousness.			
Disagree	110	32.9	40.4
Agree	162	48.5	59.6
Other response	62	18.6	--

(table continues)

Item	Frequency	%	Valid %
31. Consciousness gives meaning to reality.			
Disagree	51	15.3	16.5
Agree	259	77.5	83.5
Other response	24	7.2	--
32. Human values are the most powerful force now shaping world events.			
Disagree	108	32.3	35.4
Agree	197	59.0	64.6
Other response	29	8.7	--
33. Consciousness is more real than physical reality.			
Disagree	197	59.0	69.6
Agree	86	25.7	30.4
Other response	51	15.3	--
34. It is possible in principle to discover exact laws which govern human behavior.			
Disagree	148	44.3	47.0
Agree	167	50.0	53.0
Other response	19	5.7	--
35. Human consciousness would not exist without the brain.			
Disagree	44	13.2	14.2
Agree	266	79.6	85.8
Other response	24	7.2	--
36. There is an absolute truth which is not context-dependent.			
Disagree	147	44.0	54.0
Agree	125	37.4	46.0
Other response	62	18.6	--
37. Our culture can be viewed as a basic conspiracy against self-knowledge and awakening in which we collude together to reinforce one another's defenses and insanity.			
Disagree	192	57.5	67.1
Agree	94	28.1	32.9
Other response	48	14.4	--
38. Consciousness is proof of the reality of mental existence.			
Disagree	70	21.0	26.2
Agree	197	59.0	73.8
Other response	67	20.1	--
39. Science necessarily involves personal beliefs.			
Disagree	58	17.4	17.7
Agree	269	80.5	82.3
Other response	7	2.1	--
40. Human consciousness is derived from language.			
Disagree	203	60.8	67.9
Agree	96	28.7	32.1
Other response	35	10.5	--

(table continues)

Item	Frequency	%	Valid %

41. There are modes of understanding latent within a person which are superior to rational thought.

Disagree	99	29.6	35.0
Agree	184	55.1	65.0
Other response	51	15.3	--

42. We are morally obligated to reduce pain and suffering in the world.

Disagree	59	17.7	18.3
Agree	263	78.7	81.7
Other response	12	3.6	--

43. Mind and body, though separate, act causally on each other.

Disagree	147	44.0	49.7
Agree	149	44.6	50.3
Other response	38	11.4	--

44. It is possible for there to be consciousness in which there is awareness but no object of awareness.

Disagree	111	33.2	39.8
Agree	168	50.3	60.2
Other response	55	16.5	--

45. Science will never be fully able to explain human nature.

Disagree	71	21.3	24.5
Agree	219	65.6	75.5
Other response	44	13.2	--

46. Human consciousness is an emergent property of complex neural activity.

Disagree	63	18.9	22.0
Agree	223	66.8	78.0
Other response	48	14.4	--

47. Consciousness is the key to personal growth.

Disagree	54	16.2	19.0
Agree	230	68.9	81.0
Other response	50	15.0	--

48. Consciousness plays a causal role in determining neural activity and behavior.

Disagree	82	24.6	29.8
Agree	193	57.8	70.2
Other response	59	17.7	--

49. Death is simply part of the process of life.

Disagree	26	7.8	8.2
Agree	290	86.8	91.8
Other response	18	5.4	--

50. Someday we will be able to say that computers are conscious.

Disagree	198	59.3	72.8
Agree	74	22.2	27.2
Other response	62	18.6	--

(table continues)

Item	Frequency	%	Valid %

51. There are some truths concerning reality which, in principle, are not amenable to scientific investigation.

Disagree	106	31.7	35.0
Agree	197	59.0	65.0
Other response	31	9.3	--

52. Consciousness is self-evident; it does not require further proof for its existence.

Disagree	78	23.4	24.7
Agree	238	71.3	75.3
Other response	18	5.4	--

53. Even though we are not yet able to explain mental events in terms of physical processes, an explanation is, in principle, possible.

Disagree	81	24.3	27.1
Agree	218	65.3	72.9
Other response	35	10.5	--

54. The harmony of nature reflects the existence of an original creator.

Disagree	174	52.1	61.5
Agree	109	32.6	38.5
Other response	51	15.3	--

55. Conscious experience is experience that is, at least in principle, reportable.

Disagree	44	13.2	13.6
Agree	280	83.8	86.4
Other response	10	3.0	--

56. Consciousness transcends time.

Disagree	100	29.9	40.7
Agree	146	43.7	59.3
Other response	88	26.3	--

57. Knowledge of people achieved through literature is more profound than any knowledge of people that can be achieved using the scientific method.

Disagree	202	60.5	69.2
Agree	90	26.9	30.8
Other response	42	12.6	--

58. Personal consciousness continues after physical death.

Disagree	155	46.4	63.8
Agree	88	26.3	36.2
Other response	91	27.2	--

59. The subject of consciousness is a legitimate subject of study.

Disagree	9	2.7	2.8
Agree	317	94.9	97.2
Other response	8	2.4	--

(*table continues*)

Item	Frequency	%	Valid %
60. Science is not value free.			
Disagree	19	5.7	5.8
Agree	308	92.2	94.2
Other response	7	2.1	--
61. There is a universal consciousness of which individual consciousness is but a part.			
Disagree	144	43.1	52.9
Agree	128	38.3	47.1
Other response	62	18.6	--
62. The question of the real physical existence or non-existence of objects of experience cannot be answered.			
Disagree	176	52.7	66.7
Agree	88	26.3	33.3
Other response	70	21.0	--
63. All thought and behavior is caused by the operation of biological and environmental events and does not occur freely.			
Disagree	199	59.6	67.5
Agree	96	28.7	32.5
Other response	39	11.7	--
64. The meaning of life is inherent in the world around us.			
Disagree	101	30.2	38.7
Agree	160	47.9	61.3
Other response	73	21.9	--
65. Consciousness cannot be defined or explained.			
Disagree	245	73.4	79.0
Agree	65	19.5	21.0
Other response	24	7.2	--
66. Reality is the result of an interaction between consciousness and the physical domain.			
Disagree	93	27.8	30.8
Agree	209	62.6	69.2
Other response	32	9.6	--
67. A process of psychological change is necessary in order to fully experience human consciousness.			
Disagree	106	31.7	40.9
Agree	153	45.8	59.1
Other response	75	22.5	--

General comments by respondents

Written comments by respondents			
Negative	15	4.5	12.7
Miscellaneous	78	23.4	66.1
Positive	25	7.5	21.2

(*table continues*)

Item	Frequency	%	Valid %
Ambiguity in questionnaire			
No reference to ambiguity	303	90.7	90.7
Reference to ambiguity	31	9.3	9.3
Name given			
No name given	118	35.3	35.3
Name given	216	64.7	64.7

Note. N=334 except for section entitled "Psychologists."

[a]This section is based on the subgroup of respondents who indicated psychology as their discipline (n=140). The experimental/physiological entry combines the "exp/animal", physiological and statistics entries for psychologists in the discipline section of this table. The clinical/applied entry combines the clinical, "ind/commer/org" and psychometrics entries for the psychologists in the discipline section of this table. The "soc/pers/commun/dev" entry combines the developmental and "soc/pers/commun" entries for the psychologists in the discipline section of this table.

[b]The level of rigidity for each respondent was calculated by adding the number of "3"s and twice the number of "4"s endorsed by the respondent for above questionnaire items 4, 10, 17 and 22. These four items are modified items from Budner's Intolerance of Ambiguity Scale taken from Kirton (1981).

Table C.2

Crosstabulation of Demographic Data and Endorsed Definitions with Factor Scores

Place of return vs factor scores of cluster 1

	I		II		III		IV	
	Lo	Hi	Lo	Hi	Lo	Hi	Lo	Hi
University of Sask								
Cell count	18.0	22.0	23.0	17.0	23.0	17.0	12.0	28.0
Expected value	20.0	20.0	20.0	20.0	20.0	20.0	20.0	20.0
Reply mail								
Cell count	95.0	90.0	102.0	83.0	77.0	108.0	100.0	85.0
Expected value	92.5	92.5	92.5	92.5	92.5	92.5	92.5	92.5

(table continues)

	I		II		III		IV	
	Lo	Hi	Lo	Hi	Lo	Hi	Lo	Hi
San Francisco								
Cell count	8.0	25.0	5.0	28.0	23.0	10.0	21.0	12.0
Expected value	16.5	16.5	16.5	16.5	16.5	16.5	16.5	16.5
United States								
Cell count	10.0	11.0	8.0	13.0	13.0	8.0	8.0	13.0
Expected value	10.5	10.5	10.5	10.5	10.5	10.5	10.5	10.5
E-mail								
Cell count	36.0	19.0	29.0	26.0	31.0	24.0	26.0	29.0
Expected value	27.5	27.5	27.5	27.5	27.5	27.5	27.5	27.5
χ^2(4, N=334)	14.595**		20.236¶		13.297**		11.425*	

Place of return vs factor scores of cluster 2

	I		II		III	
	Lo	Hi	Lo	Hi	Lo	Hi
University of Sask						
Cell count	30.0	10.0	17.0	23.0	21.0	19.0
Expected value	20.0	20.0	20.0	20.0	20.0	20.0
Reply mail						
Cell count	106.0	79.0	113.0	72.0	104.0	81.0
Expected value	92.5	92.5	92.5	92.5	92.5	92.5
San Francisco						
Cell count	4.0	29.0	5.0	28.0	5.0	28.0
Expected value	16.5	16.5	16.5	16.5	16.5	16.5
United States						
Cell count	6.0	15.0	6.0	15.0	7.0	14.0
Expected value	10.5	10.5	10.5	10.5	10.5	10.5
E-mail						
Cell count	21.0	34.0	26.0	29.0	30.0	25.0
Expected value	27.5	27.5	27.5	27.5	27.5	27.5
χ^2(4, N=334)	39.810§		30.038§		21.778¶	

Age vs factor scores of cluster 1

	I		II		III		IV	
	Lo	Hi	Lo	Hi	Lo	Hi	Lo	Hi
Up to 29 years								
Cell count	22.0	16.0	18.0	20.0	17.0	21.0	21.0	17.0
Expected value	19.1	18.9	19.1	18.9	19.1	18.9	19.1	18.9
30 to 44 years								
Cell count	72.0	77.0	65.0	84.0	78.0	71.0	74.0	75.0
Expected value	74.7	74.3	74.7	74.3	74.7	74.3	74.7	74.3

(table continues)

	I		II		III		IV	
	Lo	Hi	Lo	Hi	Lo	Hi	Lo	Hi
45 to 59 years								
Cell count	60.0	55.0	67.0	48.0	57.0	58.0	57.0	58.0
Expected value	57.7	57.3	57.7	57.3	57.7	57.3	57.7	57.3
60 to 99 years								
Cell count	13.0	18.0	17.0	14.0	15.0	16.0	15.0	16.0
Expected value	15.5	15.5	15.5	15.5	15.5	15.5	15.5	15.5
χ^2(3, N=333)	2.136		5.955		.788		.466	

Age vs factor scores of cluster 2

	I		II		III	
	Lo	Hi	Lo	Hi	Lo	Hi
Up to 29 years						
Cell count	17.0	21.0	19.0	19.0	20.0	18.0
Expected value	19.1	18.9	19.1	18.9	19.1	18.9
30 to 44 years						
Cell count	64.0	85.0	65.0	84.0	71.0	78.0
Expected value	74.7	74.3	74.7	74.3	74.7	74.3
45 to 59 years						
Cell count	66.0	49.0	64.0	51.0	61.0	54.0
Expected value	57.7	57.3	57.7	57.3	57.7	57.3
60 to 99 years						
Cell count	20.0	11.0	19.0	12.0	15.0	16.0
Expected value	15.5	15.5	15.5	15.5	15.5	15.5
χ^2(3, N=333)	8.504*		5.470		0.889	

Sex vs factor scores of cluster 1

	I		II		III		IV	
	Lo	Hi	Lo	Hi	Lo	Hi	Lo	Hi
Female								
Cell count	32.0	57.0	45.0	44.0	48.0	41.0	47.0	42.0
Expected value	44.6	44.4	44.6	44.4	44.4	44.6	44.6	44.4
Male								
Cell count	135.0	109.0	122.0	122.0	118.0	126.0	120.0	124.0
Expected value	122.4	121.6	122.4	121.6	121.6	122.4	122.4	121.6
χ^2(1, N=333)	9.790**		0.008		0.810		0.343	

(*table continues*)

Sex vs factor scores of cluster 2

	I Lo	I Hi	II Lo	II Hi	III Lo	III Hi
Female						
Cell count	44.0	45.0	28.0	61.0	35.0	54.0
Expected value	44.6	44.4	44.6	44.4	44.4	44.6
Male						
Cell count	123.0	121.0	139.0	105.0	131.0	113.0
Expected value	122.4	121.6	122.4	121.6	121.6	122.4
$\chi^2(1, N=333)$	0.025		16.971§		5.381*	

Education vs factor scores of cluster 1

	I Lo	I Hi	II Lo	II Hi	III Lo	III Hi	IV Lo	IV Hi
No doctorate								
Cell count	43.0	67.0	42.0	68.0	65.0	45.0	59.0	51.0
Expected value	55.2	54.8	55.2	54.8	55.2	54.8	55.2	54.8
Doctorate								
Cell count	124.0	99.0	125.0	98.0	102.0	121.0	108.0	115.0
Expected value	111.8	111.2	111.8	111.2	111.8	111.2	111.8	111.2
$\chi^2(1, N=333)$	8.036**		9.412**		5.252*		0.799	

Education vs factor scores of cluster 2

	I Lo	I Hi	II Lo	II Hi	III Lo	III Hi
No doctorate						
Cell count	45.0	65.0	40.0	70.0	43.0	67.0
Expected value	55.2	54.8	55.2	54.8	55.2	54.8
Doctorate						
Cell count	122.0	101.0	127.0	96.0	124.0	99.0
Expected value	111.8	111.2	111.8	111.2	111.8	111.2
$\chi^2(1, N=333)$	5.611*		12.488¶		8.036**	

Discipline vs factor scores of cluster 1

	I Lo	I Hi	II Lo	II Hi	III Lo	III Hi	IV Lo	IV Hi
Hard sciences								
Cell count	67.0	42.0	67.0	42.0	42.0	67.0	55.0	54.0
Expected value	54.3	54.7	54.3	54.7	54.3	54.7	54.7	54.3

(table continues)

	I		II		III		IV	
	Lo	Hi	Lo	Hi	Lo	Hi	Lo	Hi
Human sciences								
Cell count	61.0	88.0	72.0	77.0	79.0	70.0	69.0	80.0
Expected value	74.3	74.7	74.3	74.7	74.3	74.7	74.7	74.3
Humanities								
Cell count	38.0	37.0	27.0	48.0	45.0	30.0	43.0	32.0
Expected value	37.4	37.6	37.4	37.6	37.4	37.6	37.6	37.4
χ^2(2, N=333)	10.637**		11.779**		9.275**		2.432	

Discipline vs factor scores of cluster 2

	I		II		III	
	Lo	Hi	Lo	Hi	Lo	Hi
Hard sciences						
Cell count	65.0	44.0	60.0	49.0	68.0	41.0
Expected value	54.3	54.7	54.7	54.3	54.7	54.3
Human sciences						
Cell count	74.0	75.0	64.0	85.0	68.0	81.0
Expected value	74.3	74.7	74.7	74.3	74.7	74.3
Humanities						
Cell count	27.0	48.0	43.0	32.0	31.0	44.0
Expected value	37.4	37.6	37.6	37.4	37.6	37.4
χ^2(2, N=333)	9.930**		5.680		10.073**	

Psychological specialty vs factor scores for cluster 1

	I		II		III		IV	
	Lo	Hi	Lo	Hi	Lo	Hi	Lo	Hi
Exp/physiol								
Cell count	14.0	12.0	21.0	5.0	9.0	17.0	11.0	15.0
Expected value	10.9	15.1	12.9	13.1	14.5	11.5	11.3	14.7
Clinical/applied								
Cell count	14.0	39.0	22.0	31.0	34.0	19.0	24.0	29.0
Expected value	22.3	30.7	26.3	26.7	29.5	23.5	23.1	29.9
Social/personality								
Cell count	7.0	12.0	12.0	7.0	10.0	9.0	10.0	9.0
Expected value	8.0	11.0	9.4	9.6	10.6	8.4	8.3	10.7
Cognitive								
Cell count	15.0	4.0	10.0	9.0	6.0	13.0	5.0	14.0
Expected value	8.0	11.0	9.4	9.6	10.6	8.4	8.3	10.7

(*table continues*)

	I		II		III		IV	
	Lo	Hi	Lo	Hi	Lo	Hi	Lo	Hi
Transpersonal								
Cell count	6.0	10.0	1.0	15.0	15.0	1.0	8.0	8.0
Expected value	6.7	9.3	7.9	8.1	8.9	7.1	7.0	9.0
$\chi^2(4, N = 133)$	17.757¶		24.987§		20.153¶		3.284	

Psychological specialty vs factor scores of cluster 2

	I		II		III	
	Lo	Hi	Lo	Hi	Lo	Hi
Experimental/physiol						
Cell count	13.0	13.0	13.0	13.0	16.0	10.0
Expected value	10.4	15.6	10.9	15.1	12.3	13.7
Clinical/applied						
Cell count	22.0	31.0	22.0	31.0	17.0	36.0
Expected value	21.1	31.9	22.3	30.7	25.1	27.9
Social/pers/comm/dev						
Cell count	8.0	11.0	8.0	11.0	10.0	9.0
Expected value	7.6	11.4	8.0	11.0	9.0	10.0
Cognitive						
Cell count	9.0	10.0	11.0	8.0	16.0	3.0
Expected value	7.6	11.4	8.0	11.0	9.0	10.0
Transpersonal						
Cell count	1.0	15.0	2.0	14.0	4.0	12.0
Expected value	6.4	9.6	6.7	9.3	7.6	8.4
$\chi^2(4, N=133)$	9.203		8.369		20.833¶	

Religious affiliation vs factor scores for cluster 1

	I		II		III		IV	
	Lo	Hi	Lo	Hi	Lo	Hi	Lo	Hi
None								
Cell count	62.0	20.0	67.0	15.0	22.0	60.0	34.0	48.0
Expected value	41.0	41.0	40.7	41.3	40.2	41.8	41.3	40.7
Traditional								
Cell count	56.0	85.0	51.0	90.0	78.0	63.0	78.0	63.0
Expected value	70.5	70.5	70.0	71.0	69.1	71.9	71.0	70.0
Own beliefs								
Cell count	38.0	51.0	37.0	52.0	53.0	36.0	45.0	44.0
Expected value	44.5	44.5	44.2	44.8	43.6	45.4	44.8	44.2
$\chi^2(2, N=312)$	29.376§		46.280§		22.346§		3.985	

(table continues)

Religious affiliation vs factor scores of cluster 2

	I		II		III	
	Lo	Hi	Lo	Hi	Lo	Hi
None						
Cell count	56.0	26.0	62.0	20.0	60.0	22.0
Expected value	42.3	39.7	42.3	39.7	40.5	41.5
Traditional						
Cell count	78.0	63.0	73.0	68.0	56.0	85.0
Expected value	72.8	68.2	72.8	68.2	69.6	71.4
Own beliefs						
Cell count	27.0	62.0	26.0	63.0	38.0	51.0
Expected value	45.9	43.1	45.9	43.1	43.9	45.1
$\chi^2(2, N=312)$	26.042§		36.789§		25.426§	

Frequency of religious practice vs factor scores for cluster 1

	I		II		III		IV	
	Lo	Hi	Lo	Hi	Lo	Hi	Lo	Hi
Daily								
Cell count	27.0	57.0	16.0	68.0	55.0	29.0	57.0	27.0
Expected value	40.3	43.7	41.2	42.8	43.1	40.9	41.2	42.8
Occasionally								
Cell count	34.0	48.0	33.0	49.0	40.0	42.0	39.0	43.0
Expected value	39.4	42.6	40.2	41.8	42.1	39.9	40.2	41.8
Never								
Cell count	84.0	52.0	99.0	37.0	60.0	76.0	52.0	84.0
Expected value	65.3	70.7	66.6	69.4	69.8	66.2	66.6	69.4
$\chi^2(2, N=302)$	20.189§		63.483§		9.774**		18.327§	

Frequency of religious practice vs factor scores of cluster 2

	I		II		III	
	Lo	Hi	Lo	Hi	Lo	Hi
Daily						
Cell count	18.0	66.0	33.0	51.0	19.0	65.0
Expected value	41.2	42.8	40.3	43.7	41.4	42.6
Occasionally						
Cell count	43.0	39.0	36.0	46.0	37.0	45.0
Expected value	40.2	41.8	39.4	42.6	40.5	41.5

(*table continues*)

	I		II		III	
	Lo	Hi	Lo	Hi	Lo	Hi
Never						
Cell count	87.0	49.0	76.0	60.0	93.0	43.0
Expected value	66.6	69.4	65.3	70.7	67.1	68.9
$\chi^2(2, N=302)$	38.137§		6.492*		44.308§	

Rigidity scores[a] vs factor scores for cluster 1

	I		II		III		IV	
	Lo	Hi	Lo	Hi	Lo	Hi	Lo	Hi
Tolerant								
Cell count	118	102	122	98	115	105	108	112
Expected value	110	110	110	110	110	110	110	110
Rigid								
Cell count	49	65	45	69	52	62	59	55
Expected value	57	57	57	57	57	57	57	57
$\chi^2(1, N=334)$	3.409		7.671**		1.332		0.213	

Rigidity scores[a] vs factor scores of cluster 2

	I		II		III	
	Lo	Hi	Lo	Hi	Lo	Hi
Tolerant						
Cell count	103	117	113	107	112	108
Expected value	110	110	110	110	110	110
Rigid						
Cell count	64	50	54	60	55	59
Expected value	57	57	57	57	57	57
$\chi^2(1, N=334)$	2.610		0.479		0.213	

Endorsement of definition 2 vs factor scores for cluster 1

	I		II		III		IV	
	Lo	Hi	Lo	Hi	Lo	Hi	Lo	Hi
Not emergent								
Cell count	76.0	95.0	68.0	103.0	123.0	48.0	93.0	78.0
Expected value	85.5	85.5	85.5	85.5	85.5	85.5	85.5	85.5
Emergent								
Cell count	91.0	72.0	99.0	64.0	44.0	119.0	74.0	89.0
Expected value	81.5	81.5	81.5	81.5	81.5	81.5	81.5	81.5
$\chi^2(1, N=334)$	4.326*		14.679§		67.404§		2.696	

(table continues)

Endorsement of definition 2 vs factor scores of cluster 2

	I		II		III	
	Lo	Hi	Lo	Hi	Lo	Hi
Not emergent						
Cell count	69.0	102.0	74.0	97.0	72.0	99.0
Expected value	85.5	85.5	85.5	85.5	85.5	85.5
Emergent						
Cell count	98.0	65.0	93.0	70.0	95.0	68.0
Expected value	81.5	81.5	81.5	81.5	81.5	81.5
$\chi^2(1, N=334)$	13.049¶		6.339**		8.736**	

Endorsement of definition 3 vs factor scores of cluster 1

	I		II		III		IV	
	Lo	Hi	Lo	Hi	Lo	Hi	Lo	Hi
Not information								
Cell count	128	142	129	141	149	121	142	128
Expected value	135	135	135	135	135	135	135	135
Information								
Cell count	39	25	38	26	18	46	25	39
Expected value	32	32	32	32	32	32	32	32
$\chi^2(1, N=334)$	3.788*		2.783		15.154§		3.788*	

Endorsement of definition 3 vs factor scores of cluster 2

	I		II		III	
	Lo	Hi	Lo	Hi	Lo	Hi
Not information						
Cell count	128	142	131	139	128	142
Expected value	135	135	135	135	135	135
Information						
Cell count	39	25	36	28	39	25
Expected value	32	32	32	32	32	32
$\chi^2(1, N=334)$	3.788*		1.237		3.788*	

Endorsement of definition 4 vs factor scores of cluster 1

	I		II		III		IV	
	Lo	Hi	Lo	Hi	Lo	Hi	Lo	Hi
No states								
Cell count	131.0	114.0	125.0	120.0	112.0	133.0	123.0	122.0
Expected value	122.5	122.5	122.5	122.5	122.5	122.5	122.5	122.5

(table continues)

	I		II		III		IV	
	Lo	Hi	Lo	Hi	Lo	Hi	Lo	Hi
States								
Cell count	36.0	53.0	42.0	47.0	55.0	34.0	44.0	45.0
Expected value	44.5	44.5	44.5	44.5	44.5	44.5	44.5	44.5
$\chi^2(1, N=334)$	4.427*		0.383		6.755**		0.015	

Endorsement of definition 4 vs factor scores of cluster 2

	I		II		III	
	Lo	Hi	Lo	Hi	Lo	Hi
No states						
Cell count	131.0	114.0	137.0	108.0	125.0	120.0
Expected value	122.5	122.5	122.5	122.5	122.5	122.5
States						
Cell count	36.0	53.0	30.0	59.0	42.0	47.0
Expected value	44.5	44.5	44.5	44.5	44.5	44.5
$\chi^2(1, N=334)$	4.427*		12.882¶		0.383	

Endorsement of definition 6 vs factor scores of cluster 1

	I		II		III		IV	
	Lo	Hi	Lo	Hi	Lo	Hi	Lo	Hi
No stream								
Cell count	76	48	54	70	67	57	62	62
Expected value	62	62	62	62	62	62	62	62
Stream								
Cell count	91	119	113	97	100	110	105	105
Expected value	105	105	105	105	105	105	105	105
$\chi^2(1, N=334)$	10.056**		3.284		1.283		0.000	

Endorsement of definition 6 vs factor scores of cluster 2

	I		II		III	
	Lo	Hi	Lo	Hi	Lo	Hi
No stream						
Cell count	57	67	65	59	60	64
Expected value	62	62	62	62	62	62
Stream						
Cell count	110	100	102	108	107	103
Expected value	105	105	105	105	105	105
$\chi^2(1, N=334)$	1.283		0.462		0.205	

(table continues)

Endorsement of definition 7 vs factor scores of cluster 1

	I		II		III		IV	
	Lo	Hi	Lo	Hi	Lo	Hi	Lo	Hi
Not knowledge								
Cell count	65	67	67	65	71	61	64	68
Expected value	66	66	66	66	66	66	66	66
Knowledge								
Cell count	102	100	100	102	96	106	103	99
Expected value	101	101	101	101	101	101	101	101
$\chi^2(1, N=334)$	0.050		0.050		1.253		0.200	

Endorsement of definition 7 vs factor scores of cluster 2

	I		II		III	
	Lo	Hi	Lo	Hi	Lo	Hi
No knowledge						
Cell count	51	81	54	78	76	56
Expected value	66	66	66	66	66	66
Knowledge						
Cell count	116	86	113	89	91	111
Expected value	101	101	101	101	101	101
$\chi^2(1, N=334)$	11.274¶		7.215**		5.011*	

Endorsement of definition 8 vs factor scores of cluster 1

	I		II		III		IV	
	Lo	Hi	Lo	Hi	Lo	Hi	Lo	Hi
No intentionality								
Cell count	108	102	103	107	115	95	96	114
Expected value	105	105	105	105	105	105	105	105
Intentionality								
Cell count	59	65	64	60	52	72	71	53
Expected value	62	62	62	62	62	62	62	62
$\chi^2(1, N=334)$	0.462		0.205		5.131*		4.156*	

Endorsement of definition 8 vs factor scores of cluster 2

	I		II		III	
	Lo	Hi	Lo	Hi	Lo	Hi
No intentionality						
Cell count	105	105	93	117	114	96
Expected value	105	105	105	105	105	105

(table continues)

	I		II		III	
	Lo	Hi	Lo	Hi	Lo	Hi
Intentionality						
Cell count	62	62	74	50	53	71
Expected value	62	62	62	62	62	62
$\chi^2(1, N=334)$	0.000		7.388**		4.156*	

Endorsement of definition 9 vs factor scores of cluster 1

	I		II		III		IV	
	Lo	Hi	Lo	Hi	Lo	Hi	Lo	Hi
No subjective comp								
Cell count	134.0	115.0	124.0	125.0	128.0	121.0	121.0	128.0
Expected value	124.5	124.5	124.5	124.5	124.5	124.5	124.5	124.5
Subjective comp								
Cell count	33.0	52.0	43.0	42.0	39.0	46.0	46.0	39.0
Expected value	42.5	42.5	42.5	42.5	42.5	42.5	42.5	42.5
$\chi^2(1, N=334)$	5.697*		0.016		0.773		0.773	

Endorsement of definition 9 vs factor scores of cluster 2

	I		II		III	
	Lo	Hi	Lo	Hi	Lo	Hi
No subjective component						
Cell count	128.0	121.0	119.0	130.0	132.0	117.0
Expected value	124.5	124.5	124.5	124.5	124.5	124.5
Subjective component						
Cell count	39.0	46.0	48.0	37.0	35.0	50.0
Expected value	42.5	42.5	42.5	42.5	42.5	42.5
$\chi^2(1, N=334)$	0.773		1.909		3.551	

Endorsement of definition 10 vs factor scores of cluster 1

	I		II		III		IV	
	Lo	Hi	Lo	Hi	Lo	Hi	Lo	Hi
No subjective existence								
Cell count	114	94	99	109	104	104	101	107
Expected value	104	104	104	104	104	104	104	104
Subjective existence								
Cell count	53	73	68	58	63	63	66	60
Expected value	63	63	63	63	63	63	63	63
$\chi^2(1, N=334)$	5.098*		1.274		0.000		0.459	

(table continues)

Endorsement of definition 10 vs factor scores of cluster 2

	I		II		III	
	Lo	Hi	Lo	Hi	Lo	Hi
No subjective existence						
Cell count	105	103	111	97	112	96
Expected value	104	104	104	104	104	104
Subjective existence						
Cell count	62	64	56	70	55	71
Expected value	63	63	63	63	63	63
χ^2(1, N=334)	0.051		2.498		3.263	

Endorsement of definition 11 vs factor scores of cluster 1

	I		II		III		IV	
	Lo	Hi	Lo	Hi	Lo	Hi	Lo	Hi
No transformation								
Cell count	153	113	146	120	127	139	125	141
Expected value	133	133	133	133	133	133	133	133
Transformation								
Cell count	14	54	21	47	40	28	42	26
Expected value	34	34	34	34	34	34	34	34
χ^2(1, N=334)	29.544§		12.483¶		2.659		4.727*	

Endorsement of definition 11 vs factor scores of cluster 2

	I		II		III	
	Lo	Hi	Lo	Hi	Lo	Hi
No transformation						
Cell count	148	118	144	122	155	111
Expected value	133	133	133	133	133	133
Transformation						
Cell count	19	49	23	45	12	56
Expected value	34	34	34	34	34	34
χ^2(1, N=334)	16.619§		8.937**		35.749§	

Endorsement of definition 12 vs factor scores of cluster 1

	I		II		III		IV	
	Lo	Hi	Lo	Hi	Lo	Hi	Lo	Hi
Physical								
Cell count	132.0	93.0	122.0	103.0	99.0	126.0	104.0	121.0
Expected value	112.5	112.5	112.5	112.5	112.5	112.5	112.5	112.5

(*table continues*)

	I		II		III		IV	
	Lo	Hi	Lo	Hi	Lo	Hi	Lo	Hi
Non-physical								
Cell count	35.0	74.0	45.0	64.0	68.0	41.0	63.0	46.0
Expected value	54.5	54.5	54.5	54.5	54.5	54.5	54.5	54.5

$\chi^2(1, N=334)$	20.714§		4.916*		9.928**		3.936*	

Endorsement of definition 12 vs factor scores of cluster 2

	I		II		III	
	Lo	Hi	Lo	Hi	Lo	Hi
Physical						
Cell count	129.0	96.0	139.0	86.0	133.0	92.0
Expected value	112.5	112.5	112.5	112.5	112.5	112.5
Non-physical						
Cell count	38.0	71.0	28.0	81.0	34.0	75.0
Expected value	54.5	54.5	54.5	54.5	54.5	54.5

$\chi^2(1, N=334)$	14.831§		38.255§		22.893§	

Presence of written definition vs factor scores of cluster 1

	I		II		III		IV	
	Lo	Hi	Lo	Hi	Lo	Hi	Lo	Hi
No definition								
Cell count	130.0	133.0	137.0	126.0	133.0	130.0	128.0	135.0
Expected value	131.5	131.5	131.5	131.5	131.5	131.5	131.5	131.5
Definition								
Cell count	37.0	34.0	30.0	41.0	34.0	37.0	39.0	32.0
Expected value	35.5	35.5	35.5	35.5	35.5	35.5	35.5	35.5

$\chi^2(1, N=334)$	0.161		2.164		0.161		0.876	

Presence of written definition vs factor scores of cluster 2

	I		II		III	
	Lo	Hi	Lo	Hi	Lo	Hi
No definition						
Cell count	143.0	120.0	130.0	133.0	136.0	127.0
Expected value	131.5	131.5	131.5	131.5	131.5	131.5
Definition						
Cell count	24.0	47.0	37.0	34.0	31.0	40.0
Expected value	35.5	35.5	35.5	35.5	35.5	35.5

$\chi^2(1, N=334)$	9.462**		0.161		1.449	

(*table continues*)

Respondents' written comments vs factor scores of cluster 1

	I		II		III		IV	
	Lo	Hi	Lo	Hi	Lo	Hi	Lo	Hi
Negative								
Cell count	8.0	7.0	8.0	7.0	8.0	7.0	6.0	9.0
Expected value	8.4	6.6	7.0	8.0	7.4	7.6	7.6	7.4
Miscellaneous								
Cell count	49.0	29.0	41.0	37.0	38.0	40.0	37.0	41.0
Expected value	43.6	34.4	36.4	41.6	38.3	39.7	39.7	38.3
Positive								
Cell count	9.0	16.0	6.0	19.0	12.0	13.0	17.0	8.0
Expected value	14.0	11.0	11.7	13.3	12.3	12.7	12.7	12.3
$\chi^2(2, N=118)$	5.572		6.519*		0.124		4.012	

Respondents' written comments vs factor scores of cluster 2

	I		II		III	
	Lo	Hi	Lo	Hi	Lo	Hi
Negative						
Cell count	8.0	7.0	8.0	7.0	7.0	8.0
Expected value	6.5	8.5	7.8	7.2	6.7	8.3
Miscellaneous						
Cell count	36.0	42.0	40.0	38.0	39.0	39.0
Expected value	33.7	44.3	40.3	37.7	35.0	43.0
Positive						
Cell count	7.0	18.0	13.0	12.0	7.0	18.0
Expected value	10.8	14.2	12.9	12.1	11.2	13.8
$\chi^2(2, N=118)$	3.259		0.022		3.725	

Request for results vs factor scores of cluster 1

	I		II		III		IV	
	Lo	Hi	Lo	Hi	Lo	Hi	Lo	Hi
No								
Cell count	65	53	66	52	61	57	52	66
Expected value	59	59	59	59	59	59	59	59
Yes								
Cell count	102	114	101	115	106	110	115	101
Expected value	108	108	108	108	108	108	108	108
$\chi^2(1, N=334)$	1.887		2.568		0.210		2.568	

Request for results vs factor scores of cluster 2

	I		II		III	
	Lo	Hi	Lo	Hi	Lo	Hi
No						
Cell count	72	46	57	61	66	52
Expected value	59	59	59	59	59	59
Yes						
Cell count	95	121	110	106	101	115
Expected value	108	108	108	108	108	108
χ^2(1, N=334)	8.858**		0.210		2.568	

Note. In each case, the factor scores were split at the median value, with "Lo" designating scores below the median and "Hi" scores above the median. The first and fifth definitions of Section 3 were omitted from this table because there were no significant interactions between them and the factor scores. Similarly there were no statistically significant interactions between the presence of comments concerning ambiguity and the factor scores, so that these data were left out of the table. Cluster 1, Factor I: Meaning; Cluster 1, Factor II: Religiosity; Cluster 1, Factor III: Physicalism; Cluster 1, Factor IV; Determinism; Cluster 2, Factor I: Extraordinary experiences; Cluster 2, Factor II: Extraordinary beliefs; Cluster 2, Factor III: Inner growth.

[a]A respondent was classified as "tolerant" if they scored in the range 0 to 2 for the rigidity items, and "rigid" if they scored in the range 3 to 8.

* $p<.05$ ** $p<.01$ ¶ $p<.001$ § $p<.0001$

REFERENCES

Abbagnano, N. (1967). Positivism. In P. Edwards (Ed.), *The encyclopedia of philosophy*. New York: Macmillan and Free.

Alexander, J. B. (1980). The new mental battlefield: 'Beam me up, Spock'. *Military Review, 60*, 47 – 54.

Appleton, T. (1976). Consciousness in animals. *Zygon, 11*(4), 337 – 345.

Arbib, M. A. (1972). Consciousness: The secondary role of language. *The Journal of Philosophy, 69*(17), 579 – 591.

Arkle, W. (1974). *A geography of consciousness*. London: Neville Spearman.

Armstrong, D. M. (1987). Mind-body problem: Philosophical theories. In R. L. Gregory (Ed.), *The Oxford companion to the mind*. Oxford: Oxford University.

Assagioli, R. (1965). *Psychosynthesis: A manual of principles and techniques*. New York: Penguin.

Bakan, P. (1978). Two streams of consciousness: A typological approach. In K. S. Pope & J. L. Singer (Eds.). *The stream of consciousness: Scientific investigations into the flow of human experience*. New York: Plenum.

Baker, D. (1975). *Meditation (The theory and practice)*. Hertsfordshire, England: Little Elephant.

Ballentine, L. E. (1986). What is the point of the quantum theory of measurement? In L. M. Roth and A. Inomata (Eds.), *Fundamental questions in quantum mechanics: Proceedings of a conference, Albany, New York, April 12 – 14, 1984*. London, England: Gordon and Breach.

Barrell, J. J., Aanstoos, C., Richards, A. C. & Arons, M. (1987). Human science research methods. *Journal of Humanistic Psychology, 27*(4), 424 – 457.

Barrett, W. (1978, Autumn). The faith to will. *The American Scholar, 525* – 536.

Baruss, I. (1986). Quantum mechanics and human consciousness. *Physics in Canada/La Physique au Canada, 42*(1), 3 – 5.

Barwise, J. (1986). Information and circumstance. *Notre Dame Journal of Formal Logic, 27*(3), 324 – 338.

Battista, J. R. (1978). The science of consciousness. In K. S. Pope & J. L. Singer (Eds.), *The stream of consciousness: Scientific investigations into the flow of human experience*. New York: Plenum.

Beaumont, J. G. (1981). Split brain studies and the duality of consciousness. In G. Underwood & R. Stevens (Eds.), *Aspects of consciousness. Volume 2. Structural issues.* New York: Academic.

Beck, A. T. (1976). *Cognitive therapy and the emotional disorders.* New York: International Universities.

Berger, R. (1977). *Cyclosis: The circularity of experience.* San Francisco: W. H. Freeman.

Berman, M. (1986). The recovery of participating consciousness. *Institute of Noetic Sciences Newsletter, 14*(2), 17 – 21.

Bindra, D. (1970). The problem of subjective experience: Puzzlement on reading R. W. Sperry's "A modified concept of consciousness". *Psychological Review, 77*(6), 581 – 584.

Blanpied, W. A. (1969). *Physics: Its structure and evolution.* Toronto: Blaisdell.

Block, R. A. (1979). Time and consciousness. In G. Underwood and R. Stevens (Eds.), *Aspects of consciousness. Volume 1. Psychological issues.* New York: Academic.

Bohm, D. (1980). *Wholeness and the implicate order.* London: Ark.

Boring, E. G. (1929). *A history of experimental psychology.* New York: D. Appleton-Century.

Bowers, K. S. (1987). Revisioning the unconscious. *Canadian Psychology/ Psychologie Canadienne, 28*(2), 93 – 104.

Brams, S. J. (1983). *Superior beings: If they exist, how would we know? Game-theoretic implications of omniscience, omnipotence, immortality, and incomprehensibility.* New York: Springer-Verlag.

Brennan, J. F. (1985). *History and systems of psychology* (2nd ed.). Englewood Cliffs, New Jersey: Prentice-Hall.

Brentano, F. (1960). The distinction between mental and physical phenomena. (D. B. Terrell, Trans.). In R. M. Chisholm (Ed.), *Realism and the background of phenomenology.* Glencoe, Illinois: The Free Press. (Reprinted from *Psychologie vom empirischen standpunkt,* 1874, Vol. I, Book II, Chap. i.)

Briggs, J. P. & Peat, F. D. (1984). *Looking glass universe: The emerging science of wholeness.* New York: Simon and Schuster.

Broughton, R. (1986). Human consciousness and sleep/waking rhythms. In B. B. Wolman and M. Ullman (Eds.), *Handbook of states of consciousness.* New York: Van Nostrand Reinhold.

Brown, D. (1988). The transformation of consciousness in meditation. *Noetic Sciences Review, 6,* 14 – 16.

Budzynski, T. H. (1986). Clinical applications of non-drug-induced states. In B. B. Wolman and M. Ullman (Eds.), *Handbook of states of consciousness.* New York: Van Nostrand Reinhold.

Buss, A. R. (1978). The structure of psychological revolutions. *Journal of the History of the Behavioral Sciences, 14,* 57 – 64.

Caird, D. (1987). Religiosity and personality: Are mystics introverted, neurotic, or psychotic? *British Journal of Social Psychology, 26,* 345 – 346.

Carr, T. H. (1979). Consciousness in models of human information processing: Primary memory, executive control and input regulation.

In G. Underwood and R. Stevens (Eds.), *Aspects of consciousness. Volume 1. Psychological issues.* London: Academic.

Carrington, P. (1986). Meditation as an access to altered states of consciousness. In B. B. Wolman and M. Ullman (Eds.), *Handbook of states of consciousness.* New York: Van Nostrand Reinhold.

Chang, S. C. (1978). The psychology of consciousness. *American Journal of Psychotherapy, 32,* 105 – 116.

Child, I. L. (1986). Reply to Clemmer. *American Psychologist, 41*(10), 1174 – 1175.

Churchland, P. M. (1984). *Matter and consciousness: A contemporary introduction to the philosophy of mind.* Cambridge, Massachusetts: MIT.

Churchland, P. S. (1980). A perspective on mind-brain research. *The Journal of Philosophy, 77*(4), 185 – 207.

Churchland, P. S. (1983). Consciousness: The transmutation of a concept. *Pacific Philosophical Quarterly, 64,* 80 – 95.

Clemmer, E. J. (1986). Not so anomalous observations question ESP in dreams. *American Psychologist, 41*(10), 1173 – 1174.

Coan, R. W. (1968). Dimensions of psychological theory. *American Psychologist, 23,* 715 – 722.

Coan, R. W. (1979). *Psychologists: Personal and theoretical pathways.* New York: Irvington.

Csikszentmihalyi, M. (1978). Attention and the holistic approach to behavior. In K. S. Pope & J. L. Singer (Eds.), *The stream of consciousness: Scientific investigations into the flow of human experience.* New York: Plenum.

Dancy, J. (1988). Contemplating one's Nagel. *Philosophical Books, 29*(1), 1 – 16.

Dane, J. R. & DeGood, D. E. (1987). [Review of *Handbook of states of consciousness*]. *Journal of Parapsychology, 51,* 91 – 98.

Davidson, J. M. & Davidson, R. J. (Eds.), (1980). *The psychobiology of consciousness.* New York: Plenum.

Dawson, L. L. (1987). On references to the transcendent in the scientific study of religion: A qualified idealist proposal. *Religion, 17*(3), 227 – 250.

Dennett, D. C. (1978). *Brainstorms: Philosophical essays on mind and psychology.* Montgomery, Vermont: Bradford.

Dennett, D. C. (1982). How to study human consciousness empirically or nothing comes to mind. *Synthese, 53,* 159 – 180.

Dennett, D. C. (1987). Consciousness. In R. L. Gregory (Ed.), *The Oxford companion to the mind.* Oxford: Oxford University.

Dennett, D. C. (1988). Quining qualia. In A. J. Marcel and E. Bisiach (Eds.), *Consciousness in contemporary science.* Oxford, England: Oxford University.

Denzin, N. K. (1982). On time and mind. *Studies in Symbolic Interaction, 4,* 35 – 42.

Dilley, F. B. (1975). The irrefutability of belief systems. *American Academy of Religion – Journal, 43,* 214 – 223.

Dreyfus, H. L. (1982). Introduction. In H. L. Dreyfus (Ed.), *Husserl: Intentionality and cognitive science*. Cambridge, Massachusetts: MIT.

Eccles, J. C. (Ed.). (1966). *Brain and conscious experience: Study week September 28 to October 4, 1964, of the Pontificia Academia Scientiarum*. New York: Springer-Verlag.

Eccles, J. C. (1976a). Brain and free will. In G. G. Globus, G. Maxwell & I. Savodnik (Eds.), *Consciousness and the brain: A scientific and philosophical inquiry*. New York: Plenum.

Eccles, J. C. (1976b). How dogmatic can materialism be? In G. G. Globus, G. Maxwell & I. Savodnik (Eds.), *Consciousness and the brain: A scientific and philosophical inquiry*. New York: Plenum.

Eccles, J. (Ed.). (1982). *Mind and brain: The many-faceted problems*. Washington: Paragon.

Eccles, J. & Robinson, D. N. (1984). *The wonder of being human: Our brain and our mind*. New York: Macmillan.

Ellenberg, L. & Sperry, R. W. (1980). Lateralized division of attention in the commissurotomized and intact brain. *Neuropsychologia, 18*, 411 – 418.

Factor, D. (Ed.). (1985). *Unfolding meaning: A weekend of dialogue with David Bohm*. Mickleton, Gloucestershire, England: Foundation.

Farrell, J. B. (1985 – 86). The firewalk: Stepping over a belief system – An interview with Ange Stephens. *Institute of Noetic Sciences Newsletter, 13*(3), 12 – 15.

Feagin, J. R. (1964). Prejudice and relegious [*sic*] types: A focused study of southern fundamentalists. *Journal for the Scientific Study of Religion, 4*(1), 3 – 13.

Fischer, R. (1978-79). Narcissus looks into the mirror: Self-conscious descriptions of conscious states. *Journal of Altered States of Consciousness, 4*(2), 157 – 170.

Fischer, R. (1986a). On the remembrance of things present: The flashback. In B. B. Wolman and M. Ullman (Eds.), *Handbook of states of consciousness*. New York: Van Nostrand Reinhold.

Fischer, R. (1986b). Toward a neuroscience of self-experience and states of self-awareness and interpreting interpretations. In B. B. Wolman and M. Ullman (Eds.), *Handbook of states of consciousness*. New York: Van Nostrand Reinhold.

Flanagan, O. W., Jr. (1984). *The science of the mind*. Cambridge, Massachusetts: MIT.

Flor-Henry, P. (1983). *Cerebral basis of psychopathology*. Boston: John Wright, PSG.

Fodor, J. A. (1981). The mind-body problem. *Scientific American, 244*(1), 114 – 123.

Foss, J. (1985). A materialist's misgivings about eliminative materialism. *Canadian Journal of Philosophy, Supplementary Volume 11*, 105 – 133.

Foss, J. (1986). Critical notice: John Heil, *Perception and cognition* and Stephen P.Stich, *From folk psychology to cognitive science*. *Canadian Journal of Philosophy, 16*(2), 303 – 322.

Frank, J. D. (1977). Nature and functions of belief systems: Humanism and transcendental religion. *American Psychologist, 32*(7), 555 – 559.

Frith, C. D. (1981). Schizophrenia: An abnormality of consciousness. In G. Underwood & R. Stevens (Eds.), *Aspects of consciousness. Volume 2. Structural issues.* New York: Academic.

Galin, D. (1976). The two modes of consciousness and the two halves of the brain. In P. R. Lee, R. E. Ornstein, D. Galin, A. Deikman & C. T. Tart (Eds.), *Symposium on consciousness.* New York: Plenum.

Gardner, M. & Baruss, I. (1988). [Conceptions of the afterlife]. Unpublished raw data.

Gemes, K. (1987). The world in itself: Neither uniform nor physical. *Synthese, 73,* 301 – 318.

Gergen, K. J. (1985). The social constructionist movement in modern psychology. *American Psychologist, 40*(3), 266 – 275.

Globus, G. & Franklin, S. (1980). Prospects for the scientific observer of perceptual consciousness. In J. M. Davidson & R. J. Davidson (Eds.), *The psychobiology of consciousness.* New York: Plenum.

Globus, G. G., Maxwell, G. & Savodnik, I. (Eds.). (1976). *Consciousness and the brain: A scientific and philosophical inquiry.* New York: Plenum.

Goodman, N. (1984). *Of mind and other matters.* Cambridge, Massachusetts: Harvard University.

Greeley, A. (1987). The "impossible": It's happening. *Noetic Sciences Review, 2,* 7 – 9.

Green, C. M. (1956). *Eli Whitney and the birth of American technology.* Boston: Little, Brown and Company.

Green, E. E. & Green, A. M. (1986). Biofeedback and states of consciousness. In B. B. Wolman and M. Ullman (Eds.), *Handbook of states of consciousness.* New York: Van Nostrand Reinhold.

Greenman, M. A. (1987). Intuition and the limits of philosophical insight. *Metaphilosophy, 18*(2), 125 – 135.

Gregory, R. L. (1980). Regarding consciousness. In B. D. Josephson & V. S. Ramachandran (Eds.), *Consciousness and the physical world: Edited proceedings of an interdisciplinary symposium on consciousness held at the University of Cambridge in January 1978.* Toronto: Pergamon.

Grinspoon, L. & Bakalar, J. B. (1979). *Psychedelic drugs reconsidered.* New York: Basic.

Groeger, J. A. (1987). Computation: The final metaphor? An interview with Philip Johnson-Laird. *New Ideas in Psychology, 5*(2), 295 – 304.

Grosso, M. (1981). Toward an explanation of near-death phenomena. *The Journal of the American Society for Psychical Research, 75,* 37 – 60.

Guillen, M. A. (1984, February). The center of attention. *Psychology Today,* pp. 74 – 75, 79.

Gurwitsch, A. (1964). *The field of consciousness.* Pittsburgh, Pennsylvania: Duquesne University.

Hall, B. P. (1976). *The development of consciousness: A confluent theory of values.* New York: Paulist.

Hanson, N. R. (1963). The dematerialization of matter. In E. McMullin (Ed.), *The concept of matter.* Notre Dame, Indiana: University of

Notre Dame.

Harman, W. W. (1981a). Broader implications of recent findings in psychological and psychic research. In R. G. Jahn (Ed.), *The role of consciousness in the physical world*. Boulder, Colorado: Westview.

Harman, W. W. (1981b). *Human consciousness research: Problems and promises of an emerging science*. Invited address to Division 32, American Psychological Association, 1981 Annual Convention.

Harman, W. W. (1987a). Survival of consciousness after death: A perennial issue revisited. In J. S. Spong (Ed.), *Consciousness and survival: An interdisciplinary inquiry into the possibility of life beyond biological death*. Sausalito, California: Institute of Noetic Sciences.

Harman, W. (1987b). Further comments on ". . . an extended science." *Noetic Sciences Review, 4*, 22 – 25.

Harnad, S. (1987). Methodological epiphenomenalism vs methodological behaviorism. *Psychnet Newsletter, 2*(7). [Machine-readable data file]. EPSYNET @ UHUPVM1 (Producer & Distributor)

Harre, R. (1984). *Personal being. A theory for individual psychology.* Cambridge, Massachusetts: Harvard.

Harvey, O. J., Hunt, D. E. & Schroder, H. M. (1961). *Conceptual systems and personality organization.* New York: John Wiley & Sons.

Heidegger, M. (1962). *Being and time.* (J. Macquarrie & E. Robinson, Trans.). New York: Harper & Row. (Original work published 1926)

Helminiak, D. A. (1984). Consciousness as a subject matter. *Journal for the Theory of Social Behaviour, 14*(2), 211 – 230.

Hilgard, E. R. (1979). Altered states of awareness. In D. Goleman and R. J. Davidson (Eds.), *Consciousness: brain, states of awareness, and mysticism.* New York: Harper and Row.

Hilgard, E. R. (1980). Consciousness in contemporary psychology. *Annual Review of Psychology, 31*, 1 – 26.

Hilgard, E. R. (1987). *Psychology in America: A historical survey.* San Diego: Harcourt Brace Jovanovich.

Hill, O. W. (1986). Further implications of anomalous observations for scientific psychology. *American Psychologist, 41*(10), 1170 – 1172.

Hillner, K. P. (1985). *Psychological reality.* Amsterdam: North-Holland.

Hofstadter, D. R. (1979). *Godel, Escher, Bach: An eternal golden braid.* New York: Basic.

Holt, E. B. (1914). *The concept of consciousness.* London: George Allen.

Hsu, Sung-Peng (1972). Belief, knowledge, and the personal. *Philosophical Review (Taiwan)*, 95 – 110.

Hurley, T. J. III. (1988). The greater self: New frontiers in exceptional abilities research. *Noetic Sciences Review, 6*, 3 – 4.

Izutsu, T. (1984). Matter and consciousness in oriental philosophies. In M. Cazenave (Ed.), *Science and consciousness: Two views of the universe.* New York: Pergamon.

Jackendoff, R. (1987). *Consciousness and the computational mind.* Cambridge, Massachusetts: MIT.

Jahn, R. G. (1981). Introduction. In R. G. Jahn (Ed.), *The role of consciousness in the physical world.* Boulder, Colorado: Westview.

Jahn, R. G. & Dunne, B. J. (1986). On the quantum mechanics of consciousness, with application to anomalous phenomena. *Foundations of Physics, 16*(8), 721 – 772.

Jahn, R. G. & Dunne, B. J. (1987). *Margins of reality: The role of consciousness in the physical world.* San Diego: Harcourt Brace Jovanovich.

James, W. (1904a). Does "consciousness" exist? *The Journal of Philosophy, Psychology and Scientific Methods, 1*(18), 477 – 491.

James, W. (1904b). A world of pure experience. I. *The Journal of Philosophy, Psychology and Scientific Methods, 1*(20), 533 – 543.

James, W. (1904c). A world of pure experience. II. *The Journal of Philosophy, Psychology and Scientific Methods, 1*(21), 561 – 570.

James, W. (1958). *The varieties of religious experience.* N. Y.: NAL Penguin. (Original work published 1902)

James, W. (1983) *The principles of psychology.* Cambridge, Massachusetts: Harvard University. (Original work published 1890)

Jarvik, M. E. (1979). The psychopharmacological revolution. In D. Goleman and R. J. Davidson (Eds.), *Consciousness: Brain, states of awareness, and mysticism.* New York: Harper and Row.

Jaynes, J. (1976). *The origin of consciousness in the breakdown of the bicameral mind.* Boston: Houghton Mifflin.

Jaynes, J. (1986). Consciousness and the voices of the mind. *Canadian Psychology/Psychologie Canadienne, 27*(2), 128 – 139.

John, E. R. (1976). A model of consciousness. In G. E. Schwartz & D. Shapiro (Eds.), *Consciousness and self-regulation: Advances in research (Vol. 1).* New York: Plenum.

John, E. R. (1980). Multipotentiality: A statistical theory of brain function – Evidence and implications. In J. M. Davidson & R. J. Davidson (Eds.), *The psychobiology of consciousness.* New York: Plenum.

Josephson, B. D. (1980). Some hypotheses concerning the role of consciousness in nature. In B. D. Josephson & V. S. Ramachandran (Eds.), *Consciousness and the physical world: Edited proceedings of an interdisciplinary symposium on consciousness held at the University of Cambridge in January 1978.* New York: Pergamon.

Keen, E. (1975). *A primer in phenomenological psychology.* Lanham, Maryland: University Press of America.

Kelly, E. F. (1979). Converging lines of evidence on mind/brain relations. In B. Shapin and L. Coly (Eds.), *Brain/mind and parapsychology: Proceedings of an international conference held in Montreal, Canada, August 24 – 25, 1978.* New York: Parapsychology Foundation.

Kelly, G. (1955). *The psychology of personal constructs.* New York: Norton.

Kimble, G. A. (1984). Psychology's two cultures. *American Psychologist, 39*(8), 833 – 839.

Kirton, M. J. (1981). A reanalysis of two scales of tolerance of ambiguity. *Journal of Personality Assessment, 45*(4), 407 – 414.

Klein, D. B. (1984). *The concept of consciousness: A survey.* Lincoln: University of Nebraska.

Klein, G. S. (1959). Consciousness in psychoanalytic theory: Some implications for current research in perception. *American Psychoanalytic Association Journal, 7*, 5 – 34.

Kornblith, H. (1987). Some social features of cognition. *Synthese, 73*, 27 – 41.

Krasner, L. & Houts, A. C. (1984). A study of the "value" systems of behavioral scientists. *American Psychologist, 39*(8), 840 – 850.

Kurtzman, H. S. (1987). Deconstruction and psychology: An introduction. *New Ideas in Psychology, 5*(1), 33 – 71.

Leary, T. (1983). *Flashbacks: An autobiography.* Los Angeles: J. P. Tarcher.

LeShan, L. & Margenau, H. (1982). *Einstein's space and Van Gough's sky: Physical reality and beyond.* New York: Macmillan.

Lester, D., Thinschmidt, J. S. & Trautman, L. A. (1987). Paranormal belief and Jungian dimensions of personality. *Psychological Reports, 61*, 182.

Levison, A. B. (1987). Rorty, materialism, and privileged access. *Nous, 21*, 381 – 393.

Llinas, R. & Pellionisz, A. (1984). La mente in quanto proprieta tensoriale dei circuiti cerebrali. In M. P. Palmarini (Ed.), *Livelli di realta.* Italy: Feltrinelli. [English-language preprint obtained from authors]

Lowenhard, P. (1981). Consciousness. A biological view. *Goteborg Psychological Reports,* (No. 10, Vol. 11).

Lunzer, E. A. (1979). The development of consciousness. In G. Underwood & R. Stevens (Eds.), *Aspects of consciousness. Volume 1. Psychological issues.* New York: Academic.

Lycan, W. G. (1987). *Consciousness.* Cambridge, Massachusetts: MIT.

Lyons, W. (1986). *The disappearance of introspection.* Cambridge, Massachusetts: MIT.

MacKay, D. M. (1966). Cerebral organization and the conscious control of action. In J. C. Eccles (Ed.), *Brain and conscious experience.* New York: Springer-Verlag.

Mandell, A. J. (1980). Toward a psychobiology of transcendence: God in the brain. In J. M. Davidson & R. J. Davidson (Eds.), *The psychobiology of consciousness.* New York: Plenum.

Mandler, G. (1975). Consciousness: Respectable, useful, and probably necessary. In R. L. Solso (Ed.), *Information processing and cognition: The Loyola Symposium.* Hillsdale, New Jersey: Lawrence Erlbaum.

Mandler, G. (1985). *Cognitive psychology: An essay in cognitive science.* Hillsdale, New Jersey: Lawrence Erlbaum.

Marcel, G. (1976). *Being and having: An existentialist diary.* Gloucester, Massachusetts: Peter Smith.

Mark, V. H., Ervin, F. R. & Yakovlev, P. I. (1962). The treatment of pain by stereotaxic methods. *Confina Neurologica, 22*, 238 – 245.

Marks, C. E. (1981). *Commissurotomy, consciousness and unity of mind.* Cambridge, Massachusetts: MIT.

Marras, A. (1972). Introduction. In A. Marras (Ed.), *Intentionality, mind, and language.* Urbana, Illinois: University of Illinois.

Martindale, C. (1977 – 78). Theories of the evolution of consciousness. *Journal of Altered States of Consciousness, 3*(3), 261 – 278.

Maslow, A. (1966). *The psychology of science: A reconnaissance.* New York: Harper and Row.

Maslow, A. (1968). *Toward a psychology of being (2nd Ed).* New York: Van Nostrand Reinhold.

Mavromatis, A. (1987). On shared states of consciousness and objective imagery. *Journal of Mental Imagery, 11*(2), 125 – 130.

Maxwell, G. (1976). Scientific results and the mind-brain issue: Some afterthoughts. In G. G. Globus, G. Maxwell & I. Savodnik (Eds.), *Consciousness and the brain: A scientific and philosophical inquiry.* New York: Plenum.

McLaughlin, S. C. (1986). Dimensionality and states of consciousness. In B. B. Wolman and M. Ullman (Eds.), *Handbook of states of consciousness.* New York: Van Nostrand Reinhold.

Medin, D. L. & Smith, E. E. (1984). Concepts and concept formation. *Annual Review of Psychology, 35,* 113 – 138.

Merrell-Wolff, F. (1973a). *Pathways through to space: A personal record of transformation in consciousness.* New York: Julian.

Merrell-Wolff, F. (1973b). *The philosophy of consciousness without an object: Reflections on the nature of transcendental consciousness* (2nd ed.). New York: Julian.

Messer, S. B. (1985). Choice of method is value laden too. *American Psychologist, 40*(12), 1414.

Miller, G. A. & Buckhout, R. (1973). *Psychology: The science of mental life (2nd ed.).* New York: Harper and Row.

Moody, R. Jr. (1979). The experience of dying. In D. Goleman and R. J. Davidson (Eds.), *Consciousness: Brain, states of awareness, and mysticism.* New York: Harper and Row.

Morrow, F. (1984). William James and John Dewey on Consciousness: Suppressed writings. *Journal of Humanistic Psychology, 24*(1), 69 – 79.

Muses, C. (1968a). Hypernumber and metadimension theory: Mathematical models for a science of consciousness (noetics) with an historical note on higher kinds of number. *The Journal for the Study of Consciousness, 1*(1), 29 – 48.

Muses, C. (1968b). Unusual states of consciousness: A new objective approach. *The Journal for the Study of Consciousness, 1*(2), 149 – 157.

Muses, C. (1970). Altering states of consciousness by mathematics, with applications to education. *Journal for the Study of Consciousness, 3*(1), 43 – 50.

Nagel, T. (1986). *The view from nowhere.* New York: Oxford University.

Natsoulas, T. (1978a). Consciousness. *American Psychologist, 33,* 906 – 914.

Natsoulas, T. (1978b). Residual subjectivity. *American Psychologist, 33,* 269 – 283.

Natsoulas, T. (1980). Against phenomenal objects. *Journal for the Theory of Social Behaviour, 10*(2), 97 – 114.

Natsoulas, T. (1981). Basic problems of consciousness. *Journal of Personality and Social Psychology, 41*(1), 132 – 178.

Natsoulas, T. (1983a). Concepts of consciousness. *The Journal of Mind and Behavior, 4*(1), 13 – 59.

Natsoulas, T. (1983b). The experience of a conscious self. *The Journal of Mind and Behavior, 4*(4), 451 – 478.

Natsoulas, T. (1986). Consciousness: Consideration of a self-intimational hypothesis. *Journal for the Theory of Social Behaviour, 16*(2), 197 – 207.

Natsoulas, T. (1986-87). The six basic concepts of consciousness and William James's stream of thought. *Imagination, Cognition and Personality, 6*(4), 289 – 319.

Needleman, J. (1965). *A sense of the cosmos: The encounter of modern science and ancient truth.* New York: E. P. Dutton.

Neusner, J. (1988). The theological enemies of religious studies: Theology and secularism in the trivialization and personalization of religion in the west. *Religion, 18*(1), 21 – 35.

Newell, R. W. (1986). *Objectivity, empiricism and truth.* London: Routledge & Kegan Paul.

O'Regan, B. (1983). Psychoneuroimmunology: The birth of a new field. *Investigations: A Bulletin of the Institute of Noetic Sciences, 1*(2), 1 – 2.

O'Regan, B. (1985, Summer). Consciousness and survival: Life, death and science. *Institute of Noetic Sciences Newsletter, 13*(2), pp. 1, 9.

Ornstein, R. E. (1972). *The psychology of consciousness.* New York: Viking.

Osborne, J. W. (1979). The status of the psychology of consciousness within Canadian academic psychology. *Canadian Psychological Review/Psychologie Canadienne, 20*(2), 92 – 94.

Osborne, J. (1981). Approaches to consciousness in North American academic psychology. *The Journal of Mind and Behavior, 2*(3), 271 – 291.

Otis, L. P. & Kuo, E. C. Y. (1984). Extraordinary beliefs among students in Singapore and Canada. *The Journal of Psychology, 116*, 215 – 226.

Ouspensky, P. D. (1972). In search of the miraculous. In J. White (Ed.), *The highest state of consciousness.* Garden City: Doubleday.

Oxley, W. (1982). *Of human consciousness: A philosophical discourse.* Salzburg, Austria: Institut fur Anglistik und Amerikanistik, Universitat Salzburg.

Pattison, E. M. & Kahan, J. (1986). Personal experience as a conceptual tool for modes of consciousness. In B. B. Wolman and M. Ullman (Eds.), *Handbook of states of consciousness.* New York: Van Nostrand Reinhold.

Peacock, E. J. & Reker, G. T. (1982). The life attitude profile (LAP): Further evidence of reliability and empirical validity. *Canadian Journal of Behavioural Science, 14*(1), 92 – 95.

Pekala, R. J. & Levine, R. L. (1981-82). Mapping consciousness:

Development of an empirical-phenomenological approach. *Imagination, Cognition and Personality, 1*(1), 29 – 47.

Pelletier, K. R. (1978). *Toward a science of consciousness.* New York: Dell.

Pelletier, K. R. (1985a). *A new age: Problems and potential.* San Francisco: Robert Briggs Associates.

Pelletier, K. R. (1985b). *Toward a science of consciousness.* Berkeley, California: Celestial Arts.

Penfield, W. (1969a). Consciousness, memory, and man's conditioned reflexes. In K. H. Pribram (Ed.), *On the biology of learning.* New York: Harcourt, Brace & World.

Penfield, W. (1969b). Epilepsy, neurophysiology, and some brain mechanisms related to consciousness. In H. H. Jasper, A. A. Ward & A. Pope (Eds.), *Brain mechanisms of the epilepsies.* Boston: Little, Brown and Company.

Penfield, W. (1975). *The mystery of the mind: A critical study of consciousness and the human brain.* Princeton, New Jersey: Princeton University.

Place, U. T. (1962). Is consciousness a brain process? In V. C. Chappell (Ed.), *The philosophy of mind.* Englewood Cliffs, New Jersey: Prenctice-Hall.

Polanyi, M. (1974). Scientific thought and social reality: Essays by Michael Polanyi. (F. Schwartz, editor). *Psychological Issues, 8* (4, Serial No. 32).

Pope, K. S. & Singer, J. L. (1978). Introduction: The flow of human experience. In K. S. Pope & J. L. Singer (Eds.), *The stream of consciousness: Scientific investigations into the flow of human experience.* New York: Plenum.

Pribram, K. H. (1976). Problems concerning the structure of consciousness. In G. G. Globus, G. Maxwell & I. Savodnik (Eds.), *Consciousness and the brain: A scientific and philosophical inquiry.* New York: Plenum.

Pribram, K. H. (1980). Mind, brain, and consciousness: The organization of competence and conduct. In J. M. Davidson & R. J. Davidson (Eds.), *The psychobiology of consciousness.* New York: Plenum.

Pribram, K. H. (1982). What the fuss is all about. In K. Wilber (Ed.), *The holographic paradigm and other paradoxes.* Boulder, Colorado: Shambhala.

Pribram, K. H. (1986). The cognitive revolution and mind/brain issues. *American Psychologist, 41*(5), 507 – 520.

Pugh, G. E. (1976). Human values, free will, and the conscious mind. *Zygon, 11*(1), 2 – 24.

Rama, S. (1981). Energy of consciousness in the human personality. In R. S. Valle & R. von Eckartsberg (Eds.), *The metaphors of consciousness.* New York: Plenum.

Ramachandran, V. S. (1980). Introduction. In B. D. Josephson & V. S. Ramachandran (Eds.), *Consciousness and the physical world: Edited proceedings of an interdisciplinary symposium held at the University of Cambridge in January, 1978.* Oxford, England: Pergamon.

Reker, G. T. & Peacock, E. J. (1981). The life attitude profile (LAP): A multidimensional instrument for assessing attitudes toward life. *Canadian Journal of Behavioural Science, 13*(3), 264 – 273.

Restivo, S. P. (1978). Parallels and paradoxes in modern physics and eastern mysticism: I. A critical reconnaissance. *Social Studies of Science, 8*, 143 – 181.

Restivo, S. (1982). Parallels and paradoxes in modern physics and eastern mysticism: II. A sociological perspective on parallelism. *Social Studies of Science, 12*(1), 37 – 71.

Rheingold, H. (1982). The changing mind of America: Emerging human needs in the '80s. *Institute of Noetic Sciences Newsletter, 10*(2), 8 – 12.

Ring, K. (1974). A transpersonal view of consciousness: A mapping of farther regions of inner space. *The Journal of Transpersonal Psychology, 6*(2), 125 – 155.

Ring, K. (1987). Near-death experiences: Intimations of immortality? In J. S. Spong (Ed.), *Consciousness and survival: An interdisciplinary inquiry into the possibility of life beyond biological death.* Sausalito, California: Institute of Noetic Sciences.

Roberts, T. B. (1983). New learning. In L. Grinspoon & J. B. Bakalar (Eds.), *Psychedelic reflections.* New York: Human Sciences.

Roberts, T. B. (1984). *The concept state-of-consciousness and an SOC model of psychology.* Unpublished manuscript, Northern Illinois University, Department of Learning, Development & Special Education, DeKalb.

Roberts, T. B. (1985). States of consciousness: A new intellectual direction, a new teacher education direction. *Journal of Teacher Education, 36*(2), 55 – 59.

Roberts, T. B. (1986). *Brainstorm*: A psychological odyssey. *Journal of Humanistic Psychology, 26*(1), 126 – 136.

Robinson, H. M. (1976). The mind-body problem in contemporary philosophy. *Zygon, 11*(4), 346 – 360.

Rogers, C. R. (1961). *On becoming a person: A therapist's view of psychotherapy.* Boston: Houghton Mifflin.

Rogers, C. R. & Stevens, B. (1967). *Person to person: The problem of being human – A new trend in psychology.* Moab, Utah: People Press.

Rokeach, M. (1960). *The open and closed mind: Investigations into the nature of belief systems and personality systems.* New York: Basic.

Rokeach, M. (1976). *Beliefs, attitudes, and values: A theory of organization and change.* San Francisco: Jossey-Bass.

Rosenthal, R. & Rosnow, R. L. (1984). *Essentials of behavioral research: Methods and data analysis.* New York: McGraw-Hill.

Rossi, E. L. (1986). Altered states of consciousness in everyday life: The ultradian rhythms. In B. B. Wolman and M. Ullman (Eds.), *Handbook of states of consciousness.* New York: Van Nostrand Reinhold.

Russell, E. W. (1986). Consciousness and the unconscious: Eastern meditative and Western psychotherapeutic approaches. *The Journal of Transpersonal Psychology, 18*(1), 51 – 72.

Rychlak, J. F. (1978). The stream of consciousness: Implications for a humanistic psychological theory. In K. S. Pope and J. L. Singer (Eds.), *The stream of consciousness: Scientific investigations into the flow of human experience.* New York: Plenum.

Salk, J. (1984). Anatomy of reality: Merging intuition and reason. *Institute of Noetic Sciences Newsletter, 12*(1), 8 – 9.

Sartre, J. P. (1960). *Critique de la raison dialectique, precede de question de methode.* Paris: Gallimard.

Savage, C. W. (1976). An old ghost in a new body. In G. G. Globus, G. Maxwell & I. Savodnik (Eds.), *Consciousness and the brain: A scientific and philosophical inquiry.* New York: Pleı um.

Searle, J. R. (1981). Minds, brains, and programs. In D. R. Hofstadter and D. C. Dennett (Eds.), *The mind's I: Fantasies and reflections on self and soul.* New York: Bantam.

Searle, J. R. (1983). *Intentionality: An essay in the philosophy of mind.* Cambridge, England: Cambridge University.

Shallice, T. (1972). Dual functions of consciousness. *Psychological Review, 79*(5), 383 – 393.

Sheikh, A. (1988, June). *Healing images: From ancient wisdom to modern science.* Paper presented at the meeting of the American Association for the Study of Mental Imagery, New Haven, Connecticut.

Shotter, J. (1982). Consciousness, self-consciousness, inner games, and alternative realities. In G. Underwood (Ed.), *Aspects of consciousness. Volume 3. Awareness and self-awareness.* New York: Academic.

Sidman, M., Stoddard, L. T. & Mohr, J. P. (1968). Some additional quantitative observations of immediate memory in a patient with bilateral hippocampal lesions. *Neuropsychologia, 6*, 245 – 254.

Sloan, D. (1980). Science and consciousness: Some problems and possibilities. Paper presented at the Spring Hill Conference on the Assessment of Consciousness Research, Wayzata, Minneapolis, October, 1980.

Smith, D. W. & McIntyre, R. (1982). *Husserl and intentionality: A study of mind, meaning, and language.* Boston: D. Reidel.

Spanos, N. P. & Moretti, P. (1988). Correlates of mystical and diabolical experiences in a sample of female university students. *Journal for the Scientific Study of Religion, 27*(1), 105 – 116.

Sperry, R. W. (1982). Bridging science and values: A unifying view of mind and brain. In J. Eccles (Ed.), *Mind and brain: The many-faceted problems.* Washington: Paragon.

Sperry, R. W. (1983). Changed concepts of brain and consciousness: Some value implications. *Southern Methodist University, Dallas, Perkins School of Theology. Journal, 36*, 21 – 32.

Sperry, R. (1986). The new mentalist paradigm and ultimate concern. *Perspectives in Biology and Medicine, 29*(3), Part 1, 413 – 422.

Sperry, R. W. (1987). Structure and significance of the consciousness revolution. *The Journal of Mind and Behavior, 8*(1), 37 – 65.

Stapp, H. P. (1985). Consciousness and values in the quantum universe.

Foundations of Physics, 15(1), 35 – 47.

Stapp, H. P. (1986). *Quantum measurement theory and the place of man in nature.* Paper presented at the conference: Science and the boundaries of knowledge, Venice, Italy, March 4 – 7, 1986.

Sternberg, C. F. (1979). Belief systems and the conceptualization of God. *Dissertation Abstracts International, 40,* 4034B - 4035B. (University Microfilms No. 80-03,018)

Stich, S. P. (1983). *From folk psychology to cognitive science: The case against belief.* Cambridge, Massachusetts: MIT.

Straker, S. M. (1985). What is the history of theories of perception the history of? In M. J. Osler and P. L. Farber (Eds.), *Religion, science, and worldview: Essays in honor of Richard S. Westfall.* New York: Cambridge University.

Strange, J. R. (1978). A search for the sources of the stream of consciousness. In K. S. Pope & J. L. Singer (Eds.), *The stream of consciousness: Scientific investigations into the flow of human experience.* New York: Plenum.

Szentagothai, J. (1984). Downward causation? *Annual Review of Neuroscience, 7,* 1 – 11.

Tapper, M. (1986). The priority of being or consciousness for phenomenology: Heidegger and Husserl. *Metaphilosophy, 17*(2 & 3), 153 – 161.

Tart, C. T. (Ed.). (1969). *Altered states of consciousness.* New York: John Wiley & Sons.

Tart, C. (1980). States of consciousness and state-specific sciences. In R. N. Walsh and F. Vaughan (Eds.), *Beyond ego: Transpersonal dimensions in psychology.* Los Angeles: Jeremy P. Tarcher.

Tart, C. T. (1985). Altered states of consciousness and the possibility of survival of death. *Institute of Noetic Sciences: Special Report for Members,* 1 – 8.

Taylor, C. (1982). Consciousness. In P. F. Secord (Ed.), *Explaining human behaviour.* London, England: Sage.

Taylor, E. (1978). Asian interpretations: Transcending the stream of consciousness. In K. S. Pope & J. L. Singer (Eds.), *The stream of consciousness: Scientific investigations into the flow of human experience.* New York: Plenum.

Taylor, E. (1981). The evolution of William James's definition of consciousness. *Revision: Journal of Knowledge and Consciousness, 4*(2), 40 – 47.

Taylor, E. (1982). *William James on exceptional mental states: The 1896 Lowell lectures.* Amherst, Massachusetts: The University of Massachusetts.

Thomas, L. (1983). Debating the unknowable: When the scientific method won't work. *Institute of Noetic Sciences Newsletter, 11*(1), 6 – 8, 20.

Thomas, L. E. & Cooper, P. E. (1980). Incidence and psychological correlates of intense spiritual experiences. *The Journal of Transpersonal Psychology, 12*(1), 75 – 85.

Toulmin, S. (1982). The genealogy of "consciousness". In P. F. Secord

(Ed.), *Explaining human behaviour*. London, England: Sage.

Tucker, D. M. & Williamson, P. A. (1984). Asymmetric neural control systems in human self-regulation. *Psychological Review, 91*(2), 185 – 215.

Turing, A. M. (1950). Computing machinery and intelligence. *Mind, 59*(238), 433 – 460.

Tyler, L. E. (1981). More stately mansions: Psychology extends its boundaries. *Annual Review of Psychology, 32*, 1 – 20.

Ujhely, G. B. (1982). *Psychotherapy and consciousness*. Unpublished manuscript, Graduate Psychiatric Nursing Center, Adelphi, New York.

Unger, R. K. (1983). Through the looking glass: No wonderland yet! (The reciprocal relationship between methodology and models of reality.) *Psychology of Women Quarterly, 8*(1), 9 – 32.

Unger, R. K., Draper, R. D. & Pendergrass, M. L. (1986). Personal epistemology and personal experience. *Journal of Social Issues, 42*(2), 67 – 79.

Van Dusen, W. (1967). The natural depth in man. In C. R. Rogers and B. Stevens (Eds.), *Person to person: The problem of being human – A new trend in psychology*. Moab, Utah: Real People.

Walker, E. H. (1970). The nature of consciousness. *Mathematical Biosciences, 7*, 131 – 178.

Walker, E. H. (1974). Consciousness and quantum theory. In J. White (Ed.), *Psychic exploration: A challenge for science*. New York: G. P. Putnam's Sons.

Walker, E. H. (1977). Quantum mechanical tunneling in synaptic and ephaptic transmission. *International Journal of Quantum Chemistry, 11*, 103 – 127.

Walsh, R. N. (1976). Reflections on psychotherapy. *Journal of Transpersonal Psychology, 8*(2), 100 – 111.

Walsh, R. N. (1980). The consciousness disciplines and the behavioral sciences: Questions of comparison and assessment. *American Journal of Psychiatry, 137*(6), 663 – 673.

Walsh, R. N.: (1984a). Journey beyond belief. *Journal of Humanistic Psychology, 24*(2), 30 – 65.

Walsh, R. N. (1984b, Spring). World at risk. *Association for Transpersonal Psychology Newsletter*, pp. 10 – 14.

Walsh, R. (1988). Asian psychotherapies. In R. Corsini and D. Wedding (Eds.), *Current psychotherapies (4th ed.)*. Itasca, Illinois: F. E. Peacock. [Prepublication copy obtained from author]

Walsh, R. N. & Vaughan, F. (1980). A comparison of psychotherapies. In R. N. Walsh and F. Vaughan (Eds.), *Beyond ego: Transpersonal dimensions in psychology*. Los Angeles: Jeremy P. Tarcher.

Walter, E. (1974). The psychoanalytic method of argumentation. *Midwestern Journal of Philosophy*, Spring, 45 – 51.

Wassermann, G. D. (1983). Quantum mechanics and consciousness. *Nature and System, 5*, 3 – 16.

Watson, J. B. (1919). *Psychology from the standpoint of a behaviorist*. Philadelphia: J. B. Lippincott.

Watson, R. I. (1967). Psychology: A prescriptive science. *American Psychologist, 22,* 435 – 443.

Webb, W. B. (1981). The return of consciousness. *G. Stanley Hall Lecture Series, 1,* 129 – 152.

Weinland, J. D. (1974). *Consciousness, freedom and dignity.* Philadelphia: Dorrance.

Wetherick, N. E. (1979). The foundations of psychology. In N. Bolton (Ed.), *Philosophical problems in psychology.* New York: Methuen.

Wheeler, J. A. (1981). Not consciousness but the distinction between the probe and the probed as central to the elemental quantum act of observation. In R. G. Jahn (Ed.), *The role of consciousness in the physical world.* Boulder, Colorado: Westview.

Wheeler, J. A. & Zurek, W. H. (Eds.). (1983). *Quantum theory and measurement.* Princeton, New Jersey: Princeton University.

White, P. (1982). Beliefs about conscious experience. In G. Underwood (Ed.), *Aspects of consciousness. Volume 3. Awareness and self-awareness.* New York: Academic.

White, P. A. (1986). On consciousness and beliefs about consciousness: Consequences of the physicalist assumption for models of consciousness. *Journal of Social Behavior and Personality, 1*(4), 505 – 524.

White, P. A. (1988). Knowing more about what we can tell: 'Introspective access' and causal report accuracy 10 years later. *British Journal of Psychology, 79,* 13 – 45.

Wilber, K. (1977). *The spectrum of consciousness.* Wheaton, Illinois: Theosophical.

Wilber, K. (1979). A developmental view of consciousness. *The Journal of Transpersonal Psychology, 11*(1), 1 – 21.

Wilber, K. (1980). *The atman project: A transpersonal view of human development.* Wheaton, Illinois: Theosophical.

Wolf, F. A. (1984). *Star wave: Mind, consciousness and quantum physics. An original interpretation of what quantum physics tells us about the human mind.* New York: Macmillan.

Wolman, B. B. (1986). Protoconscious and psychopathology. In B. B. Wolman and M. Ullman (Eds.), *Handbook of states of consciousness.* New York: Van Nostrand Reinhold.

Wolman, B. B. & Ullman, M. (Eds.). (1986). *Handbook of states of consciousness.* New York: Van Nostrand Reinhold.

Yates, F. E. (1980). Two minds about brain asymmetries. *American Journal of Physiology, 238,* R1 – R2.

Ziemelis, U. O. (1986). Quantum mechanical reality, consciousness, and creativity. *Canadian Research, 19*(7), 62, 64, 67 – 68.

Zweig, C. (1985-86). Mind and healing: The debate intensifies. *Institute of Noetic Sciences Newsletter, 13*(3), 9 – 11.